G000026770

GREAT POWER RELATIONS IN ARGENTINA, CHILE AND ANTARCTICA

Great Power Relations in Argentina, Chile and Antarctica

Edited by
Michael A. Morris

Professor of Political Science
Clemson University
South Carolina

MACMILLAN

First published 1990

Published by
THE MACMILLAN PRESS LTD
Houndmills, Basingstoke, Hampshire RG21 2XS
and London
Companies and representatives
throughout the world

Printed in Hong Kong

British Library Cataloguing in Publication Data
Great power relations in Argentina, Chile and
Antarctica
1. Antarctic. International political
aspects
2. Argentina. Foreign relations.
3. Chile. Foreign relations
I. Morris, Michael A.
320.1′2′09989
ISBN 0-333-46035-9

Contents

List of Tables and Figures

Tables

Figures

Notes on the Contributors

Ricardo Alagia is Professor of Public International Law at the Catholic University of La Plata, Argentina, and at the National University of Mar del Plata. During 1983–1987, he was a representative in the Argentine Congress (*Camara de Diputados*), when he authored more than forty declarations, resolutions and laws. When a member of the Argentine Congress, Dr Alagia was on the Foreign Relations, Penal Law and General Legislation Committees. He is the author of articles and monographs on international law and international political economy, about which he also has given over seventy visiting lectures in Argentina, Latin America and the USA.

Peter J. Beck is Reader in International History at Kingston Polytechnic, Kingston-upon-Thames, England, where he has lectured since 1968. Educated at the London School of Economics, University of London, he has researched since the late 1970s on historical and contemporary aspects of the Antarctic and Falklands questions. He has published extensively in Britain and overseas, including Argentina, and his book, *The International Politics of Antarctica*, appeared in 1986. Recently he completed *The Falkland Islands as an International Problem* (1988), and he contributed to the forthcoming work *La Antartida en el Sistema Internacional del Futuro: Problemas y Perspectivas* edited by Carlos Moneta. He is a member of the Royal Institute of International Affairs' Latin American Study Group.

Jan Knippers Black is Research Professor of Public Administration at the University of New Mexico, where she also teaches in the Department of Political Science. Previously, she was Senior Research Scientist and Chairman of the Latin American Research Team in the Foreign Area Studies Division of American University. A former Peace Corps Volunteer in Chile, she holds a PhD in international studies from the American University in Washington, DC. Professor Black has authored, edited, or co-authored more than two dozen books on Latin America and on United States foreign policy. Her most recent books are *Latin America, Its Problems and Its Promise: a Multidisciplinary Introduction* (1984), *Sentinels of Empire: The United States and Latin American Militarism* (1986), and *The Dom-*

inican Republic: Politics and Development in an Unsovereign State (1986).

Peter Calvert is Professor of Comparative and International Politics at the University of Southampton, England. His most recent publications include *Guatemala, a Nation in Turmoil* (Boulder, Colorado: Westview Press, 1985) and *The Foreign Policy of New States* (Brighton: Wheatsheaf Books, 1986), and he is co-author (with Susan Milbank) of *The Ebb and Flow of Military Government in Latin America* (London: The Centre for Security and Conflict Studies, 1987, Conflict Study No. 198).

Ruben de Hoyos is Professor, Department of Political Science, University of Wisconsin/Oshkosh, where he was Co-ordinator of Latin American Studies for more than a decade. His visiting appointments include Visiting Professor in Iran (1970–1971) and Visiting Scholar at the Institute for Latin American Studies, Chinese Academy of Social Sciences, Beijing (1987). A native of Argentina, he wrote his doctoral dissertation (Department of Government, New York University) on the second administration of President Juan D. Peron, who he interviewed personally. Professor de Hoyos has written extensively on the geopolitics of hydroelectric developments among the nations of the River Plate (La Plata) basin, as well as on conflict control and resolution among Southern Cone countries.

Joaquin Fermandois is Professor of Contemporary History at the Catholic University of Valparaiso and at the Catholic University of Santiago, Chile, specialising in the history of contemporary political ideas and in the history of international relations. He studied history at the Catholic University of Valparaiso, at Marburg and Berlin (West Germany) and in Seville, Spain. His publications include a recent book, *Chile y el Mundo 1970–1973. La Politica Exterior del Gobierno de la Unidad Popular y el Sistema Internacional* (Santiago: Ediciones Universidad Catolica de Chile, 1985).

Michael A. Morris is Professor of Political Science at Clemson University, South Carolina, and during 1987–1989 is Fulbright Exchange Professor in Great Britain. He is the author or editor of a number of books, the most recent of which are *Expansion of Third-World Navies* (London: Macmillan, 1987 and New York: St.Martin's Press, 1987) and (editor) *North–South Perspectives on Marine Policy*

(Boulder, Colorado: Westview Press, 1988). His published books, as well as numerous articles, focus on the international relations of Third World countries especially those of Latin America.

Fred Parkinson is a professor emeritus at the Faculty of Laws, University College London and the Institute of Latin American Studies of the University of London. His teaching and research interests have been international law and Latin American international relations. His many publications about Latin American and world affairs include two books, *Latin America, the Cold War and the World Powers* (Sage, 1974) and *The Philosophy of International Relations* (Sage, 1978). For over a decade, he was Managing Editor of the *Year Book of World Affairs*.

Camilo Rodriguez Berrutti is Professor of International Public Law at the Universidad del Salvador, Buenos Aires, Argentina and Professor of International Law at the National University of La Plata. Dr Rodriguez Berrutti is also a foreign affairs adviser to the Argentine Congress. He is the author of numerous articles and monographs and a book on the Malvinas/Falklands crisis, *Malvinas: Ultima Frontera del Colonialismo* (1975).

Cynthia Watson teaches in the Political Science faculty and Latin American Program at Loyola University in Chicago. She holds an MA in Latin American Studies from the London School of Economics and a PhD in Government and International Studies from the University of Notre Dame. Her research centres on strategic issues and on Latin America, with particular emphasis on nuclear developments in the Southern Cone. Her publications have appeared in several journals on Latin American affairs and she edited *Military Interest Groups* (Greenwood Press, 1988).

1 Introduction
Michael A. Morris

OVERVIEW

The great powers (Great Britain, the Soviet Union and the United
States) have been entangled in local South American rivalries between Argentina and Chile, and this maze of competing interests has
increasingly extended to Antarctica. Co-operation has been evident,
as in the case of relations between the United States and Chile,
Argentina and the Soviet Union and most recently Argentina and
Chile. However, local rivalry continues, great power involvement is
frequently condemned by one side or the other as intrusion and the
emergence of Antarctica as a major international issue threatens to
add to strains. Apparently irreconcilable great power disputes with
local states include the continuing Anglo-Argentine clash over the
Falklands/Malvinas and Antarctica and longstanding Chilean–Soviet
antagonism, and a variety of problems have continued to dog US
relations with both Argentina and Chile.

A changing setting adds to the fluidity of great power relations in
Argentina, Chile and Antarctica. The international system is evolving from a predominantly bipolar order towards a more multipolar
one, with complex effects for the great powers, South America as a
region and Argentina and Chile in particular. Every one of the five
state actors of concern here (Great Britain, the Soviet Union, the
United States, Argentina and Chile) either is undergoing or is vulnerable to major change. US hegemony in the Western hemisphere has
been receding; the Soviet Union has been experiencing important
changes in domestic and foreign policy, with implications for relations with Argentina and Chile; British staying power in the South
Atlantic and Antarctica remains questionable; and Argentine and
Chilean political and economic life remain under much stress with the
potential for rapid change. All these changes converge in Antarctica,
and the Antarctic Treaty System is subject to review in 1991.

At the same time, momentum is strong in international relations,
and national foreign policies – including those of the great powers as
well as Argentina and Chile – continue to cling to traditions even

1

when they may no longer be appropriate. The longevity of disputes in the area is a case in point.

A FIVE-CORNERED RELATIONSHIP

The terms 'superpowers' and 'great powers' are used here somewhat interchangeably because of the distinctive setting. In international relations parlance, a 'great power' refers to countries such as Britain and France near the upper tier of the international power hierarchy but with less national power and international influence than the two superpowers (the Soviet Union and the United States). Great powers as well as the superpowers rank well above regional (or 'middle') powers such as Brazil and sub-regional or local powers such as Argentina. Lower still in the international hierarchy of power yet well above the bottom rungs is a small power such as Chile, whose national cohesion and military power have given the country considerable prominence within South America.

While these hierarchical distinctions broadly hold in South America as elsewhere, the British presence and influence is more pronounced in the southern portion of South America and environs than in almost any other part of the Third World. In this sizable area from Argentina and Chile to the South Pole, the British presence is reinforced by territorial sovereignty (over the Falkland/Malvinas Islands and the Dependencies of South Georgia and South Sandwich Islands, all contested by Argentina) and a related territorial claim (over a portion of Antarctica and adjacent waters and islands fronting South America, contested by both Argentina and Chile). The 1982 Falklands/Malvinas war tended to intensify longstanding British involvement in the area.

This relatively prominent British position is paralleled by a rising Soviet presence in Argentina, the Southern Ocean and Antarctica. The US presence in South America, including Argentina and Chile, has suffered a relative decline in recent years, but the United States retains considerable influence. This unusual panoply of one great power and the two superpowers, all with a substantial presence, justifies relaxing the generally strict distinction between great powers and superpowers for the purpose of assessing their relations in Argentina, Chile and Antarctica.

The states and areas which are the object of great power concern and interest here (Argentina, Chile and offshore areas and portions of Antarctica fronting South America) are not easily categorised. The term 'Southern Cone' refers to the affinity between Argentina, Chile and Uruguay, and sometimes includes Paraguay and part of southern Brazil as well. For certain purposes, this distinction is useful, although the perspective here is different. This book posits that great power relations with Argentina and Chile are distinctive and that this distinctive web of relationships extends to Antarctica. Other regional and extra-regional actors impinge in varying degrees on issues in this area, but the key local states are Argentina and Chile and the most prominent external countries are Great Britain, the Soviet Union and the United States. A five-cornered relationship has resulted, with three great powers interacting over issues involving the two local states and portions of Antarctica including adjacent off-shore areas.

The prominent involvement of three great powers in interlocking issues involving Argentina, Chile and Antarctica is distinctive. This distinctive involvement of the three great powers in Argentina, Chile and Antarctica involves a variety of relationships, both conflictive and collaborative, with each other and with the two local states. The great power presence in the area has been especially prominent in politico-strategic affairs, although economic involvement has been substantial as well. Britain was long the primary external economic influence on the area and was later displaced by the United States, whose position in turn has experienced relative decline in recent decades. The United States has continued to play a central role in the external debt situation of Argentina and Chile, and growing Argentine–Soviet relations have been predominantly economic in nature.

The relationship of Argentina and Chile to the great powers is in many ways distinctive as well. All Latin American states have been troubled by dependency on the United States during this century, but South American countries and especially those in the distant Southern Cone have been relatively less affected by US influence. Over the past several decades, as US influence in the region has tended to decline, Latin American states have become more assertive and self-confident in international affairs. This shifting constellation of great and lesser powers has resulted from declining US will and capability to sustain traditional hegemonial responsibilities in the Western hemisphere, a concomitant rise in Latin American will and capabilities, and a receptivity by other developed and developing states to respond to Latin American efforts to diversify their international ties. These opportunities for greater foreign policy leeway or autonomy, while subject to constraints and qualifications, have been reinforced for Argentina and Chile by geographical isolation and national traditions.

Argentina has long been distinctive in aspiring to be a commercial and political rival to the United States, but in recent decades Argentine economic power and political influence have experienced a relative decline. Traditional aspirations to regional leadership have been undercut by Brazil's rise as a regional power, and pretensions to hemispheric leadership have been even more elusive. At the same time, Argentina has stood out over the past decade in forging a mutually beneficial economic relationship with the Soviet Union. Longstanding disputes with Great Britain over the Falkland/Malvinas Islands and Antarctica (the latter dispute involving Chile as well) paralleled these developments and culminated in the 1982 war. In the aftermath of the war, Anglo-Argentine and US–Argentine relations have remained strained, while the Argentine–Soviet economic relationship survived intact. However, an Argentine–Soviet military dimension was not added as some had expected.

Chile was distinctive in South America in achieving national unity and cohesion at a fairly early date following independence at the beginning of the nineteenth century. By the latter part of the century, Chile had emerged in a dominant position on the west coast of South America and rivalled Argentina. During the twentieth century, Chilean economic power and political influence have declined relative to that of Argentina, although Chile has remained a viable small power with ambitious aspirations, like Argentina, to control extensive off-shore areas as well as a portion of Antarctica opposite the South American continent. Unlike Argentina, Chile has resisted the region-wide trend towards democracy and has retained a military dictatorship whose harshness has attracted global attention.

The intrinsic importance of the issues involved justifies a book-length study. The five-cornered relationship, being distinctive, requires particular attention, since findings elsewhere cannot easily be transferred here. Previous studies have examined various angles or parts of the five-cornered relationship, and provide an essential foundation for the present study. Much relevant research has examined US relations with individual South American countries or groups of them, including the Southern Cone. Studies on US–Latin American, US–Argentine and US–Chilean relations have included overall surveys as well as more specific analyses of periods and issues. Argentine and Chilean foreign policies have also received attention, including assessment of different periods and issues as well as their respective pretensions in Antarctica. There are also studies of British and Soviet relations with Latin and South America. However, none of these studies squarely and fully addresses great power relations in Argentina, Chile and Antarctica. This book constitutes the only systematic, comprehensive treatment of the five-cornered relationship.

BOOK ORGANISATION AND ORIENTATION

Argentine and Chilean authors have collaborated with British and US scholars to analyse all aspects of the troubled great power relations in Argentina, Chile and Antarctica and explore prospects for reconciliation. Both local and great power perspectives are assured full representation, as the contributors are nearly equally divided between these two groups of countries (see Notes on 'Contributors' section at the front of this volume). Some sharply diverging views may be observed, for example, regarding the Malvinas/ Falklands situation, although sustained analysis of interlocking issues from multiple perspectives does, it is believed, help promote mutual understanding. For all the differences that have remained, sustained collaboration between authors from Argentina, Chile and the great powers constitutes an important step beyond the usual formula of edited books whereby representatives from a single perspective reinforce one another.

Part I surveys the troubled legacy of great power relations with Argentina and Chile. Following this introductory chapter, *Jan Black* highlights past and present trends in US relations with Latin America and especially with Argentina and Chile, and suggests that a changing context is not resolving longstanding problems. *Camilo Rodriguez Berrutti* examines the British and US impact on the formation of Argentine borders, which, while at times constructive, more often has produced resentment.

Part II examines the various facets of interaction between the great powers, Argentina and Chile. *Peter Calvert* surveys British relations with the Southern Cone countries, and in exploring prospects recommends how these relations might be less conflictive. Argentine–Soviet relations have become increasingly close, and *Ruben de Hoyos* links past and prospective trends in these relations by positing three stages in their development. *Joaquin Fermandois* traces the tortuous interaction of conflict and co-operation in Chilean relations with the great powers, and concludes that while the military government has some foreign policy achievements the international record of a civilian government would likely be better.

Part III focuses on key issues. While Antarctica is an issue of global dimensions and import, *Peter Beck* shows that relations there between Argentina, Chile and the great powers are distinctive and important. With particular emphasis on Argentina, *Ricardo Alagia* indicates that the external debt poses dilemmas for the great powers as well as Latin American states. *Michael Morris* assesses great power military relations with Argentina and Chile, including both conventional military affairs and nuclear proliferation.

Part IV compares great power relations with Argentina and Chile to those with the other South American countries and offers some conclusions. *Cynthia Watson* analyses great power relations with Brazil, while *Fred Parkinson* focuses on South America as a whole in assessing great power relations. *Michael Morris* extends and synthesises the findings of the previous articles in the volume.

The editor of this volume chaired a panel on Great Power Relations in Argentina, Chile and Antarctica at the XIII International Congress of the Latin American Studies Association, Boston, Massachusetts, 23–25 October 1986. Initial discussions on that occasion generated some general and specific guidelines for revision of the panel papers. Successive drafts helped integrate the essays. Some other papers were subsequently recruited to fill in gaps, and these too went through successive drafts. Steady correspondence helped tie the various parts of the project together, as did visits between the editor and nearly all the contributors in either Britain or the United States.

There is still some overlap between the essays, but this deepens the analysis rather than duplicates it. For example, Antarctica is the subject of sustained attention as an issue (P. Beck), but it also has been the object of great power pressure opposing Argentine and Chilean territorial pretensions (C. Rodriguez Berrutti). The external debt has become an especially prominent issue (R. Alagia) and surfaces in a variety of different settings (J. Black and C. Watson). Great power military relations are surveyed with particular emphasis on Argentina and Chile (M. Morris), in a South American context (F. Parkinson) and with reference to apparent emerging trends in Argentine–Soviet relations (R. de Hoyos).

The Editor wishes to thank Simon Winder of The Macmillan Press for his help and patience in shepherding this volume from a rough draft to publication. The Editor also wishes to express appreciation for support of this project from Clemson University (USA) as well as the Hatfield Polytechnic (UK), where he was Fulbright Exchange Professor during the academic year, 1987–1988. Library facilities of the London School of Economics and Political Science, where the Editor was a Visiting Fellow, 1987–8, were also very helpful.

Part I
Background

2 The Passing of Pax Americana
Jan Knippers Black

The Reagan Administration seems now to be presiding – probably unwittingly and certainly unwillingly – like Great Britain's Churchill some while back – over the liquidation of an empire. The vehicles of access, leverage and control that served for a decade or so to bend even the more distant and more developed Latin American countries to the will of the United States are no longer available or adequate for that purpose. Trends within and outside Latin America have converged to produce this result.

The impact of such post Second World War trends as economic growth, mechanisation and the decline of home industry and subsistence farming, urbanisation, the spread of mass communications and labour and political organisation has been felt throughout the Western hemisphere, but the consequences have varied in accordance with national and regional idiosyncrasies and with levels of economic and political development. In the more highly developed South American countries such trends increased pressures on limited democracies for expansion of effective political participation and on poorly regulated, externally-oriented capitalist systems for increased regulation, redistribution and local control. Defenders of the status quo, with the United States and its loyalists among Latin American military factions weighing in on their side, were able between the mid-1960s and the mid-1970s to roll back the tide of change, but only temporarily.

In most of Central America the tidal waves of change were lashing against an even older social order, a rigidly stratified, pre-democratic one built on conquest. The United States might have learned from its experience in South America the high cost and ultimate futility of standing firm against the course of history. In Central America, it might have loosened its grip and accommodated the changes. But institutional memories are short and perspectives are narrow. Sensing, perhaps, that the country was losing its grip on its more distant clients – even in the Western hemisphere – a cadre of US leaders drawn together in part by frustrated chauvinism decided instead to

11

draw the wagons around the backyard and to dare any pretenders –
domestic or foreign – to challenge its authority there.

Whether or not the United States should continue to exercise the
control implicit in a hegemonic relationship is a question that has not
been openly raised by any US administration since the country's
Western hemisphere sphere of influence began to be demarcated.
The only remaining question has been whether or not the United
States would also assume the responsibilities implicit in a colonial
relationship. In that sense, liberal presidents have generally been
more nearly colonialist than conservative ones, more likely to offer
carrots along with sticks and to assume some measure of responsibility for the quality of life in client states. While conservative
presidents have generally limited their concerns to the protection of
US investments and other economic interests and the prevention of
'destabilising' political developments, liberal presidents have sometimes promoted – at least during their first years in office – democratic
and egalitarian reforms.

Latin American leaders, therefore, particularly those of democratic inclination, have regularly been caught in a vise as US policy
shifted from one US administration to the next. In fact, however, in
the mix of US instruments of control, the stick has become ever more
prominent and the carrot has correspondingly shrunk. It is hardly
surprising that a new generation of leaders, given a choice, would
now look elsewhere for aid and trade to offset the costs and risks of
heavy dependence on the United States.

In the 1980s there has been a virtual replay of some of the
controversies and conflicts that characterised hemispheric relations
more than half a century ago. The United States is once again
intervening militarily to crush insurgencies and topple governments
in Central America and the Caribbean; and the larger and, for the
most part, more distant Latin American states, enjoying a new
measure of independence, are once again taking collective initiatives
to counter that intervention.

It was inevitable that the degree of US hegemonic control exercised over Latin American and other client states in the immediate
postwar period would diminish as the devastation wrought by that
war on Europe and Japan was overcome and as Latin American
states themselves became modernised. Had the United States chosen,
however, to adapt itself to those changes through a diplomacy of
mutual accommodation rather than one of force and intrigue, its
prospects for exercising a positive influence over the affairs of the

Western hemisphere as the twentieth-first century approaches would have been brighter.

NATIONALISM AND THE HEGEMONIC ORDER

More than a half century ago, when a new hegemonic order was taking shape in the Western hemisphere, the United States was intervening militarily, almost at will, throughout Central America and the Caribbean. Such intervention sparked a pattern of collective protest on the part of the more nearly independent states of South America, strengthening a regional approach to international law and nurturing the idea of a collective approach to conflict resolution. As US hegemony spread southward in the wake of the Second World War, facilitated by the military links deriving from wartime experience, nationalistic resentment, previously directed against Spain or Portugal, Great Britain, or neighbouring states, began to focus on this new hegemonic power. And US decision-makers generally chose to view such nationalism as a manifestation of foreign influence.

As nationalism in Latin America has grown, nurtured by education, urbanisation, and the development of modern labour organisations and political parties, so, too, has the perception on the part of US officials of a security threat and of the need to maintain a veto over policy and the selection of policy-makers in the region. Thus, Latin American nationalism and the US compulsion to maintain control have been ever more at loggerheads, generating increasing volatility.

By the mid-1960s, the contradictions inherent in US policy towards Latin America (and in varying degrees, towards other client states) could no longer be controlled facilely. It became clear that it was not possible to promote economic development, even to the limited degree necessary to expand markets for US overseas investors, without at the same time promoting the spread of mass communication and social organisation, thus giving rise to demands for more nearly open and participatory politics. Such democratising trends, in turn, feed upon and strengthen nationalism and consequently place limits on the ability of the hegemonic power to control the choices of policies and policy-makers.

The Kennedy administration tried to hedge this dilemma by promoting economic development and democracy, within limits, while strengthening military establishments and paramilitary and police organisations more or less under US control to ensure that those limits were maintained. Not surprisingly, political leaders of Latin America's era of burgeoning democracy chafed at the limits. Some rejected them and came to be seen by US policy-makers as dangerous subversives. Others grudgingly accepted the limits and, unable to cater to their domestic constituencies, lost their political bases to the 'subversives'.

The consequent political fluidity was viewed with alarm in Washington as well as in the corporate suites and country clubs of Latin America. Kennedy administration liberals, feeling betrayed, began to back away from their erstwhile democratic allies in Latin America. After Kennedy's assassination, the Johnson adminis- tration, seeking to pull the Latin American drama back to the US script, turned enthusiastically to the area's armed forces – forces that had been carefully groomed for political leadership.

THE RISE AND DECLINE OF MILITOCRACY

In the 1960s and 1970s, limited participatory democracy in Latin America carried the seeds of its own destruction. The wave of militarism that gathered momentum during that era swept the whole of the region. Whereas in 1961 there were only three Latin American governments that were generally considered dictatorial, by 1976 there were only three or four that were generally considered democ- ratic.

It was in the Southern Cone, where links with the new hegemonic power developed late and economic growth and political infrastruc- ture developed early, that military counter-revolution was most violent and economically devastating. The relatively large middle classes in those countries, seeing their interests threatened by the increasingly effective demands of lower income groups, enlisted their own military establishments and at least some agencies of the US government in their defence against the 'communist menace'. As political mobilisation and economic self-determination had achieved higher levels of development in those countries, more extreme measures were required to demobilise and denationalise them.

Many of the changes in the institutional characteristics and am- bitions of the Latin American armed forces that became apparent during the 1960s can be explained by changes in the nature and extent of training that accompanied the incorporation of those forces into the hemispheric strategy of the United States. Prior to the Second World War, most of the military establishments in South America had been exposed to European training and strategic theory. European strategy was based on the premise that ally and adversary relationships were of a temporary nature. The focus was on the protection or extension of national borders.

With the onset of the Second World War, the United States acquired a near monopoly on the training and equipping of the Latin American armed forces. In the postwar period, the United States began to teach a new global strategy, based on the need for a permanent alliance in the face of a presumably permanent war. The Cold War worldview held that the enemy was not merely a nation, nor even a group of nations, but rather an ideology, and that the enemy was not external, but internal. Thus, the protection of national security appeared to call for maintaining control over all aspects of national life. Training was expanded to include economic planning, systems analysis, psychological operations, management and other aspects of the art of governing.

Through its programmes of training and material assistance in the 1960s and early 1970s, therefore, the United States contributed to the budgetary autonomy, the repressive capability, and the managerial self-confidence of Latin American military establishments. But the United States was not prepared to settle for indirect influence on the course of events; it engaged in direct reinforcement of the political ambitions of the military as well. The best documented cases of direct US encouragement of military seizures of power in Latin America in the 1960s and 1970s are the cases of Brazil (1964) and Chile (1973); but the general pattern of strengthening the Right, including military and paramilitary groups, dividing and weakening the Left, and frightening the middle class was played out to varying degrees in most other Latin American countries as well.[1]

By the late 1960s the optimism that had launched the decade had been overtaken by events and the idealism that had complicated policy considerations during the brief Kennedy era had given way to a more traditional stance. Like his predecessor, President Nixon concentrated on the short-term promotion and protection of US investments and the maintenance of hemispheric security as interpreted by the Cold War worldview. In that context, pressure for socioeconomic and political reform was viewed as a threat of alien inspiration.

The military regimes nurtured by US moral and material support

tended to be of the 'institutional' category (as opposed to the previously more common personal dictatorships), governing in the name
of the armed forces as a whole. While a few regimes of the period
flirted briefly with redistributive domestic policies and more nearly
independent foreign policies, most were slavishly pro-American, at
least initially, and economic policies were designed to promote
reconcentration rather than redistribution of wealth. Credit, tax, and
tariff policies commonly favoured foreign businesses over domestic
ones. Domestic enterprises were absorbed at a fast rate by transnational ones and a general denationalisation and oligopolisation
occurred. While some regimes were able to do little more than hold
the line against labour demands, others – those of Argentina, Chile,
Uruguay, in particular – brought about a major transfer of income
from wage-earning to capitalist classes. Brazil was able to generate an
impressive rate of economic growth and modernise its economic
system; the benefits, however, did not trickle down to the working
classes.

Meanwhile, in some countries, particularly those that had previously enjoyed the highest levels of political and economic development, internecine violence reached an all-time high. Military and
paramilitary forces occupied their own countries as if they were alien
turf and murdered tens of thousands of civilians. In such an enterprise, the military regimes of the area clearly needed each other.
Elaborate transnational intelligence networks were established.
National secret police agencies tracked their prey across international
borders with the greatest of ease, and political refugees often met
violent deaths in their newly adopted countries.

The strengths of military rule, however, proved to have been
overrated. By the late 1970s, several factors tended to make government by sheer force of arms untenable and converged with factors
that would tend to weaken any government – factors not unlike those
that had weakened previous civilian regimes and cleared the way for
military seizures of power.

Military elites are even more prone to cleavage than civilian ones,
particularly because of difficulties in establishing an orderly means of
succession to the highest office. Thus the preservation of the unity of
the armed forces, often cited as a rationale for seizing power, later
came to be cited as a rationale for the withdrawal from power. In
some cases the actions of the prevailing faction were viewed by other
factions as dragging the institution as a whole into disrepute. In other
instances, a new generation of officers with new ideas and ripe

ambitions sought to displace the existing hierarchy. Most often the call to unity meant that power had become highly concentrated in the hands of an individual or a clique and that other factions or branches of the armed forces had ceased to profit adequately from military rule. For military governments, as for civilian ones, patronage has its limits; for every individual or group rewarded or co-opted by high office there were many others left disappointed. Competition among officers from different regions of the country and differences of perspective or interest among the three services and the various specialised branches also placed strains on the façade of unity.

Questions of succession in these military regimes and issues such as whether to seize power or to withdraw from it were generally resolved by formal or informal polling among upper echelon officers. Military elections, however, were not simulations of democracy but rather simulated battles, as votes were generally weighted in terms of command of firepower. And battles, even simulated ones, proved an inefficient means of regulating competition. This failure to routinise succession to power meant continual instability and vulnerability. Once internal cleavage became pronounced, military dissidents sought support from influential civilian groups in order to displace the ruling faction, or the ruling faction sought civilian support to bulwark it against the plotting of military dissidents. In either case, the price of civilian support was likely to be a commitment to return the government to civilian hands eventually.

The health of the economy and the nature of economic policy have a strong bearing on the survivability of military governments, as of civilian ones. Economic stress in the late 1970s and early 1980s sharpened the competition and conflict among classes and economic sectors, creating a climate of instability. Such a climate undermined the claims of military governments to superiority over civilians in the maintenance of law and order. Some regimes were forced to choose between adopting more repressive measures, which might generate an irrepressible reaction, and making concessions that might appear to demonstrate weakness. The crisis also exacerbated competition between military officers and institutions who had taken advantage of their governmental roles to establish profit-making enterprises or to extend their control over the economy and their erstwhile supporters in the business community.

Those military officers most concerned about the image of the military institution wanted to avoid presiding over a complete collapse of the economy. Whether recognising the inadequacies of the institution or simply seeking to shift the blame, they advocated an orderly transfer of power before it was too late. By the late 1970s, it had become clear to several of the military governments that the hour of economic reckoning was approaching. Even reasonably healthy economies, like that of Brazil, had reeled under the energy crisis, and most Latin American economies were suffering from negligible growth along with soaring debt, inflation and unemployment.

Finally, several military regimes found that there are limits to the effectiveness of brutality and terror in controlling the population. In the 1970s, the abuse by governments supported by the United States of their own citizens (and in some cases of US citizens as well) became so flagrant and extensive as to include not only the inarticulate poor but also legislators, academicians, clergymen, and others with ties to politically articulate groups in the United States. This brought the US Congress under intense pressure to terminate certain activities and programmes, such as the arming and training of Latin American military establishments and police forces.

The legislative foundation for a human rights policy had been laid well in advance of President Carter's inauguration, but the Carter administration was quick to grasp an idea whose time had come around again. Military assistance was terminated to several states flagrantly violating human rights, and other regimes preemptively renounced their interest in such assistance. The Military Assistance Program, under which 7000 US advisers had been stationed in Latin America in 1960, was trimmed in both function and personnel until by 1978 there were fewer than 1000 US officers assigned to Military Assistance Advisory Groups in Latin America.[2]

Thus, while other factors contributed to the trend, it was not coincidental that the retreat of the generals began with Carter's assumption of power. In mid-1978 military intervention in the Dominican Republic to nullify the election of Antonio Guzman, of the centre-left Dominican Revolutionary Party (PRD), was thwarted, in part by the timely intercession of American diplomats and military officers expressing the displeasure of the Carter administration with the initiative of the Dominican military. In July 1979, the Somoza dynasty, which with the support of the National Guard, its combined military and police force, had plundered Nicaragua for more than forty years, was felled in a revolution led by the Sandinistas. In August 1979, Ecuador, after seven years of military rule, inaugurated a popularly elected civilian president. In Peru, where the military had held power since 1968, a popularly elected civilian president was inaugurated in July 1980. The Bolivian government changed hands eight times in four years, as civilians, with help from some military officers, made a heroic effort to reinstate democratic rule; that effort, frustrated, in particular, by a coup in 1980, bore fruit in 1982.

REDEMOCRATISATION IN BRAZIL AND THE SOUTHERN CONE

The Brazilian Lead

'We know that as Brazil goes, so will go the rest of that Latin American continent.' So said President Nixon in 1971 in lavishing praise on General Medici, the least charming in Brazil's twenty-year parade of military presidents. And so, in certain grisly respects, it did. The militarisation of Brazil in 1964 was not an aberration, but a harbinger. In Latin America in the years that followed, one constitutional government after another fell victim to military coups.

Brazil also led the trend toward redemocratisation, with its *abertura*, or opening, for free expression and free assembly in the late 1970s. Democracy, with some yet to be determined level of participation and representation, will have its day; but the apparatus of the national security state has not been dismantled. Much of the debris of the authoritarian period remains in the law books and in the bureaucracy, and the economic questions that must now be raised will surely be threatening to those who have something to lose. It is not entirely clear that the new or newly-invigorated civilian institutions can overwhelm and contain an extensive and still ambitious intelligence and security network.

Now in the late 1980s, Brazilian leadership, at least of South America if not of the whole Latin American region, promises to become ever more pronounced; but that prospect no longer gladdens the hearts of US officials. The Brazilian lead, at this point, portends independent foreign policies, competition rather than complementarity in trade, and, most unnerving of all, suspension of payments – maybe even default – on external debts.

For all its weaknesses and uncertainties, there is no denying that Brazil has achieved the status of a mid-level power and that it has ceased to be a 'client' of the United States. In the 1980s, the United States remained Brazil's most important single trading partner, though it no longer accounted for nearly half of Brazil's trade, as had

been the case in the early 1960s. The intimate ties and the patron–
client relationship between US and Brazilian military establishments
that had been so apparent and so destructive in the 1960s had
dissolved in the 1970s. The dissolution came about in part because of
discord on specific issues: territorial waters claims; Brazil's nuclear
power accord with West Germany; and Carter's human rights policy.
But, more importantly, strains in bilateral relations came about
because once in power the military, like other sectors of Brazilian
society, came to be resentful of occupying a subordinate position in
an unequal relationship, of being expected to subordinate national
interests to US interests. Finally, strains came about because Brazil's
accelerated process of industrialisation had set in relief the very real
conflicts of economic interest between the two countries.

By 1987, Brazil's major concerns in its dealings with the United
States were with tariffs and quotas, with mutual charges of protectionism, and with the high US interest rates that had helped
plunge Brazil into an abyss of debt. Meanwhile the Reagan administration had failed miserably in its attempts to interest Brazilian
leaders in its Central American exploits and its Cold War agenda.
Brazil has its own foreign policy agenda, and it is not necessarily in
consonance with that of the United States. With its newly representative political system and its more assertive relationship with the
United States, Brazil now seems prepared to play a weightier role not
only in South America but in global diplomacy as well.

A Measured Retreat in the Southern Cone

Since the inception of the Reagan administration in early 1981, two
of Latin America's most offensive military regimes have fallen –
victims of their own poor judgement and economic mismanagement.
The military establishments of Argentina and Uruguay have withdrawn, but not to a distance safe enough to allow the forces of
democracy a completely free rein.

The Argentine junta of General Galtieri was hounded out of the
Casa Rosada after foolishly provoking an unwinnable war with Great
Britain over the Malvinas/Falkland Islands. The generals had
gambled that in a surge of patriotic fervor the population would
forget about the approximately 30 000 'disappeared' persons and
cope passively with an inflation rate of more than 200 per cent. But
military defeat coupled with political and economic failures finally
rendered their position untenable.

Elections in October 1983, the first after the coup of 1976, gave the presidency to Raul Alfonsin of the Radical Civic Union and appeared to launch a new era of civic peace and reconciliation. However, the economy and civil–military relations continued to pose serious problems for the government. Difficulties in meeting the conditions of the International Monetary Fund (IMF) and creditor banks had left the country in a chronic credit crisis.

Relations between the Alfonsin government and the Reagan administration, always somewhat uneasy, were further strained by reverberations of the debt crisis. Alfonsin has railed against the 'ridiculous prescriptions' of the IMF and has attempted to place the plight of debtor nations on the agendas of international gatherings.[3]

In late 1984, Uruguay celebrated the end of an eleven-year period of brutalising military rule. After suffering humiliating defeat in a constitutional referendum in 1980, the military government, headed by General Gregorio Alvarez, promised to schedule elections. Two of the country's most popular political figures, Retired General Liber Seregni of the Frente Amplio (Board Front) and Wilson Ferreira of the Blanco (White) Party, were barred from seeking the presidency. The elections, which took place in November, were to choose a president, vice-president, 130 members of the national legislature, nineteen mayors, and hundreds of city councillors. The victor in the presidential election, Julio Sanguinetti of the Colorado (Red) Party, which had held power during most of the twentieth century, was inaugurated on 1 March.

US relations with Uruguay have never been particularly close, but US assistance, both economic and military, rose very sharply between the late 1960s and the mid-1970s. This period, which saw the Nixon and Ford administrations presiding in Washington, coincided in Uruguay with the military takeover and the beginnings of a reign of terror. All US military aid and most economic aid as well were suspended by the Carter administration in 1977. Military assistance was renewed by the Reagan administration in 1981, despite human rights requirements in legislation that remained in effect.[4]

Having thus proved itself a friend to the Uruguayan military command, the Reagan administration was not able to enjoy unqualified trust among the democratic forces trying to establish ascendancy. Furthermore, the Uruguayan government is not likely to enjoy the most amiable of relations with a major creditor country while Uruguay staggers under an external debt that greatly complicates economic recovery.

The regime of Chile's General Pinochet, an international pariah since its bloody inception in 1973, found itself beginning its second decade in power faced with serious domestic economic and political problems as well. The failure to topple the dictatorship has been due in large part to the fact that while Pinochet has managed to keep the armed forces united behind him, the civilian opposition has remained divided.

US support for the Pinochet government began to waver in 1986, after the fall of the Marcos regime in the Philippines caused the spotlight to fall on other oppressive dictatorships. Stealing credit for the triumph of Cory Aquino, the Reagan administration found itself under popular and congressional pressures publicly to advocate democracy for Chile as well. The administration has responded to such pressures with ambivalence. While it has become uncomfortable with the dictatorship, fearing that its tenacity strengthens the Left, it cannot sanction an opposition coalition broad enough to have any chance of success. In November and December of 1986, the administration abstained on votes for World Bank and Inter-American Development Bank loans to Chile. Abstention, however, was merely a gesture to pacify Congress while allowing the loans to go through; a 'no' vote would have killed the loans.

OLD DIPLOMACY IN A NEW CONTEXT

Of Carrots and Sticks

For most of South America, at least, it is possible to believe that the traumatic era of the divine right of generals has passed. The problems facing the continent's old and new democratic regimes in the 1980s are staggering, but they are not necessarily the same problems that most preoccupied national leaders during the last interlude of optimism a generation ago. That earlier generation of civilian leaders pondered the means of modernising their economies at minimal cost to traditional and marginal sectors. As it happened, the cost has been scandalous, but a very great deal of modernisation has indeed taken place. The overriding problems now are not those associated with traditionalism but rather those of the flotsam of modernisation.

Leading the list of these seemingly insurmountable problems is the external debt, which for Latin America as a whole exceeded $400 billion in 1986 and claimed almost half of the area's export earnings for interest payments alone. The debts of Mexico and Brazil, each in the $100 billion range, though dwarfed now in absolute terms by the US debt, were the highest in the Third World; and those of several other Latin American states were even higher in per capita terms.

Latin American economies were also being wrenched by inflation rates averaging more than 100 per cent and in some cases rising into the stratosphere of four or five digits. As if to spite those economists who had posed a choice between inflation and unemployment, the latter was also mushrooming, reaching a third or more of the work-force in several countries.

These problems, along with declining rates of production and of productivity, had been exacerbated by the sharp rise in energy costs in the 1970s and the global recession of the early 1980s. They were in large part also a consequence of the modern international version of debt peonage and of the punishment creditors and their collection agency, the IMF, were able to inflict on delinquents. That punishment generally included currency devaluation, higher interest rates, lower wages and longer working hours, a slashing of government services, subsidies, and welfare programmes, and a veritable fire sale of government assets. As the rich made the usual negative choice as to whether or not to accept sacrifice, the additional load of sacrifice was being borne mainly by the underprivileged who had no choice.

Unable to withstand the threatened cut-off of international credit, Latin American countries remain dependent on loans from US and international banks and thus to some extent, on the goodwill of the US government. But these stop-gap loans extended to cover interest payments on previous loans are by no means viewed as 'development assistance'. Latin American leaders may have little choice, but they no longer look to the United States for guidance.

A generation ago a sometimes generous, paternalistic US government was telling its Latin American clients that the problem was underdevelopment and the solution was modernisation. Now the United States can only look upon those countries devastated by modernisation and say, with the IMF, that they will have to destroy their economies in order to save them. Thus, from the perspectives of Latin American leaders in the 1980s, the United States, so much a part of the problem, is not likely to be a part of the solution.

It is also clear enough that the solution is not to be found in the existing system. For the time being the very fragility of the international financial system gives the Latin American debtor countries a certain leverage of their own. The foreign banks are forced to continue to extend bad loans in order to maintain the facade of the system in good working order. But debtors and creditors alike know very well that the debts will never be paid in full.

For a brief period in the 1960s, the United States was generally able to work its will with minimal bloodshed, using a combination of carrots and sticks. Since then, however, the Japanese and European economies destroyed by the Second World War have rebounded and modernised and have ended the near monopoly of the United States on aid to, investment in and trade with Latin America. Obsessed with the military aspects of its presumed global mission, the United States has weakened its own economy, leaving it with more sticks but fewer carrots with which to pursue its goals. Meanwhile, even as previously promising Latin American economies slumped, Latin American populations have become better educated, better organised and less patient with leaders who would seek to accommodate hegemonic pretenders at the expense of their domestic constituencies.

The willingness of the US government to purchase influence with economic aid has declined steadily over the last two decades while its inclination, excepting the Carter years, to seek to control events through the direct or indirect use of force has increased. The militarisation of South America in the 1960s and 1970s might be seen at least in part as an extension of the constabulary solution that had served since the 1930s to keep certain Central American and Caribbean countries submissive. But having played the military card so heavy-handedly, the US now finds itself short on trumps as it seeks to deal with a new, shrewder set of civilian leaders.

Furthermore, it is unlikely that the United States still commands the loyalty of large proportions of Latin American military elites, as it did in the early post-war years. By the early 1980s the United States had lost its near-monopoly position as a supplier of arms to Latin American governments. Some individual decisions on the part of Latin American governments to look to Western European countries, to Israel, or even to the Soviet Union for arms were idiosyncratic – the advent of new governments in Latin America, new, restrictive policies in the United States or some particularly attractive terms offered by extra-hemispheric suppliers. On the whole, however, this shift in the arms trade has simply been a part of a larger trend, notable since the early 1970s, of expanding relations of trade and aid between Latin America and other parts of the world, particularly Western Europe. Finally, with military as well as with civilian leaders throughout Latin America, the reliability of the United States as an ally was called into question by US alignment with Great Britain in the Malvinas/Falkland War of 1982.

A New Agenda

With the fallback of US hegemony in South America and a new assertiveness on the part of some national leaders, it is likely that a new set of issues will come to the fore. Newly democratic governments have very real and pressing problems to deal with and no incentive to give credence to a 'communist menace'. Economic problems will have top priority, but that focus will not necessarily preclude the revival of old contentions and the emergence of new sources of friction.

Economic crisis, of course, makes more acute the need for new resources – resources in particular, like oil and gas, that may be found in remote, poorly demarcated, and contested border regions. Such resource hunger contributed to a brief flare-up of hostilities between Peru and Ecuador in a contested area of the Amazon Basin in 1981. Other clashes of that type are to be expected; virtually all of the Latin American countries have on-going border disputes with at least one neighbour.

Economic crises also often call for scapegoats, and if 'communists' are no longer viable for that role the new scapegoats might be illegal aliens. In several areas the flood of would-be-workers across national borders has accelerated in recent years. In South America, the most porous border has been that between Colombia and Venezuela. Venezuelans have long blamed the influx from Colombia for a host of problems from unemployment to crime. Elsewhere, Argentina, even with its formidable economic problems, continually draws from its poorer neighbouring states, Bolivia and Paraguay. Ecuadorians have moved in large numbers across their northern border into Colombia, and Brazilians have spilled over borders in several areas, particularly into Paraguay and the Rio de la Plata basin to the south and into Venezuela and the Guianas in the north.

COMING FULL CIRCLE

'Until now Central America has always understood that governments which we recognize and support stay in power while those which we do not recognize and support fall. Nicaragua has become a test case.

It is difficult to see how we can afford to be defeated.'[5]

Those words, spoken by US Under Secretary of State Robert Olds about a half century ago, faithfully reflect the attitude of the Reagan administration. But whereas in the early twentieth century that attitude – accompanied by the buying and selling of presidents and direct intervention and occupation by US marines – reflected the audacity of a rising imperial power in its adolescence, the same attitude in the late 1980s reflects the desperation of an empire in retreat.

The United States has come full circle. A half century ago US intervention in Central America and the Caribbean provoked or reinforced insurrection. Rebels then were called bandits and were accused of fronting for the Mexicans or the Germans. Today's rebels are called subversives and are accused of fronting for the Cubans or the Soviets. Then, as now, rebels were above all nationalists, but the nationalism of today's rebels has been intensified by a half century in which US power has lurked behind the pretensions of every local tyrant. Today's rebels are also better organised and better connected with the outside world, and they draw upon a better informed populace.

A half century ago, US pretensions and interventions in the Caribbean Basin served to draw together more distant and less vulnerable Latin American countries in a chorus of protest. That protest was not wholly silenced until the post-war wave of militarism swept through to the southernmost extremes of the hemisphere.

With the new US stance of belligerence in the Caribbean Basin, that chorus is being heard from again. The lead voices this time have been those of the so-called Contadora countries – Colombia, Mexico, Panama and Venezuela. Their ministers met in early 1983 on the Panamanian island of Contadora to seek a means of containing Central American conflict and of countering the US pursuit of a military solution. While Contadora goals have been modest – the promotion of negotiation and peaceful resolution of conflict – the Reagan administration did not fail to recognise that such regional collaboration in itself stems from and tends to advance one of the major motives of rebellion in Central America, that of diluting the hegemony of the United States in the Western hemisphere. Thus, the United States, while feigning co-operation, sought to sabotage the process launched by the Contadora states. It succeeded to a point, and yet momentum remained with the Contadora states and other complementary peace-makers. In August 1985, the governments of Argentina, Brazil, Peru and Uruguay formally offered their support to the efforts of the original four Contadora countries. At a meeting of Contadora and Support Group countries in December 1986 in Rio de Janeiro, the eight countries agreed to establish a process of regular consultation, meeting three times a year to consider issues including but not limited to Central America.[6]

Meanwhile, both the United Nations and the Organization of American States passed resolutions in support of Contadora initiatives and the Secretaries-General of those two organisations offered their services in support of the peace efforts. In January 1987 those Secretaries-General, Javier Perez de Cuellar of the UN and Joao Baena Soares of the OAS, accompanied the eight foreign ministers of the Contadora and Support Group countries on a mission to Central America. Finally, in August 1987, the Central American states themselves seized the initiative. At a meeting hosted by Guatemala's new civilian president, Vinicio Cerezo, a peace plan drawn up by Costa Rican President Oscar Arias was signed by the presidents of all five Central American countries.

US military might in the 1980s is truly awesome, incomparably greater both absolutely and relatively than it was a half century ago, but this time history is not on its side. The United States can inflict unspeakable punishment on its adversaries, but it cannot draw the whole of Latin America back into a system of rigid hegemonic control. Some, at least, of its Latin American adversaries and would-be-allies have learned some of the lessons of history; the United States has not.

Notes

1. For elaboration of these themes, see Jan Knippers Black, *United States Penetration of Brazil* (Philadelphia: University of Pennsylvania Press, 1977) and *Sentinels of Empire: The United States and Latin American Militarism* (Westport, Connecticut: Greenwood Press, 1986).
2. Paul Y. Hammond, David J. Louscher and Michael D. Salomon, 'Growing Dilemmas for the Management of Arms Sales', *Armed Forces and Society*, Vol. 6, No. 1 (Fall 1979) pp. 1–21.
3. *Latin American Debt Chronicle*, 1, 3 and 10 September 1987.
4. Diego Abente, 'Uruguay and Paraguay', Chapter 26 in Jan Knippers

Black (ed.), *Latin America: Its Problems and Its Promise* (Boulder, Colorado: Westview Press, 1984) p. 459.
5. Robert Olds, US Undersecretary of State, quoted in Eduardo Crawley, *Dictators Never Die* (London: Hurst, 1979) pp. 52–3.
6. Embassy of Mexico, Press Release, 18 December 1986.

3 Diplomacy of the United States and Great Britain in the History of Argentine Borders*
Camilo Rodriguez Berrutti

INTRODUCTION

The definition and maintenance of international borders is an especially sensitive political question, and on numerous occasions in the history of Argentina this has drawn in great powers especially Great Britain and the United States. Some of these problems found amicable solutions. Over the last century, there were instances in which Great Britain and the United States were involved in definition and settlement of Argentine borders through arbitrations that were respectfully accepted. At the same time, both of these great powers have affected Argentina's position adversely in the Malvinas and its territorial waters, as well as in its portion of Antarctica. Disagreements and resentments about frontiers have continued to upset relations both between regional states and between them and the great powers up to the present. Diplomacy relating to borders then tends to merge with general diplomatic trends and reflect overall relations between Argentina and the great powers.

Especially since the 1982 Malvinas/Falklands war, considerable attention has been given to the longstanding, adverse impact of Britain on the formation of Argentine borders. This impact will be reviewed here, but particular attention will be given to the more neglected, yet important, counterpart US impact – likewise predominantly negative.

US–Argentine relations have been burdened by difficulties, in spite of a long parallel tradition of co-operation since 1816 when the United Provinces of the River Plate proclaimed their independence from Spain. In the struggle for this independence, the United States

* Translated by Michael A. Morris.

29

showed a benevolent neutrality and was the first non-European country to recognise Argentina. The US Constitution and constitutional practice have been so important and influential as a model – not only for Argentina but also for the entire hemisphere – that the Argentine Supreme Court relies in part on US texts and jurisprudence. This constitutes an important feature of affinity that has led to reciprocal sympathies.

However, from the start trade policy has created difficulties due to the application of protectionist measures. Argentina squarely raised the issue of intervention and non-intervention with the Drago Doctrine, after having prevented US intervention in Paraguay for which Congress had authorised President Buchanan to use force. And in 1831 the US frigate *Lexington* attacked the Argentine military garrison that guarded the Malvinas/Falkland Islands, which facilitated the British invasion of 1833 and tended to poison the subsequent course and contents of the bilateral relationship.

On the Argentine side, stress was generally placed on law, while in Britain and the United States opportunism and power politics were all too prevalent. A long and difficult period of cohabitation may be traced between the United States, a world power as well as regional hegemon, and an assertive Argentina. Since the first Pan American conference, Argentina has opposed the regional hegemony of the United States and held to its own positions, even to the extent of espousing Spanish as the official diplomatic language for the hemisphere.

MALVINAS/FALKLAND ISLANDS

The attack late in 1831 by the US frigate *Lexington* paved the way for the British military invasion of 1833 and caused longstanding Argentine resentment. The US Captain Silas Duncan acted on the urging of the US Consul Slacum, who demanded reprisals for the seizure of three US fishing schooners by order of Governor Luis Vernet (the Argentine political and military commander of the Malvinas at the time). Even US sources have acknowledged that the US vessels were violating Argentine laws on fishing and seal hunting.[1] Moreover, a court of Massachusetts decreed that a captain of an American warship (the *Lexington*) had no right to administer justice in the jurisdiction of a country that was on peaceful terms with the United States, and advised one of the US captains of the fishing vessels to present his case before the courts of Buenos Aires.[2] In turn, a British General Consul in Montevideo, Thomas Samuel Hood, complained to Captain Duncan about having captured a British subject in the Malvinas Islands, which he considered to belong to Argentina.[3]

Other factors reconfirm Argentine sovereignty over the Malvinas/ Falkland Islands. According to the generally recognised doctrine of the legitimate succession of states, Argentina had inherited the Malvinas from Spain.[4] Argentina continued what had been continuous Spanish possession of the islands throughout the eighteenth and early nineteenth centuries. Treaties with Britain had reinforced a system through which Spanish sovereignty over territories already occupied was insured. These treaties included the Nootka Sound Convention (1790) and the conventions of 1783 and 1786, which explicitly referred without exception to islands that were adjacent to the American continent.

At the critical time of 1833, Argentina was at total peace and the Treaty of Friendship, Trade and Navigation of 1825 with Britain was in force and made no reservation whatsoever about the Malvinas Islands. All official measures taken by Buenos Aires up to that time in administering the islands were legitimate. Consequently, the British invasion, which devastated the economic activity of a prosperous colony and expelled the Argentine garrison, was an unjustified act of aggression. Even official and unofficial British sources have occasionally acknowledged the unfairness and illegality of the British presence in the Malvinas.[5]

The injustice and illegality of the British presence in the Malvinas has not only tended to sour Argentine relations with Britain. The United States generally has accepted a distorted British version of the history of the Malvinas as well as the one-sided British legal case derived from this. Largely on this basis, the US government has defined and implemented its own policy towards the Malvinas. Relations with Argentina have suffered accordingly.

This unfortunate legacy was evident in a note of 4 December 1841 of US Secretary of State Webster, in which he took for granted that Great Britain, in seizing the Malvinas in 1833, had done so 'adjusting itself to the existence of a previous right'. Again, Secretary of State Bayard, in his note of 18 March 1886, concluded that 'it is a matter of non-controversial history that the claim on the part of Great Britain regarding sovereignty over the Falkland Islands was categorically declared and sustained throughout the discussions with Spain in 1770 and 1771'.

To correct this US misconception based on British rewriting of history, it will suffice to cite the work of a distinguished US writer, Julius Goebel.[6] The text of the agreement of 22 January 1771 contains no British invocation of rights over the islands. The British concern at this time was to obtain reparation for offended British honour because of the expulsion of a British enclave from the islands in 1770 by Spanish military forces, not to oppose continuing Spanish efforts to uphold sovereignty.

Argentines would like to believe US Secretary of State Forsyth's affirmation to General Alvear:

> It is not for the United States to judge on the right of the islands, I mean, if they belong to you or to England. We would prefer that you owned them, but you can count on the fact that we shall never allow a European nation to take possession of a single inch of land in any region of the Americas.

However, US policy still remains deferential to British views, including continuing abstentions in United Nations General Assembly votes on the Malvinas. US support also continues for the British-inspired application of the principle of self-determination to the Malvinas. However, the inhabitants of the Malvinas do not technically constitute a population, inasmuch as habitation occurred to suit a long-term colonial policy while Argentine nationals generally have been deterred from settling on the islands. Moreover, the United Nations has considered it inadmissible to grant the right of veto to a group of inhabitants in a dispute over sovereignty (Resolution 2065, XXth General Assembly).

Concurrent with Argentine protests about the attack of the *Lexington* were US–Argentine discussions regarding the alleged right of American seamen to carry out fishing and seal hunting along the coasts of the South Atlantic including the Malvinas. The subject long since had been regulated through prohibitions contained in Anglo-Spanish treaties, in particular the 1790 Convention, which prevented those activities within less than ten leagues from the coasts. Subsequent laws and regulations of the Argentine government had created an entire legal system regulating fisheries, and a competent coastguard was in charge of their enforcement. In fact, American ships had asked Buenos Aires for authorisation of their fishing operations, thereby reflecting recognition of Argentine sovereignty over the Malvinas.

Fishing around the Malvinas continued to some extent, and in 1854 led to a crisis between the United States and Great Britain, which had strengthened its position in the islands. During the discussions, Great Britain held that it would not discuss the issue of sovereignty with any other country, and the United States acknowledged British ownership of the islands. British commitment to sovereignty over the Malvinas still vacillated. The terms of the Anglo-Argentine agreement of 1968, which was negotiated but not ratified, provided for restoration of the islands to Argentina in not less than four years nor more than ten.

Sovereignty over the Malvinas and concomitant control of the rich fisheries grounds there of course remain hotly contested between Argentina and Britain. Most recently, Argentina protested a 29 October 1986 British 150-mile fishing conservation zone around the islands. This measure, Argentina feared, would make the British presence on the islands economically viable though remaining legally untenable and militarily costly.

In light of the historical background, the pro-British behaviour of the United States on the occasion of the 1982 Anglo-Argentine war over the Malvinas is perhaps not surprising. The so-called Anglo-American special relationship was influential in shaping US policy, although there have been longstanding areas of friction in the bilateral relationship and, with specific reference to the Malvinas, the United States was pulled into support of a self-serving, legally tenuous British presence. There existed in the United States, as in almost the entire world, a great lack of knowledge regarding the Malvinas, and, in a crisis, they chose the side that offered more complete and accessible, though biased, information. Few were acquainted with the juridical and moral power of the Argentine case, nor was it generally known that throughout 17 years of fruitless Anglo-Argentine negotiations prior to the war the United Kingdom had tried to parry the mandate of the United Nations General Assembly – to end its illegal colonial presence there. At least there is consolation that the great majority of states in the world have supported Argentine sovereignty over the Malvinas in the United Nations and other international fora.

THE 1881 AND 1984 TREATIES

The involvement of US diplomacy in determining the limits of Argentine territory was especially positive in an Argentine–Chilean

1881 treaty. The Argentine–Chilean border is one of the world's longest, and by mutual accord was considered to be the Andes range since Spanish times, when the Viceroyalty of the River Plate was established. However, ambiguities in the direction of the mountain range led to recurring misunderstandings and tension between the two countries. The presence in Buenos Aires and Santiago of the US ministers, respectively, Thomas O. Osborne and Thomas A. Osborne, provided the framework for the diplomatic activity that made it possible to reach a boundary agreement. Through the good offices of the US ministers, difficulties were overcome in a few months of intense telegraphic exchanges.

The core of the compromise expressed in the 1881 treaty specified that 'the boundary-line shall run in that extent over the highest summits of said Cordilleras which divide the waters, and shall pass between the sources (of streams) flowing down to either side'. The resulting treaty has lasted for over 100 years.

Another treaty between Argentina and Chile, this time achieved in 1984 through papal mediation, clarified the disposition of the 1881 treaty about islands and offshore areas near the Beagle Channel. Britain had been involved in a previous, abortive arbitration of the Beagle Channel issue during the 1970s, whose outcome was accepted by Chile but not Argentina. Argentine resentment at the time included criticism of alleged British manipulation and incompetence of domestic officials in accepting a British role. Argentina and Chile then futilely tried to resolve this pressing boundary difference through bilateral channels in the late 1970s. In the tense aftermath, the United States helped prevent conflict between Argentina and Chile and encouraged the subsequent papal mediation.

PARAGUAY

At the end of the Paraguayan War or War of the Triple Alliance (1865–1870, Argentina/Brazil/Uruguay versus Paraguay), Argentina had proclaimed the principle that 'victory does not grant rights'. A new and harsh confrontation none the less subsequently arose between Argentina and Paraguay over the Chaco area between the Pilcomayo and Verde rivers. A formal arbitration request was made to US President Rutherford Hayes inasmuch as his reputation for honesty justified the confidence of both parties. Although in agreements previous to the War of the Triple Alliance the allies had come to an agreement regarding all their claims, Hayes, in his arbitration (1878) on the zone in dispute, the Chaco, pronounced in favour of Paraguay. Argentina's northern border with Paraguay was fixed at the Pilcomayo river. In the same sense, the US government warned Brazil of the inconvenience of making excessive gains from military victory. US involvement therefore appeared more inspired by power politics than law.

MISIONES

The historical course of Spanish–Portuguese overseas relations turned Misiones (Missions) into a critical zone. The demarcation line of the 1494 Treaty of Tordecillas had defined and separated the claims of discovery of the two empires in the New World. Numerous infringements of this dividing line came to place Misiones at a sensitive location between Argentina and Brazil. This border dispute was further burdened with profuse details of juridical complexity, due to the succession and abrogation of various treaties and uncertainty about the location of rivers mentioned in the treaties.

The territory in dispute, almost 30 000 square kilometres, constituted a projection towards the Atlantic Ocean of strategic and economic value. Patient negotiations between Argentina and Brazil nearly led to an agreement, but due to the advent of the new republican system in Brazil it was set aside. It was then decided to submit the dispute to the arbitration of the US president, Grover Cleveland. Outstanding men of government represented each party, Minister Zeballos for Argentina and the Baron of Rio Branco for Brazil. The judgement favoured the latter country, and a scant explanation was provided. It was nevertheless accepted by Argentina as the definitive border in Misiones.

PUNA DE ATACAMA

On the occasion of the dispute involving the Puna de Atacama – a sort of Latin American Tibet, as Peterson called it – US diplomacy made a contribution through William Buchanan, a minister with great experience in international controversies. The Puna, of approximately 70 000 square kilometres, was ceded by Bolivia to Argentina in exchange for Tarija, and then came to be claimed by

Chile. Amidst serious tensions, a Joint Committee presided over by Buchanan reached a verdict that was accepted by both countries in 1899. Buchanan himself suggested the method that led to seven separate votes on different geographical sectors, in which four were in favour of Argentina and two for Chile while there was a unanimous decision in the remaining instance. In a gesture of technical correctness and political common sense, he also produced a report detailing his reasoning.

RIVER PLATE

In a Joint Statement of January 1961, Argentina and Uruguay agreed on the limits of their internal waters in the River Plate. An imaginary line was drawn from Punta del Este, Uruguay, on the eastern coast, to Punta Rasa, in Cape Antonio, province of Buenos Aires, Argentina. The territorial sea would project seawards from this line.

Through this act of sovereignty, Argentina and Uruguay excluded all possibility of establishing the River Plate boundary between them by other criteria. The United States none the less interposed a reserve arguing that legal rules concerning bays applied, so that zones near the coast closed by the 1961 line were in fact high seas. The US government concluded that 'it does not consider the Joint Statement as affecting its rights in any way, nor those of its citizens, in accord with international law'. This US reserve was in turn rejected by both governments involved (Argentina and Uruguay), and in practice their stance has prevailed.

ANTARCTICA

At a relatively early date, in 1947 US Secretary of State Dean Acheson defined US policy towards Antarctica in clear opposition to claimant states such as Argentina, Britain and Chile:

> The US government has not acknowledged any claim of other nations in Antarctica, and has reserved all rights that may correspond to it in those regions. On the other hand, the United States has never formally expressed any claim, even though American citizens have done so in their own benefit.[7]

The United States subsequently supported and achieved international status for Antarctica through the Antarctic Treaty of 1959.

The Antarctic Treaty did not require the signatories to renounce claims that had already been made, but new claims were barred and previously existing claims were 'frozen' or immobilised: 'No new acts or activities taking place while the present treaty is in force shall constitute a basis for asserting, supporting or denying a claim to territorial sovereignty.' These treaty provisions have helped prevent escalation of the dispute involving overlapping claims by Argentina, Britain and Chile in Antarctica. However, Argentina has found that 'internationalisation' tends to weaken its claim and inhibits its freedom of action to sustain its longstanding Antarctic presence.

The Argentine claim to sovereignty over the sector or portion of Antarctica adjacent to the Antarctic peninsula is strong. Discovery by seal-hunting ships from Buenos Aires preceded that by Palmer of the United States. First occupation by Argentina dates from the beginning of this century, with resulting prolonged possession. Longstanding Argentine acts of sovereignty there include administration, control, surveillance, legislation and salvage.

The sector theory in Antarctica delimits jurisdictions on the basis of projecting adjacent territories in the southern hemisphere to the South Pole. Ownership of the Malvinas, by this rule, would determine the outcome of the Anglo-Argentine territorial dispute in Antarctica. This significance, together with considerations of British colonial policy and history, have steeled British resolve to remain in the Malvinas.

Notes

1. Harold F. Peterson, *Argentina y los Estados Unidos* (Buenos Aires: EUDEBA, 1970). Spanish translation of *Argentina and the United States*. See the following section: 'An official who improperly pretended to assume a representative–diplomatic character. His personality and his lack of training.'
2. Davison-Sal/Skins, 2 Paine 324. Source: Francis Wharton, *A Digest of the International Law of the United States*, 2nd edn, Vol. I (Washington: 1887). E. Fitte, *La Agresion Norteamericana a las Islas Malvinas* (Buenos Aires: Emece edn, 1986), Document number 97.
3. Public Record Office – F.O. 118/28, *idem*, Document number 59.
4. France acknowledged that it had possessed Spanish lands (the Malvinas/ Falkland Islands) and that it had restored the islands to Spain to whom they belonged, with the official acquiescence and without objection of the

British government. Julius Goebel, *The Struggle for the Malvinas* (New Haven, Connecticut: Yale University Press, 1927). Translation and reprint by the Argentine navy in 1950.

5. Captain Onslow of the HMS *Clio* arrived in Puerto Soledad. Malvinas in 1833 and 'stated that he had come to take possession of the islands in the name of His British Majesty; he hauled down the Argentine flag, hoisted the British one, and expelled the Argentine garrison'. Note to the Chancellery, F.O. 6/500. Files of the Chancellery and of the Colonial Bureau – Public Records Bureau, Kew. Bulletin RDFS 4146/66 of the British Information Services also states that neither the discoverers nor the first occupants of the islands were British, that the first colonisation had been French, and that title was then transferred to Spain due to the fact that the latter owned the islands. It also states that Argentinians were forcibly expelled in 1833.

6. Julius Goebel, *The Struggle for the Malvinas*. The British Foreign Office could not ignore the value of Goebel's work, using it as a basic source for consultation. See Camilo Rodriguez Berrutti, 'Una obra senera de imparcialidad cierta', *Revista Universidad* (La Plata, Argentina), Vol. 22 (1982).

7. Dean Acheson, *US Department of State Bulletin*, Vol. 16 (1947).

Part II
Great Power Relations

4 British Relations with the Southern Cone States

Peter Calvert

British policy played a major role in creating the diplomatic environment for the independence of the Southern Cone countries. The expeditions of Sir Home Popham and General Beresford, however, began a period of direct intervention which resulted in both the independence of the Banda Oriental (Uruguay) and the fall of Juan Manuel de Rosas at the Battle of Monte Caseros in Argentina in 1852. Meanwhile, a consistent pattern was established in which considerations of trade and investment came to dominate British policy towards the area to the exclusion of almost all else.

Direct intervention has not taken place since 1852, since it was aimed at excluding other European colonial powers from the region and this was no longer necessary. It has since then been the accepted wisdom of successive British governments and of the Foreign Office as an institution that the prime British interest in the region is in maintaining and developing trade. However, as recent events have shown, the acceptance of this priority was the product of complex factors not all of which have been adequately understood even within Britain. It is essential therefore to begin with a few words on the British policy-making process and the wider context of its recent foreign policy.

BRITISH POLICY-MAKING AND ITS CONTEXT

Britain (properly 'the United Kingdom' – UK) is a parliamentary democracy with a strongly developed party system and an active and informed public – the British still buy more newspapers per head of population than the inhabitants of any other country in the world. The focus of political power lies within the House of Commons, but this is sharply divided on party lines and decisions of the House to an overwhelming extent are determined by party considerations. Members of the government form a substantial fraction of the majority party in the House; within this a smaller group of senior ministers,

41

the Cabinet, form the chief executive. Unlike the United States – or the presidential republics of the Southern Cone – the leader of the government is not the principal individual who conducts foreign policy. Day-to-day responsibility lies with the Secretary of State for Foreign and Commonwealth Affairs (commonly known as the Foreign Secretary). Major decisions are normally placed before the Cabinet, though some – such as the decision to undertake the development of nuclear weapons – have been regarded as too secret even for that. Hence by convention the Prime Minister of the day takes a significant and not always helpful interest in foreign policy, enhanced by the tendency of other countries erroneously to regard the prime minister as a kind of 'quasi-president'.

A second substantial difference from American practice is that foreign policy is treated not only historically but also in constitutional practice as part of the royal prerogative, exercised on behalf of the Crown by the government of the day. Hence a British government has an exceptional degree of freedom to conduct foreign policy. It can sign and even ratify a treaty without reference to parliament. The Foreign and Commonwealth Office (usually referred to for short as the FCO) is empowered to conduct these and all lesser negotiations in conditions of absolute secrecy reinforced by the extensive powers conferred by the Official Secrets Act of 1911 – a very considerable advantage when it comes to diplomacy. No advance knowledge, for example, was given or needed to be given to the British public of a 1984 Bern meeting with Argentina to discuss the Falklands issue, and hence unreasonable expectations were not aroused.

A third difference is the highly professional organisation of the permanent civil service officials of the FCO itself. Entry to the higher grades is by a stiff selection procedure, the job is highly regarded and well paid, the sense of *esprit de corps* is high, and papers available to scholars under the thirty-year rule bear witness to the regularity of its reports and the efficiency of its decision-making. Only major decisions, or those with a 'political' implication, are referred to the desk of the Foreign Secretary himself for consultation as appropriate with his cabinet colleagues.

It is an important maxim of British foreign policy-making that it is only those who are responsible for making these decisions who have the necessary information to do so. The individual ambassador naturally comes to think that his own post is the centre of the universe; in Whitehall its relative importance in the global scheme of things is seen more clearly.[1] Yet it is also historically that British foreign policy has not been marked by grand designs. It has been pragmatic to a fault.[2] It was a former Conservative Foreign Secretary, Lord Salisbury, who described British foreign policy as though floating gently down stream, putting out a hand from time to time to fend off from the bank.

It was this pragmatism which was responsible for the vast increase of the British Empire in the nineteenth century and for the much more rapid decolonisation which has taken place since 1945. British policy generally since 1945 has been determined by four factors:

(a) its relative economic decline which led to the conscious decision in 1957 to end its world-wide commitments (the retreat from 'East of Suez') and a period of compulsory disinvestment as far as Latin America was concerned;
(b) declining active involvement in the Cold War as colonial burdens were lifted but maintenance of the apparatus and armament of a great power;
(c) the strategic primacy of the North Atlantic and the sentimental 'special relationship' with the United States;
(d) suspicion of a rearmed Germany and a reunified Europe, which gave way after 1960 to a spectacular reversal of policy and an increasingly urgent desire to join the European Community (EC), which was achieved only in 1973.

Though it is possible to see the whole period in ideological terms as dominated by the doctrine of the 'three circles' – the view, epitomised by Winston Churchill, that Britain has interests in each of three circles, the Commonwealth, the Atlantic Alliance and Europe – the importance of each has clearly varied from time to time. The continuities of British foreign policy transcend the ideological division between Labour and Conservative governments, and often the breaks come within governments not between them.

THE SOUTHERN CONE

The Southern Cone is usually taken to refer to Argentina, Chile, Uruguay and Paraguay. British relations with Paraguay, however, are of little relevance in the recent period for obvious reasons, and no discussion of the area can fail to take into account the interests of Brazil, which Britain, like the United States, sees as the major power of South America and a trading partner of great potential. Within the

Southern Cone, Britain's relations with Argentina since 1945 have been of the greatest significance, and will form the main theme of the chapter. Anglo-Argentine relations referring more particularly to Antarctica are included in Chapter 7 of this book and will receive only limited attention here.

1945–64

At the end of the Second World War Britain was still a great power, but the United States had displaced it after 1940 almost everywhere in the Western Hemisphere. Britain for some years yet remained Argentina's largest trading partner, and the sale of beef to the British Empire underpinned Argentina's economy. Much of the proceeds from the wartime sales were held by Argentina in the form of 'blocked' sterling balances, and were subsequently used by the Peron government to compensate British shareholders in the Argentine railways. This was the decisive step in a process of British disinvestment which was to leave Argentina wide open to US pressures.[3] British cultural influence was still strong and a substantial British and British-descended community lived in and around Buenos Aires. At the time of the Falklands/Malvinas war in 1982, the surviving Anglo-Argentine community was thought to number somewhere between 19 000 and 100 000.

It was Peron, however, who revived the Argentine claim to the Falklands/Malvinas, and extended the claims to cover South Georgia, the South Sandwich, South Orkney and South Shetland Islands and the greater part of that sector of Antarctica claimed by the UK since 1908.[4] The early history of these claims is extremely complex, but it is sufficient to say here that as regards the Falklands themselves Britain's claim rests on prior discovery, effective occupation and acquisitive prescription, while that of Argentina is regarded as derived by succession from the claims of Spain to all lands west of the Line of Demarcation of 1494.[5] South Georgia and the South Sandwich Islands lie to the east of the Line of Demarcation and Captain Cook was the first to claim them for Britain. In the case of South Georgia, which is habitable, Britain also established effective occupation, though this too is disputed by Argentina. The Argentine and Chilean claims to overlapping sectors of Antarctica through the doctrine of continental projection are accepted neither by Britain nor generally in international law.

The Antarctic issue has not proved to be a major bone of contention, though its history is complex. Britain's offer in 1947 to refer the overlapping Antarctic claims to the International Court of Justice was rejected. Instead the Argentine government, on the occasion of Britain's post-war naval review, held naval manoeuvres in the disputed zone, and Argentine bases were set up on the South Sandwich Islands and Deception Island. Shortly afterwards a special division of the Argentine Foreign Ministry was created to pursue the claims to the Falklands and the 'Argentine Antarctic', and agreement was reached between Argentina and Chile to pursue their Antarctic claims jointly against Britain, despite the fact that those claims overlapped.[6] But in 1949 the problem of the Antarctic territories was brought under control by an agreement between all three countries to keep military forces out of the area south of latitude 60° – an agreement which was to pave the way for the freezing of all Antarctic claims under the Antarctica Treaty of 1959.[7]

In the last days of the Peron government a new wave of nationalism was generated by the President when he declared his intention of 'saturating' the disputed area with settlers. Women as well as men were encouraged to go to Graham Land so that children could be born there of Argentine nationality, who could in due course claim the right of self-determination. As a result Britain took the case unilaterally to the International Court of Justice (ICJ) in 1955, but Argentina refused to accept the Court's jurisdiction.[8]

The Antarctica Treaty, which came into effect in 1961 for a period of thirty years in the first instance, essentially deferred disputes concerning the territories south of the sixtieth parallel. It did not, unfortunately, put an end to the Falklands/Malvinas issue. Indeed it was General Aramburu who in a decree of 6 March 1957 formally declared not only the Falkland Islands but also South Georgia and the South Sandwich Islands to be part of the Argentine Territory of Tierra del Fuego, the Argentine Antarctic and the Islands of the South Atlantic, with its capital at Ushuaia. This decree made the inhabitants of the islands Argentine citizens whether they liked it or not, liable for both income tax and military service if they landed in Argentina.[9] Between 1957 and 1969 direct communications between the islands and Argentina were effectively severed, air communications being maintained between Port Stanley and Montevideo, some 800 miles away. Inevitably the inhabitants of the islands, who came from a different social background from the Anglo-Argentine community, came to see themselves as separate and distinct.

With the independence of Malaya and Ghana in 1957, Britain

entered on a rapid phase of decolonisation which in a decade was to lead to the withdrawal from 'East of Suez' and reduce the Empire that in 1945 had covered a quarter of the world's land surface to an assortment of small islands (Turks and Caicos, Ascencion, Tristan da Cunha, etc.) and enclaves (Gibraltar, Hong Kong). Preoccupied above all with the British position in the Eurostrategic context and the Atlantic Alliance, successive British governments were to fail to realise that this necessarily reduced proportionately both their power and their influence on world events. This transformation was effectively disguised by the fact that Britain remained a major industrial power and – because of its North Atlantic Treaty Organisation (NATO) commitments – a very heavily armed one. Other nations, too, continued to regard Britain as more important than she really was. Argentina was a major exception.

1964–82

By 1964 there was for the first time a substantial majority of ex-colonial territories in the United Nations (UN), and in September of that year the Committee of 24 took note of the long-running Falklands/Malvinas issue and recommended direct negotiations between Britain and Argentina over the claim. This recommendation, which specifically avoided any consideration of the legitimacy of the Argentine claim, was endorsed by the UN General Assembly in Resolution 2065 of December 1965, which called for the 'decolonisation' of all remaining colonial territories.[10] By having the issue of the Falklands/Malvinas redefined as an issue of decolonisation, however, Argentina had scored something more than a diplomatic point. For the same resolution, by specifically ruling out all traditional legal grounds for claim, would, had it constituted legislation in the international legal sense, have effectively decided the question in favour of Argentina, which then and subsequently has argued that the English-speaking inhabitants of the islands ('kelpers'), being rightfully Argentine citizens, have no separate right of self-determination.[11]

In January 1966 the British Foreign Secretary, Mr Michael Stewart, visited Buenos Aires, thus initiating a series of talks over the Falklands/Malvinas that ultimately broke down in 1982.[12] At the time, however, this move, initiated by the new Labour Government of Mr Wilson, was seen in London as the beginning of a new and outward-looking policy, which as a significant component envisaged establishing better trading relations with Latin America. Central in this strategy were to be closer relations between Britain and other Latin American states, notably Chile and Brazil.

British relations with Chile had been friendly since the nineteenth century; indeed the choice of Britain as arbitrator between Argentina and Chile in 1902 reflected Britain's close relations with both sides. Like Argentina, Chile was neutral in the Great War, in which her nitrate fields played a vital role. Like her neighbour, too, Chile entered the Second World War only at the beginning of 1945, though somewhat more enthusiastically. Argentina did so only under threat from the United States that if she did not she would not be allowed to join the new United Nations Organisation. By the mid-1960s Anglo-Chilean relations were so warm that President Frei's state visit to London was reciprocated by a royal visit to Santiago – the first occasion in which a British reigning monarch had visited South America, hence a significant development in British policy. At the same time, friendly relations were established with the new military regime in Brazil.

Brazil, despite the quasi-fascist regime of President Getulio Vargas, had entered the Second World War on its own account in 1942 and sent an Expeditionary Force to Italy which fought alongside allied troops there. A veteran of the campaign, Marshal Humberto Castello Branco, was the first president of the military government that had seized power in 1964 with a determination to bring about the economic modernisation of their country. His and successive military governments became keenly interested in purchasing from Europe to offset what they saw as excessive dependence on the United States. When the US embargo on the sale of jet aircraft to Latin America was finally breached in 1969, it was France, not Britain, that was to benefit and the Mirage (and its Israeli derivative, the Dagger) that was to become the standard for Latin American air forces.

The new climate for relations with Europe brought a change of tactics by the military government of General Ongania in Buenos Aires, where it was slowly recognised in the course of 1969 that the imposed isolation of the Falkland islanders by Argentina had been counterproductive.[13] The first consequence of this was the Argentine decision to agree to arbitration of the Beagle Channel dispute and the proposal that this be done by asking the British government, as the Arbitrator appointed under the Treaty of 1902, to constitute a commission drawn from the International Court of Justice at The Hague.[14] After the June 1970 coup, talks on the future of the

Falklands/Malvinas were also opened with the new Conservative government of Edward Heath. Within a month they resulted in an Exchange of Notes concerning Communications and a Joint Statement, explicitly stated to be without prejudice to the question of sovereignty. This enabled the islanders once again to travel to and from the islands via Argentina, and obliged Britain to provide a regular shipping service and Argentina a regular air service. Unfortunately the shipping service was not provided, and the building of the airport by Argentine contractors in 1972 was seen by the islanders as giving them a fatal dependence which prejudiced their distinctive status.[15].

In the wider context of the Southern Cone, the Heath government continued friendly relations with the leftist Union Popular (UP) regime in Chile. Britain had nationalised the major parts of its own economy in the 1940s, and despite some internal partisan bickering over the future of the British steel industry, successive British governments since 1945 had taken the view that nationalisation of British interests was no bar to continued friendly relations provided that adequate compensation was paid. As elsewhere, the savagery which followed the fall of Allende was extensively reported in the British press and the new military government received little approval from any quarter. Though diplomatic relations were maintained regardless of the change of government, according to the traditional British practice of recognising any government that demonstrates it is in actual control, they were severed by the incoming Labour government in 1975 when details became known of the torture inflicted on Dr Sheila Cassidy. Relations were not to be restored for four years. British relations with Uruguay were unaffected by the 'soft coup' of 1973, though Uruguay, like Argentina, suffered severely in economic terms from Britain's entry into the EC and the closure of the European market to imports of chilled beef (1975).

Relations with Brazil were excellent. In the late 1970s British banks vied with one another to invest in Brazil's economic miracle, somehow failing to note, like the competitors in North America, that it was hardly likely that Brazil could ever repay all of them at the same time. When in 1983 the critical economic situation of Mexico suddenly made 'the debt crisis' a headline issue, the countries of the Southern Cone were already all to a great extent in the same position.

In the mid-1970s, meanwhile, the British Labour government had been keen to liquidate all remaining colonial commitments, a well-intentioned policy which was to founder on its failure to solve the long-running Rhodesia issue and on domestic political consider-ations. It was also unlucky in its timing. The *Shackleton Report*[16] on the economy of the Falklands appeared in 1976 just in time to fuel speculation that the islands were awash on a sea of oil.[17] With a military government again in power in Argentina, any deal was difficult. At the same time the *Almirante Storni* incident, when an Argentine warship fired on HMS *Shackleton*, suggested a new Argentine belligerence over the Falklands/Malvinas issue. In 1977 Mr Callaghan's government took the prudent step of ordering naval reinforcements to the islands as a signal to Buenos Aires that Britain was prepared if necessary to defend them by force of arms.[18] The following month, however, Mr Ted Rowlands of the British Foreign Office visited both the islands and Buenos Aires and a new series of talks got under way.

The Callaghan government was in fact so anxious to divest itself of this colonial embarrassment that it was a measure of the incom-petence of Argentine military diplomacy at this critical point that no satisfactory arrangement was found. The sticking point, as for British governments before and since, was the Argentine failure to allow any say for the islanders themselves. Further complicating relations at the tip of the South American continent was the announcement in May 1977 of the arbitral decision on the ownership of the Beagle Channel Islands, when relations between Argentina and Chile deteriorated suddenly and conflict seemed imminent. In 1978 the Argentine government formally rejected the award, and only at the end of that year did the two sides accept the mediation of the Vatican.

The next round of negotiations over the future of the Falklands/ Malvinas took place with the incoming Thatcher government, which also lost no time in resuming diplomatic relations with Chile. The Thatcher government justified the Chilean measure, which was hotly criticised by the Opposition in parliament and elsewhere, by suggest-ing that the mistreatment suffered by Dr Cassidy was an insufficient reason to warrant such an unusual step as severing relations. It soon became clear that whether or not the Thatcher government really believed this, they admired the economic achievements of the Pino-chet regime and were anxious to land a major arms deal. At the same time, they were prepared to do a deal with Argentina over the Falklands/Malvinas on a leaseback basis if the islanders could be persuaded to agree to it in advance.

At the talks in New York in 1980, the Argentines were prepared for the first time to have a representative of the islanders present.[19] Unfortunately for all concerned the task of 'selling' leaseback to the islanders was given to Mr Nicholas Ridley, whose advocacy of this and subsequent cases has been unpersuasive.[20] The islanders howled him down. Eventually they were to accept, reluctantly, the alternative suggestion that Britain ask Argentina for a 25-year 'freeze' instead.[21]

The Foreign Office was left with no effective policy but to continue to negotiate with nothing to negotiate about. With the approach of the 150th anniversary of the British assumption of power in the islands in January 1833, major shifts within the Argentine armed forces brought to power a new junta under General Galtieri, pledged to 'resume' Argentine sovereignty by that date. Further fuelling Argentine belligerency, Argentine newspaper and television reports about Britain suggested that the country was in a state of near-terminal economic crisis, compounded by near civil war in Northern Ireland. Mrs Thatcher's unrestrained criticism of her political opponents helped convince others besides the Anglophile Argentine Foreign Minister, Nicanor Costa Mendez, that Britain lacked the strength to do more than make a formal diplomatic response to the forcible seizure of the islands. The Nott defence review of 1981 and the decision to withdraw the sole British Antarctic patrol vessel, HMS *Endurance*, seemed to confirm this.[22] And approaches to Argentina from emissaries of the Reagan administration seeking support for their Central American policy convinced the junta that in any conflict they could count on support from the United States. The scene was set for the Falklands War of 1982.

Since 1982

Though brief, the 1982 war cost Britain 255 service lives, more than any of the eleven conflicts in which British forces have fought since 1945 except Korea, Kenya, Malaya and Northern Ireland.[23] The impact on Britain was to inspire an unexpected revival of patriotism and to salvage the position of the Thatcher government. Not everyone feels that the success of the Conservatives in the 1983 General Election was a good thing for the country, but only a few dispute that continuing Conservative popularity since has been in large part the result of the 'Falklands Factor'. The impact on Britain's position in Latin America was initially favourable. It was widely recognised that a Latin American country, facing a similar challenge, would have responded in a similar fashion. The direct cost of the war in money terms for Britain, though considerable, was a fraction of one year's budgetary contingency reserve. Even the long-term financial consequences of maintaining a garrison in the Falklands, now that the new Mount Pleasant airport has been opened, is insignificant in terms of Britain's other military expenditure, and particularly so compared with the costs of remaining a nuclear power.

Though Britain's economy has declined since 1979 relative to those of other major industrialised nations, it is now growing again and whole orders of magnitude separate its difficulties from the much graver ones of Argentina. The Alfonsin government has had to trim the inordinate military expenditure it inherited from the years of military rule. Though the 'Plan Austral' was a bold and imaginative attempt to correct fundamental economic weaknesses, it succumbed to political pressures and the popularity of the Alfonsin government declined steeply as more and more Argentines came to regard the economic issue as the most important one facing the country.[24]

Meanwhile the British government has from an early stage made it clear that it does not wish to intervene in such a way as to arrest or even hinder the international financial community in its efforts to stabilise the Argentine economy. Trade with Argentina had already declined to low levels before the conflict, and Mrs Thatcher, who (somewhat reluctantly, it is believed) sent a good-will message to President Alfonsin on the occasion of his election, is a believer in the free market and rightly or wrongly has not chosen to use Britain's economic leverage. For Britain, economic policy and foreign policy are traditionally separate spheres of activity.

At the same time relations with the other countries of the Southern Cone have not improved. Britain's failure to link the economic and the political spheres has had a particularly bad effect on relations with Brazil, since the problem of the debt dominates Brazil's current external horizons and has placed it on a confrontation course with the countries of the Group of Five of which Britain is a member. Britain's relations with Chile have been better, but the recurring difficulties of the free-market oriented Chilean economy since 1979 have not been much of an advertisement for Thatcherism.

For Argentina, as for Brazil and Chile, the failure of the Thatcher government to realise the importance of economic factors to them is the principal reason why relations have not improved further. Mrs Thatcher has a simple old-fashioned idea that people – and countries – who have debts should pay them, and it is her view that pervades the present British cabinet. The consequences are particularly ironic in the case of Chile, since the Thatcher government is one of the few that has much ideological sympathy for the present Chilean regime. Despite official Chilean neutrality during the Falklands conflict itself and sympathy from Chilean citizens for Britain in its struggle with Argentina, since 1982 relations have been correct rather than friendly.

As and when the much hoped-for democratisation of Chile actually comes, it is, paradoxically, quite likely to have a negative effect on relations with Britain. With the ending of the Beagle Channel dispute, there is a greater premium for Chile to have friendly relations with Argentina. Chile and Colombia, which abstained in both Organisation of American States (OAS) debates on the Falklands war, have joined the other Latin American states since the war in supporting Argentina's annual resolutions in the UN General Assembly calling for the resumption of Falklands talks. On the other hand, British arms sales to Chile remain quite significant in export terms, and the delivery to Chile in 1986 of HMS *Glamorgan* – damaged by a shore-based Exocet missile in the last days of the Falklands War – is an ironic commentary on the fickleness of military glory.

With the assistance of Brazil, British and Argentine delegates were brought to the negotiating table in Bern, Switzerland, in July 1984 to discuss the Falklands issue. Almost immediately the talks broke up in acrimony – an unhappy episode which brought little credit to anyone and represented a substantial setback for the prospects of peace. Subsequently Mrs Thatcher was obdurate. 'The Falkland Islands are British territory', she said. 'It is the wishes of the Falkland Islanders that are and will continue to be paramount'.[25]

Each side blames the other for breaking a prior agreement regarding the scope of the talks, but the real problem remains that Britain is prepared to discuss anything except sovereignty and Argentina wants to discuss sovereignty or nothing. To support its negotiating position, the Alfonsin government has not been prepared to declare the war at an end; in consequence Britain continues to maintain its garrison and patrol a 150-mile 'protection zone' around the islands. Both British and (by previous arrangement) Argentine fishing vessels could have operated within this zone, but the tragedy was that because of the military situation they did not. Instead frenetic overfishing by factory ships from Poland, the Soviet Union, Spain and Japan depleted stocks to danger point before Britain, on behalf of the islanders themselves, unilaterally proclaimed a fishery protection zone around the islands on 29 October 1986.

The Alfonsin government, therefore, has missed the first chance to solve the dispute, and it has not as yet taken advantage of its success in the Beagle Channel referendum to put its prestige on the line a second time. The islanders – with some reason – fear a new Argentine military coup, but even after the abortive Easter Week uprisings of 1987 and the Aldo Rico affair in January 1988, a coup still seems an unlikely contingency. Meanwhile in Britain the Conservatives, despite trailing badly in a three-party contest for months beforehand, did much better than expected in the election of June 1987 and obtained a renewal of their mandate (for up to five years) with a very substantial majority.

Even assuming that in 1991 or 1992 a new Labour or coalition government might be returned, would there be a change in British policy? The accepted wisdom is that a Labour government might be keener on negotiation than the present one, but this in itself offers little prospect of change. It might be well to remember that it was the upwelling of nationalist sentiment among traditional Labour voters in 1982, and Mr Foot's support for the task force, that made the recovery of the islands a practical possibility.

Argentines do not have a monopoly of patriotism, and a country that once (Britain in 1739) went to war with Spain because a Spanish captain was alleged to have cut off the ear of a Captain Robert Jenkins at Havana in 1731 is capable still of behaviour as quixotic as that of any other country, and perhaps more than most. Several commentators have noted the inconsistency that has enabled Britain to respond quite differently in each case to the problems posed by Gibraltar, Hong Kong and the Falklands. But sometimes this has its political advantages.

CONCLUSIONS

The Falklands War demonstrates that crisis prevention techniques were in themselves insufficient to ensure peace in the South Atlantic. Direct diplomatic negotiation failed because the contrasting Anglo-Argentine positions permitted nothing to negotiate about. Mediation failed once hostilities began because the Argentine Junta refused to heed the warning of the Haig Mission that Britain could not concede any more, even though the British government was at that time prepared to concede almost everything the Argentine government professed to want.[26] No other mediator commanded the confidence of both sides to the dispute. A 'cooling off' period was suggested on several occasions, but the logic of the situation meant that one elapsed anyway without leading to a satisfactory diplomatic outcome. As Britain has not been a member of the OAS, a solution could not be worked out in the regional context, and Argentina ignored UN Security Council Resolution 502 at the time and enabled Britain to ignore it subsequently. Argentine military governments have twice in the case of the Beagle Channel rejected the results of arbitration freely entered into, and as far as the Falklands are concerned not surprisingly neither side now seems confident enough of its case to put it to the test.

The attitude of the Argentine government is that the Falklands involve a colonial question, and that it is simply out of date for the islands to be governed by a power 12 000 km away. The islands themselves, it is clear, are not of great intrinsic importance to Argentina. But they are of strong negative value in foreign hands both in symbolic terms and as a fortress. As civilians, the Radicals can see the folly of the preceding military government in thinking that the issue could be solved by force, and in the process taking on a professional army with experience of many conflicts during and since the Second World War. Individually they express, as do virtually all Argentines, personal friendliness towards the UK and a sense of hurt that their position can be so misunderstood. They emphasise that the UN General Assembly wants discussion between the two countries to resolve the issue in a friendly fashion, but that talks have been blocked by the UK at every level. They further emphasise that all issues can be discussed between the two countries, including such matters as trade and the status of the kelpers, if only the question of sovereignty is included. Argentina wants sovereignty over the Falklands but they do not require it today, tomorrow, next week, or next year; it is sufficient at this stage that it should be on the agenda. Buenos Aires does not, as Britain does, see the failure of the Radical government to end the state of war between the two countries as a barrier; an example cited of negotiations between countries still formally at war with one another is that of Egypt and the UK after the joint British/French invasion of Suez in October 1956.

Some outside observers believe that the present British govern-ment should have gone further than it did in welcoming the Alfonsin government, and seeking an early Falklands settlement that would have helped stabilise democracy in Argentina. The British government believes that it did all it could and that its efforts were met with too little, too late. It does not seem to regard the stabilisation of democracy in Argentina as an important objective on its scale of values, nor does it believe that Argentine militarism has gone for good.

The decision unilaterally to declare a fisheries protection zone around the islands on 29 October 1986 was carefully calculated to end the pillage of the ocean's resources while causing as little anxiety as possible in Buenos Aires. But the decision to hold a military reinforcement exercise in the Islands in March 1988 seems to have been an initiative of the Ministry of Defence which ignored the diplomatic considerations, and was insensitively timed in the way that it ignored growing domestic military pressure on the government in Argentina.[27] Brazil's decision to support Argentina's protest about the March 1988 British military exercise and cancel the visit of a British trade delegation led by a junior Foreign Office minister, Mr Timothy Eggar, is only one measure of the growing *rapprochement* between the civilian governments of the Southern Cone and their rising irritation at what they see as Britain's continuing failure to negotiate.

The fact is that, economically, militarily and diplomatically it is recognised on both sides that a solution would be desirable. The problem is that any solution short of a complete abandonment of the islands by Britain must now necessarily involve the co-operation of other powers not merely in *ad hoc* techniques but in a long-term crisis management regime, and it is not at all clear that the other powers who would have to take on this role are in the least interested in doing so. The United States, which has most interest in the stability of the hemisphere, is particularly badly placed, as Argentines are deeply angry at what they see as US 'betrayal' over the Falklands/ Malvinas issue. Not a few Argentines believe that the United States has designs for herself in the South Atlantic, which any move to accept a role as a guarantor power would only tend to confirm in their minds.

If the Falklands War had one positive advantage, it must be that it put paid to the notion of a South Atlantic Treaty Organisation (SATO), canvassed for two decades by ultra-right-wing generals and admirals in Argentina, Uruguay and Brazil. It cannot be too strongly emphasised that before and since 1982 a prime assumption of British defence policy has been that Britain has no significant defence commitments outside Europe and the North Atlantic area. The sole reason for Britain remaining in the area is its commitment to defend the Falkland Islands against Argentina.[28] Yet the failure of both Argentina and Britain to achieve a satisfactory diplomatic resolution of the situation requires that some outside agency be involved to guarantee the security interests involved. Had the Falklands been in a part of the world where they formed part of a balance of power, like Belize, then the logic of the situation might have imposed itself, but, as it is, a positive effort seems essential.

Geography has placed the islands closed to Argentina and given her a legitimate interest in the security of the islands; history, unfortunately, gives a very uncertain response to the question of who really has the traditional rights of sovereignty. This being the case, self-determination should, on all recent legal precedent, be exercised by the people themselves in accordance with the normal standards of the twentieth century.

The one solution which has always been excluded from consideration is the most obvious one: that the islands should become independent. This follows directly from application of the principle of self-determination for the kelpers and obstacles to other proposed solutions. In a world which has given us the tiny UN member states of Nauru and Kiribati in the Pacific, there is in practice no minimum population for exercising the right to self-determination. By implication, therefore, the capacity for self-defence is not a requirement for statehood – an idea easier to accept in a Europe which still retains historic ministates such as Liechtenstein, Monaco and San Marino. For the Falklands this could lead to what has been termed 'the Aaland Islands solution'.[29] The islanders should be permitted to exercise their right of self-determination to choose either independence or annexation to Argentina. If they choose annexation, it is improbable that Britain would raise the slightest objection. If they choose independence, it could be under a regime guaranteed by American states, probably Brazil, Canada, Peru and the United States, which have had some responsibility for maintaining the peace between Peru and Ecuador since 1942. A condition of either choice should be the complete demilitarisation of the islands; a situation to which certainly Britain would raise no objection.

Despite wild speculation and eccentric claims over the years, the islands now have no great strategic significance except to Argentina, and for training purposes Britain has more than enough bogland in the north of Scotland. Even in the short term, Britain stands to gain more from the normalisation of her relations with the countries of the Southern Cone.

This solution of independence for the Falklands still appears in Argentine eyes to be unthinkable. Since 1983 there has been a significant reorientation of Argentine attention towards the South Atlantic and (in anticipation of 1991) Antarctica. The terms in which President Alfonsin proposed the move of the national capital to Viedma-Carmen de Patagones included a geopolitical element; it was in that southerly direction, he said, that Argentina would find her true destiny. The turn to the south does, of course, take Argentina away from most possible causes of confrontation with Brazil, unless in turn (as some Argentine geopoliticians fear[30]) Brazil should now advance a claim to the Antarctic on its own behalf, using some justification combining historic Portuguese voyages and the doctrine of continental projection. Until and unless that happens, it is Britain and Britain alone that blocks realisation of Argentina's territorial destiny.

Notes

Research for this chapter was carried out as part of the University of Southampton project on 'North/South Security Relations' funded by the Ford Foundation, whose support is gratefully acknowledged.

1. Cf. Sir Ernest Satow, *A Guide to Diplomatic Practice* (London: Longmans, 1957).
2. On the pragmatism of British foreign policy, see Joseph Frankel, *British Foreign Policy, 1945–75* (London: Oxford University Press for Royal Institute of International Affairs, 1975), pp. 112–17.
3. See Carlos Escude, *La Argentina vs. las Grandes Potencias*: *El precio del desafio* (Buenos Aires: Editorial de Belgrano, 1986), pp. 19–20.
4. Argentina. Comision Nacional del Antartico, *Soberania Argentina en la Antartida* (Buenos Aires: Ministerio de Relaciones Exteriores y Culto, 1948).
5. See *inter alia* Peter Calvert, 'Sovereignty and the Falklands Crisis', *International Affairs*, Vol. 59, No. 3 (Summer 1983), pp. 405–13; Peter J. Beck, 'The Anglo-Argentine Dispute over Title to the Falkland Islands: Changing British Perceptions on Sovereignty since 1910', *Millennium: Journal of International Studies*, Vol. 12, No. 1 (Spring 1983), pp. 6–24; Jeffrey D. Myhre, 'Title to the Falklands-Malvinas under International Law', ibid., pp. 25–38; Laurio H. Destefani, *The Malvinas, the South Georgias and the South Sandwich Islands, the conflict with Britain* (Buenos Aires: Edipress, 1982); Enrique Ferrer Vieyra, *Las Islas Malvinas y el Derecho Internacional* (Buenos Aires: Ediciones Depalma, 1984).

6. *The Annual Register 1948*, pp. 3, 353.
7. *The Times*, 19 January 1949.
8. *The Annual Register, 1955*, p. 144.
9. *BOLSA Fortnightly Review*, 30 March 1957, p. 235.
10. *The Times*, 17 December 1965.
11. Juan Archibaldo Lanus, *De Chapultepec al Beagle: Politica Exterior Argentina: 1945–1980* (Buenos Aires: EMECE Editores, 1984), pp. 459ff.
12. Martin Walker. 'The Give-Away Years', *Guardian Weekend*, 19 June 1982.
13. *The Times*, 22 and 25 November 1969.
14. Lanus, *De Chapultepec al Beagle*, pp. 508–9.
15. E.W. Hunter Christie, *Report* (London: Falkland Islands Committee, 1975).
16. *Economic Survey of the Falkland Islands* (London: HMSO, 1976).
17. Colin Phipps, *What Future for the Falklands?* (London: Fabian Society, July 1977).
18. *The Times*, 5 April 1982.
19. United Nations. Government. *Falkland Islands Review: Report of a Committee of Privy Counsellors*; *Chairman: The Rt Hon The Lord Franks, OM, GCMG, KCB, CBE*, Cmnd 8787 (London: HMSO, January 1983) p. 22.
20. At the time of writing in 1988, he is in charge of the government's unpopular attempt to substitute rates, a traditional form of graduated property tax to finance local government, with a flat-rate 'poll tax'.
21. Walker; *The Times*, 27 February 1981.
22. *The United Kingdom Defence Programme: The Way Forward*, Cmnd 8288 (London: HMSO, 1981); *The Economist*, 25 July 1981, p. 55 and 5 December 1981, p. 74.
23. *Daily Telegraph*, 16 June 1982; *The Times*, 23 June 1982, cited in Peter Calvert, *The Falklands Crisis: The Rights and the Wrongs* (London: Frances Pinter and New York: St Martin's Press, 1982) p. 143.
24. *The Annual Register 1985*, p. 73; cf. 'La imagen de Alfonsin', *Somos*, Vol. 11, No. 589 (6 January 1988), p. 12.
25. *The Annual Register 1984*, p. 46.
26. See Alexander M. Haig, Jr, *Caveat: Realism, Reagan, and Foreign Policy* (London: Weidenfeld & Nicolson, 1984).
27. *The Sunday Times*, 7 March 1988.
28. *The Daily Telegraph*, 5 March 1988.
29. 'Practical steps towards the resolution of the Falklands/Malvinas dispute', in Wayne H. Smith (ed.), *The Falklands/Malvinas Dispute: a Conference Report*, (Washington, DC: Argentine Studies Program, School of Advanced International Studies, The Johns Hopkins University, Occasional Paper No. 1, May 1985). For a discussion of plebiscites, see Lawrence J. Farley, *Plebiscites and Sovereignty: The Crisis of Political Illegitimacy* (Boulder, Colorado and London: Mansell, 1986).
30. For background to such fears, see Paulo Schilling, *El Expansionismo Brasileno* (Buenos Aires: El Cid Editor, 1978).

5 Argentina and the Soviet Union: International Relations in Three Stages
Ruben de Hoyos

How can the relations between Argentina and the Soviet Union, particularly since the end of the Second World War, be explained? The two countries are not only geographically at the antipodes, but ideologically they are antagonistic as well. History teaches that the great powers' geopolitical impact has a way of reaching the most distant beaches. The Southern Cone in the past was shaped by the ebb and flow of empires (Spanish, Portuguese, French, Dutch, British), and is being especially influenced now by today's great powers – the United States, United Kingdom, Soviet Union.

Relations between Argentina and the United States have been aptly described as perplexing, and those between Argentina and the United Kingdom as confusing, but relations between the Argentine Republic and the Soviet Union generally have been 'discreet'. For the Argentine military juntas, the attitude of President Carter of the United States can be classified as perplexing. At the time when the juntas were allegedly 'erasing the danger of the Marxist scourge from Argentina', they also were being condemned by the United States as violators of human rights. For North Americans, the behaviour of anti-communist Argentina, in not joining the US grain embargo against the Soviet Union in punishment for the deployment of Soviet troops in Afghanistan, was just as perplexing. Argentina's tendency to try to exercise an independent, competitive regional leadership also has been a recurrent irritation to the United States and Great Britain. While most Argentines have considered Argentina as forming part of Western (and Christian) civilisation confronting an atheistic Soviet Union, they have found themselves more than once opposed by their friends and supported discreetly but publicly by the 'enemy', as during the South–West Atlantic War (April–June 1982). The initiative on nuclear disarmament and international security by the Group of Six (of which Argentina is a member) was considered

59

by the Reagan administration as a nuisance while Gorbachev praised it as a 'responsible stance'.[1]

In 1972 Stephen Clissold[2] already recognised the increasing sophistication of Soviet foreign policy-makers, as manifested by their 'more discreet' links with local Communist parties in Latin America and elsewhere. Since the 1950s, Soviet foreign policy toward Latin America has been limited to indirect challenge to US hegemony in the region. The 1962 Cuban missile crisis, if not a personal mistake by Khrushchev, was more the exception than the rule. When Gorbachev wrote about Latin America in his book, *Perestroika*, he devoted nearly half of his exposition to identifying Soviet interests with the legitimate claims of Latin Americans, and the other half to reassuring the United States that 'we do not seek any advantage in Latin America. . . . We are not going to exploit anti-US attitudes . . . nor do we intend to erode the traditional links between Latin America and the United States'.[3]

Aldo Cesar Vacs published an excellent review of the relations between Argentina and the USSR since 1917, which he quite properly entitled *Discreet Partners*.[4] The word 'discreet' has come to epitomise the relations between the Argentina Republic and the Soviet Union, encompassing as it does 'prudence', 'circumspection', and 'judiciousness'. 'Discretion' also implies the ability to discern, to prudently separate the parts in order to deal with them. In this regard the word may be used to describe three successive, if overlapping, stages of relations between Argentina and the Soviet Union: (1) the diplomatic stage, which culminated in 1946 with mutual recognition; (2) the stage of commercial and technical co-operation which during the 1970s and the 1980s showed its most robust development so far; and, finally, (3) a third stage of military co-operation may be projected. These are not three different sets of foreign policies, but the same policy (Argentine or Soviet) conducted at different levels, under diverse circumstances and discreetly.

1. DIPLOMATIC STAGE IN ARGENTINE–SOVIET RELATIONS

This first stage in Argentine–Soviet relations (1917–1946) is called 'diplomatic' because it encompasses two key episodes of recognition involving Argentina and the Soviet Union.[5] The Soviet Union was opposed to the admission of Argentina to the United Nations, while a reluctant United States finally engineered Argentine membership as a means of consolidating the Latin American voting bloc inside the UN (1945–6). Argentina and the Soviet Union then recognised each other at the beginning of the Cold War (1946), despite the displeasure of the United States.

At the San Francisco Conference in April 1945, the Soviets forcefully opposed Argentina's admission to the United Nations on the basis of her 'pro-Fascist neutrality during the war'. While there was some truth to this Soviet allegation, the Argentines had fulfilled the demands of Chapultepec (3 March 1945) by declaring war on the Axis (27 March 1945) and were consequently received back into the hemispheric community. There were still those in the US government afraid of 'losing moral credibility' with the Russians if Argentina were admitted to the hemispheric community. Nelson Rockefeller, at that time US Assistant Secretary of State, was aware that the rest of Latin America would have been opposed or reluctant to get involved in any alliance with the United States (presumably to stop none other than the Soviets) were Argentina denied admission. Rockefeller was responsible for the compromise solution, related in part to a US promise to the Soviet Union at Yalta, allowing Argentine membership in the United Nations. (At Yalta, the United States had promised Stalin separate membership in the United Nations for two of the Soviet republics – Byelorussia and the Ukraine – and for Poland.) A trade-off involved admission of the two Soviet republics and Poland along with Argentina.

It could be said that the anti-Argentine disposition of the Soviets predated even the Second World War. At the beginning of the Bolshevik Revolution, the Argentine consul, J. Navellian, was imprisoned and maltreated for two years (1918–20). For her part, Argentina denied recognition to the new Soviet government while obstinately continuing to recognise the representative of the former Russian Imperial government.[6] While the Soviets did search with notable persistence for a bilateral *rapprochement* from the mid-1920s on, Argentine governments constantly refused to consider this. The official Argentine public explanation was the impossibility of recognising a government which had not respected the Argentine legation.[7] It is ironic that since 1973 – among other reasons – the maltreatment of Soviet diplomats during the anti-Allende coup in Chile has been given as one of the decisive reasons for the breaking of relations between the Soviets and Pinochet's administration.

These three decades of diplomatic impasse (1917–1946) were fuelled on both sides by the perception of the other. The Argentines were repelled by the physical elimination of the Russian Imperial family. The Soviets regarded the events of the 'tragic week' in Argentina (1919) as directed against Russians resident in that country, where some of them had achieved positions of leadership in labour movements. The Argentines regarded with suspicion the connection that was believed to exist between Moscow and every Communist Party around the world and, specifically, in Argentina.

In 1927 the Argentine government, without changing its policy of non-recognition, did allow a Soviet enterprise to promote trade with Argentina (the *Iuzhamtorg*), only to close it down in 1931 on the pretext that it was acting as an unauthorised consulate. Since a well established and mutual hostility was the public norm, the Argentine government requested the expulsion of the Soviet Union from the League of Nations when the former invaded Finland (December 1939).

In domestic Argentine politics, the Radical Party depicted the lack of diplomatic (and trade) contacts with the Soviet Union as a result of the pressure of US and British interests operating against the national benefit through the members of the Conservative Party.[8] The latter responded that the two main lawyers representing the interests of the Soviet Union were members of the Radical Party, which was accused of being soft on Communism.

While at the beginning of the Second World War diplomatic relations between both countries were non-existent, in the rest of Latin America, at US urging because of its wartime alliance with the Soviet Union, a wave of diplomatic recognition of the USSR occurred. The following Latin American states either established or reestablished relations with the Soviet Union during the war: Cuba (15 October 1942); Mexico (12 November 1942, reestablished relations); Colombia (3 February 1943, reestablished relations); Uruguay (18 July 1943, reestablished relations); Costa Rica (10 May 1944); Chile (11 December 1944); and Brazil (2 April 1945). The three Latin American states that reestablished relations with the Soviets at the time had previously broken relations because of alleged interference by Moscow in their domestic politics.

With the two military surprise attacks of 1941, that of Germany on the Soviet Union (22 June) and that of Japan on the United States (8 December), the Soviet Union and the United States became allies. By the end of the war, US military lend-lease aid had allocated a total of $50 billion, of which $11 billion went to the Soviet Union. A symbolic result of Soviet association with the United States during the war was to give the Soviet Union a new respectability via Latin American diplomatic recognition. Against the new mood and following her traditional independent foreign policy, Argentina abstained.

In 1945, with victory over their common enemies nearing, the US-USSR alliance of convenience started to fade, and the so-called Cold War began to emerge and pit them as rivals. This fundamental shift in international relations made an impact on Argentina.

After winning the election of February 1946, Juan D. Peron assumed the presidency on 4 June. Exactly two days later, in one of the first foreign policy acts of the Peron administration, Argentina established diplomatic relations with the Soviet Union.[9] Since then, Argentine–Soviet relations have survived and prospered under the most divergent circumstances – under *de facto* as well as constitutional governments, in peace and in war (that of the South-West Atlantic). The Soviet Union has become, if not an ally, at least a partner. A case in point is the sympathetic Soviet support of Argentina's requests in the United Nations for Britain to negotiate her differences with Argentina and to stop the militarisation of the Malvinas/ Falkland Islands – the Fortress Falklands policy being Mrs Thatcher's immediate solution.

The Soviets none the less long failed to appreciate properly Argentine resistance to external dictation of her policies, precisely by or for the convenience of those great powers – the United Kingdom, and the United States – which have been considered, rightly or wrongly, not only in nationalist sectors but in public opinion at large, as responsible for causing national problems. While possibly most Argentines during the Second World War would not have liked a decisive Nazi victory, many of them enjoyed a vicarious satisfaction at seeing the British Empire – of which they felt themselves to be a reluctant loyal colony – wavering. Lenin had portrayed Argentina as the model of a nation that, while having acquired legal independence, was practically an economic colony of the British.[10]

As soon as mutual recognition was announced in 1946 in Buenos Aires and Moscow, Washington reflected the fears of the US ambassador to Argentina, Spruille Braden.[11] Peron, who until that point had been perceived as a Nazi, was now labelled a Communist. Peron's political concern for social justice and his mobilisation of the workers and labour unions were regarded in official US circles as precursors of more radical measures. But while Peron had recognised the Soviet Union, he was still throwing Argentine communists into gaol.

Both great powers, the United States and the Soviet Union, seem at that time to have been unable to recognise the demands of lesser powers' diplomatic goals, which in the case of Argentina were ambitious. In the 1950s, John Foster Dulles moved around the world preaching to the Nehrus, to the Sukarnos and others that 'neutrality was immoral'. Moscow sent a similar message to Tito.

From 1946 on, established diplomatic relations between Argentina and the Soviet Union provided a base for further growth of bilateral ties, increasingly on trade matters and to some extent political co-operation. This diplomatic gambit, even if motivated initially as a political affirmation of independence by President Peron, was to develop in time into a multi-billion exchange of trade.

2. THE STAGE OF COMMERCIAL AND TECHNICAL CO-OPERATION IN ARGENTINE–SOVIET RELATIONS

While trade between the two countries predated diplomatic recognition of 1946, it would not achieve substantial value for several decades. Trade started long before ambassadors were exchanged, during a time when Argentina systematically refused to consider recognition despite renewed efforts by the Soviets. In 1922 Moscow sent a commercial representative to Buenos Aires to explore the purchase of grain. Two years later, the Soviet government tried to open an Argentine branch of an enterprise that it had in London for the same purpose and the Argentine Secretary of Agriculture travelled to Moscow with an identical aim. In 1927 the Soviet trade promotion enterprise, *Iuzhamtorg*, was installed in Buenos Aires. Within only eight years (1923–30), Soviet imports from Argentina rose from 4.7 to 61 million roubles (Figure 5.1). Pragmatism was therefore to be a basic characteristic of bilateral relations from the very start.

Even after diplomatic recognition in 1946, trade only grew slowly. In 1970 Soviet exports to Latin America amounted still to only 6.7 million dollars (1.9 to Argentina) and imports from Latin America in that year amounted to 78.8 million dollars (31.3 million from Argentina). It is only around 1975 that bilateral trade began to expand dramatically (Figure 5.2).

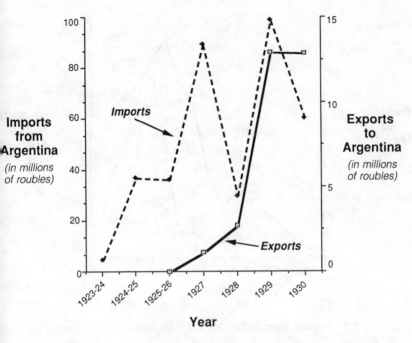

Figure 5.1   Soviet trade with Argentina 1923–1930

Source: Derived from Aldo C. Vacs, *Discreet Partners: Argentina and the USSR since 1917* (Pittsburgh, PA: University of Pittsburgh Press, 1984), p. 4.

With the return of Peron to government, the Campora adminis-tration did grant a $1.2 billion credit to Cuba despite initial US opposition, but when Peron started his presidential term he surprised his critics by adopting a mellowed attitude, including a desire to maintain good relations with both the United States and the Soviet Union. In May 1974, he dispatched a 200-strong contingent of businessmen and officials to the Socialist world after having arranged in Moscow for credits, which included the hydroelectric project at Salto Grande. Large sales of grain to the Soviet Union were arranged at the same time.

Figure 5.3 shows the comparative trade figures for 1970–84. The Third World does not bulk large in Soviet trade and, within this group, Latin America is most important for its exports to the Soviet Union. Argentine exports to the Soviet Union are especially large in this context, representing 65 per cent of all Latin American exports

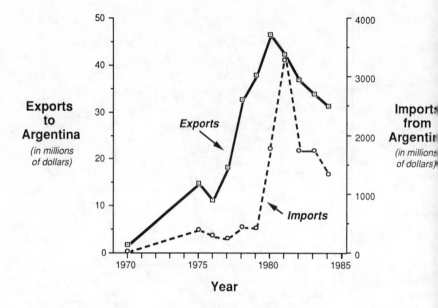

Figure 5.2   Imports from Argentina to USSR and exports to Argentina from USSR, 1970–84

Source: Derived from *Le Courier des Pays de l'East*, No. 299 (October, 1985).

to the Soviet Union. From the middle of the 1970s, the Soviet Union became one of Argentina's most important clients, thereby diluting the dominant place once occupied by Great Britain and later by the United States.

The Soviet Union also became Argentina's partner in technical ventures. Very favourable Soviet financial conditions helped finalise the first international hydroelectric dam in Latin America between Argentina and Uruguay (1 800 000 kW and $2 billion cost). The Soviets offered a loan of $50 million for the acquisition of 14 turbo-groups, to be repaid over 15 years at an interest rate of 4 per cent. Payment was to begin only when each turbine was in operation and could be rendered in the national products of Argentina and Uruguay. Moreover, these products were to be shipped to the Soviet Union in Argentine or Uruguayan bottoms. Definitive approval of these terms was granted by President Peron on 26 November 1973 after person-ally overcoming the Uruguayan government's reluctance to do busi-

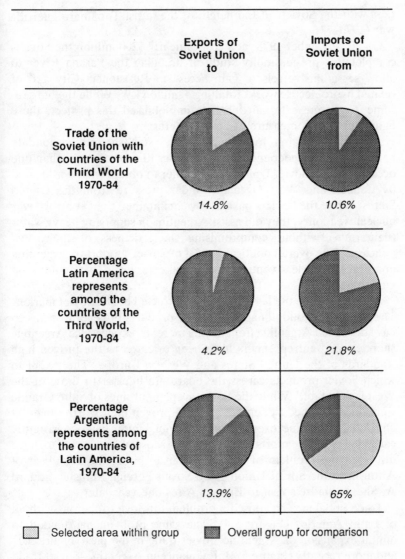

	Exports of Soviet Union to	Imports of Soviet Union from
Trade of the Soviet Union with countries of the Third World 1970-84	14.8%	10.6%
Percentage Latin America represents among the countries of the Third World, 1970-84	4.2%	21.8%
Percentage Argentina represents among the countries of Latin America, 1970-84	13.9%	65%

☐ Selected area within group ■ Overall group for comparison

Figure 5.3   Comparative trade – USSR, Third World, Latin America and Argentina

Source: Figure 5.2 of this chapter. Cuba is not included.

ness with the Soviets at the height of the leftist Tupamaro guerrilla war (1970–72).

On 20 November 1978, at a cost of nearly $200 million the Soviets completed a pre-feasibility study of dredging the Parana River to allow sea-going vessels to gain access to Resistencia City and of related hydroelectric works totalling 4 million kW. While the burdensome Argentine external debt has immobilised this project, these figures provide a measure of Soviet interest.

Argentina's search for two ways to establish and consolidate national nuclear independence has led her to turn on more than one occasion to the Soviet Union as a supplier to obtain what was denied by Canada and West Germany under pressure from the United States. While the Soviets have always maintained tight controls over nuclear weaponry, they did assist Argentina in supplying heavy water (deuterium) without compromising the strictness of their own policies.[12] The overall political impact of Soviet support to Argentina in a peaceful nuclear venture was to make her less dependent on the United States.

Argentina none the less failed to be attracted by the Soviet market. The allegedly shoddy quality of Soviet products in general seems to have dissuaded Argentina from buying more, especially since Argentine shoppers and entrepreneurs have been oriented to the proven high standards of the United States and Western Europe. The extent to which Soviet products across the board are inferior to those of the West is debatable. While the Soviet Kaplan turbines of Salto Grande were once defamed by some, they have proven their worth since. At any rate, Argentine exports to the Soviet Union have consistently exceeded Soviet exports to Argentina. Moscow is known to have discussed the problem of trade imbalance during the 1986 visit of Alfonsin to the Soviet Union[13] and Soviet Foreign Minister Eduard A. Shevardnadze's visit to Buenos Aires one year later.

Trade imbalance has posed a problem for Soviet relations with all of Latin America (Figure 5.4). The same problem has tended to inhibit expansion of Argentine–Soviet trade in the past (Figure 5.1) and more recently (Figure 5.2). Imbalance in Argentine–Soviet trade has been of particular concern to Moscow, since Argentine exports have constituted such a large percentage of overall Latin American exports to the Soviet Union. Moscow has been able to tolerate the trade imbalance with the region in general and Argentina in particular, since expansion of imports to the Soviet Union has been paralleled by some growth, although much more modest, of Soviet exports

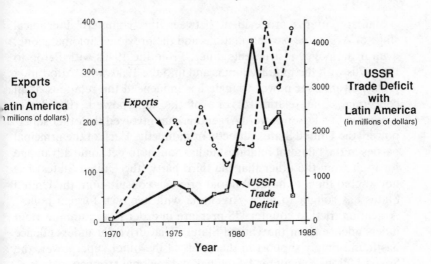

Figure 5.4   Exports to Latin America from USSR and USSR trade deficit with Latin America, 1970–84

Source: Table 5.2 of this chapter. Cuba is not included.

there. In Moscow's eyes, political objectives also may justify the burden of a chronic trade imbalance, whether through providing a beachhead into new markets or for the sake of diplomatic benefits.

Recent trade figures with both Latin America and Argentina none the less suggest that there are limits to Moscow's willingness to continue shouldering a trade imbalance weighted heavily to its disadvantage. Unless the Soviet Union can sell substantially more goods to Latin America and Argentina, it does not appear likely that Moscow will encourage sustained growth in imports from these areas.

The decline in Argentine exports to the Soviet Union during the early 1980s continued in 1985 ($1213 million), 1986 ($209 million) and 1987 ($537 million for January/September only).[14] This gradual deterioration of trade prompted the first visit of an Argentine president to Moscow in October 1986. However, it has been difficult to compete against the relatively low grain prices of the United States as it has sought to recoup lost markets, including the Soviet market. In any event, the Soviets, while reducing their purchases from Argentina, were not likely to allow this source of food and political independence to fade. With the severe US drought in 1988, market forces also may promote Argentine agricultural exports.

Similar patterns are evident between this commercial/technical stage of Argentine–Soviet relations and the previous diplomatic one, even if the policy instruments differ. From the 1940s with Peron to the 1970s with the military juntas and into the 1980s with Alfonsin, a great power/lesser power triangle has influenced the relations of all concerned. The relation of one of the superpowers (the Soviet Union) with a lesser power (Argentina) has involved the other super-power (the United States) directly or indirectly. Each of the principal parties in the bilateral relationship has sought to get some advantage for itself from the other that the third party (the United States) has not wanted them to have. Without previous consultation, the United States has sought to align Argentina with her own foreign policy. Argentina tried to counter US pressure in order to acquire a certain independence from the United States. That drive for independence has found timely support in the needs of the other superpower, the Soviet Union, to counter US global and regional strategy.

From the inception of the Cold War after the demise of the Grand Alliance, the United States did not want the Soviets to enjoy the type of international legitimacy that diplomatic recognition confers among the states of the world, and less so in her own hemisphere of influence. Containment was something more than a *cordon sanitaire*; it was also a statement of territoriality and leadership. By defying US norms in recognising the Soviet Union, Peron's Argentina aimed to stress her own traditional, independent foreign policy while benefit-ing from the domestic populist impact of the measure. By being diplomatically and commercially flexible and compliant, the Soviets were able to counter the negative attitude of the United States while challenging the latter's regional hegemony.

Growth in Argentine–Soviet trade in the second stage added a material dimension to the symbolic recognition of the first stage. By the second stage, the Soviet Union in part was able to elude the strictures of the US grain embargo – imposed by President Carter by way of a sanction for the Soviet invasion of Afghanistan – through a burgeoning trade with Argentina. Argentina consolidated her inde-pendent foreign policy in face of the pressure exercised by President Carter's envoys to join the grain embargo (February 1980). Argentine grain sales to the Soviet Union also helped compensate for falling grain exports to the countries of the European Community, its usual trading partners.

A convergence of Argentine and Soviet interests has sustained the relationship, even though deep ideological differences persist. Despite anti-communist rhetoric and Cold War commitments expressed by all postwar administrations and endorsed fully by public opinion, Argentina has adopted a highly pragmatic policy towards the Soviet Union.

Reinforcing the convergence of Argentine–Soviet interests, the commercial relationship has become institutionalised. Strong linkages between Buenos Aires and Moscow did not come about simply by accident of the US grain embargo or the Carter campaign for human rights against the Argentine military juntas or US support for Great Britain during the 1982 Malvinas/Falklands war. There was also an ongoing process of solid institutionalisation of Argentine–Soviet relations, which resulted (1) at the political level, in the adoption of the 'Third Position'; (2) at the bureaucratic level, in the setting up of the Argentine–Soviet Commission (May 1974); and (3) at the technical level, in the signing of four bilateral agreements in 1974. These four technical agreements were on Development of Trade, Economic, Scientific, and Technical Cooperation; Shipment of Machines and Equipment from the USSR to Argentina; Scientific and Technical Cooperation; and Navigation.[15]

3. A POSSIBLE MILITARY STAGE IN ARGENTINE–SOVIET RELATIONS?

It is only possible to speculate about a coming military phase in Argentine–Soviet relations. To speculate is to imagine. Only those who can envisage their future can ever be in a position to shape it. The ability to imagine the uses of political recognition (first stage) terminated an impasse that had lasted three decades between Argentina and the Soviet Union. The ability (and the need) to visualise markets other than the traditional European ones was the trigger that finally turned the Soviets into a leading client of Argentina (second stage). Given favourable conditions, a new military dimension might emerge. Among other measures, potential Soviet arms sales and involvement in the Argentine arms industry could complement and perhaps even help intensify ongoing commercial relations.

The plausibility of Argentine–Soviet military co-operation first presented itself in a stark manner during the South-West Atlantic war (April–June 1982). Regardless of which party was ultimately responsible for the military conflict in the Malvinas/Falkland Islands – the obstinacy of General Galtieri or the obduracy of Mrs Thatcher – the outcome of the war cannot be a matter of indifference to either Argentina or the Soviet Union. The Fortress Falklands policy has tended to militarise the South-West Atlantic, impacting directly on both Argentina and the Soviet Union. Not only has Argentina been confronted with a British fortress erected on the disputed islands, but also Britain has not been willing to negotiate with the democratic, moderate Alfonsin government. The Soviet Union cannot ignore the various implications of the flow of North Atlantic Treaty Organisation (NATO) forces to the South Atlantic. For example, one-third of the British nuclear submarine fleet is on average around or on its way to or from the islands.[16] Month-long British military manoeuvres in the area (March 1988), called Fire Focus, have added to existing tension.[17]

Military relations come in all types. There are those bonded publicly, like the ones that form NATO or the Warsaw Pact. There are some very close ones between a superpower and a developing country, such as between South Korea and the United States or Cuba and the Soviet Union. The military relationship between the Soviet Union and Nicaragua is at a lower level. Moscow would not go to extremes for the survival of Sandinismo, while it might do so in the Cuban case. The military relationship between the Soviets and Peru is open to various interpretations.[18]

If a military stage should ever crystallise between Argentina and the Soviet Union, it almost surely would be *sui generis*. Like the other, previous stages in both nations' dealings, this one, if it ever materialises, would have to be handled with utter discreetness, if undesirable consequences are to be avoided.

The development of Argentine–Soviet military relations is likely to be determined by three factors: (1) possible changes in Argentina's domestic and international policies; (2) Argentina's potential military needs; and (3) the willingness of the Soviet Union to co-operate.

The Potential for Change in Argentine Policies

At the time of the 1982 South-West Atlantic war, the primary obstacle to an initiation of military ties with the Soviet Union seems to have been the Argentine military junta, which displayed a hesitance to link itself militarily to the Soviets. Rumours circulated in Buenos Aires at the time about alleged Soviet pressures on Argentina to do so, which included an alleged Soviet threat to refuse to take two million tons of grain. The substance of these rumours has been difficult to verify, although the refusal of the Argentine military junta to accept Soviet military aid is on record.

It would appear that members of the junta speculated that the veto power of the Soviet Union at the United Nations Security Council could be relied on to avoid official condemnation after the Argentine landing in the Malvinas/Falkland Islands on 2 April 1982. A request to this effect was made informally within the ambit of the Security Council, but Soviet diplomats excused themselves on technical grounds from obliging (time differences with Moscow, etc.).[19] This Argentine request may be seen as an attempt to put a budding diplomatic relationship to good political use, while forgetting that diplomatic favours must spring from reciprocity.

Contradictory interpretations have been advanced about the refusal of the Argentine junta to accept Soviet military aid. Ideological reluctance of certain officers to associate militarily with the leading Communist power has been offered as the key explanation. For others, the Argentine refusal was a signal to the British and the United States of the country's conciliatory mood and disposition to negotiate an agreement. In any event, in the first days of May 1982, with President Reagan's informal but forceful association with the British war effort, Soviet military aid to Argentina could have caused a confrontation between the two superpowers.

The subsequent civilian Alfonsin administration has been another restricting factor on the development of military ties with the Soviet Union. The new administration rapidly defused the explosive situation with Chile over the Beagle Channel. Alfonsin also used major regional and global fora to obtain endorsements for a negotiated solution with the United Kingdom over the Malvinas/Falklands issue. Even the Reagan administration supported this effort. Cuts in military spending were made as well. In sum, political rather than military solutions were sought.

These restrictive walls against the widening of an Argentine–Soviet military link may collapse. Argentine efforts to negotiate a solution to the Malvinas/Falklands situation have come to nothing, while a multi-million dollar British technical fortress has been built on territory claimed as Argentine. A return to an Argentine confrontational policy *vis-à-vis* the United Kingdom would no doubt include both a more direct political role for the armed forces and greater willingness to accept Soviet military aid.

Argentina's Military Needs

Ironically, the only war that Argentina has fought in a hundred years was fought against the United Kingdom with weapons acquired in part from that same country. In the event of another round of armed confrontation over the Malvinas/Falkland Islands, Argentina would require new sources and types of weaponry. As for sources of weaponry, Argentina suffered from an arms embargo by major Western suppliers during the 1982 Malvinas/Falklands war. As for sophisticated weaponry, at an early stage in the 1982 hostilities the Thatcher administration dispatched a nuclear submarine to the South Atlantic as a deterrent. A nuclear submarine was responsible for sinking the ARA *Belgrano*, which this author considers to have been the South-West Atlantic war's point of no return.[20]

The Alfonsin administration shelved repeated demands from the armed forces for an Argentine nuclear submarine for at least three reasons – budgetary constraints, concern about unnecessarily militarising the South-West Atlantic situation and civilian control of policy. Another Argentine administration might elect to acquire or build a nuclear submarine as one way of affirming Argentine rights in the area. Options would include buying or leasing one from the Soviets. On previous occasions that would have been the way in which other ships for the Argentine navy were acquired from the United States and the United Kingdom.

The Indian navy is presently leasing a nuclear submarine from the Soviet Union. From Nehru and Peron onwards, India and Argentina have always followed parallel lines in search of independent foreign policies. More recently, both countries have developed close relations with the Soviet Union. From this perspective, the emergence of the Soviet Union as a supplier of sophisticated weaponry to Argentina would constitute a logical outgrowth of existing relations.

Possible Willingness of the Soviet Union for Military Co-operation

Assuming Argentine willingness, the Soviet Union might have several reasons for providing Argentina with significant weaponry. The opening of a military market for Soviet products to Argentina might be welcomed since the trade balance has been so unfavourable to Moscow. The emerging US–USSR accommodation of the late 1980s may serve as a brake on such a Soviet policy. However, the Fortress Falklands policy of Britain has affected geopolitically not only

Argentina, but the Soviets as well, who are forced to monitor this new military presence of a Western great power in the South-West Atlantic. A Soviet policy of supplying sophisticated arms to Argentina could be compatible with a non-provocative Soviet posture in support of Argentina including the Malvinas/Falklands dispute. In a recent study, Soviet Latin Americanists emphasised that most of the world looks upon the Soviet Union, with respect to the Malvinas/Falklands dispute, as being on the side of the weak in another 'shameful episode of an ongoing neocolonial war'.[21]

One lesson learned by Argentina and other Latin American countries from the South-West Atlantic war was the danger of depending exclusively on US and/or West European military sources for survival. The war gave a boost to Latin American arms industries, of which Argentina and Brazil have been the leaders. Foreign participation can still be important for national arms production. India's simultaneous production of Soviet and US fighters could be a pattern to be followed by Argentines and Brazilians. If presented with this opportunity, the Soviets might very well oblige. Significant involvement in the military industries of countries with the capabilities and foreign policy aspirations of Argentina, Brazil and India would be tantamount to recognising their claim for independent international action. One advantage possessed by the Soviet Union over the United States is that it may give encouragement to regional powers on a selective basis. As a superpower in dealing with its 'less powerful clients', the United States seems to have been more inflexible than the Soviet Union.[22]

Notes

1. Mikhail S. Gorbachev, *Perestroika, New Thinking for Our Country and the World* (New York: Harper & Row, 1988) p. 188.
2. Stephen Clissold, *Latin America: New World, Third World* (London: Praeger, 1972), pp. 342–3.
3. Gorbachev, *Perestroika*, p. 188.
4. Aldo Cesar Vacs, *Discreet Partners: Argentina and the USSR since 1917* (Pittsburgh, PA: University of Pittsburgh Press, 1984).
5. David Green, *The Containment of Latin America, A History of the Myths and Realities of the Good Neighbor Policy* (Chicago: Quadrangle Books, 1971); Mario Rapoport, 'Las Relaciones Argentino-Sovieticas, Comercio y Politica entre la Argentina y la URSS', *Todo es Historia*

(Buenos Aires), Vol. XVII, Number 207 (July 1984) 8–32 and Vol. XVII, Number 208 (1984) 78–95.

6. Vacs, *Discreet Partners*, p. 3.
7. Rapoport, 'Las Relaciones Argentino-Sovieticas', July 1984, pp. 9–14.
8. Vacs, *Discreet Partners*, p. 8.
9. Stephen Clissold (ed.), *Soviet Relations with Latin America, 1918–1968, A Documentary Survey* (London: Oxford University Press, 1970) p. 174. See this source for the 6 June 1946 communique on the establishment of Soviet relations with the Peron regime.
10. V.I. Lenin, *Imperialism: The Highest Stage of Capitalism* (Moscow: Institute of Marxism-Leninism, Collected Works, Vol XXVII) p. 383.
11. Green, *The Containment of Latin America*, p. 245.
12. Vacs, *Discreet Partners*, p. 90.
13. 'Argentina, Foreign Relations, USSR Disappoints Alfonsin on Grain', *Latin American Weekly Report*, WR 86–42 (30 October 1986).
14. Instituto Nacional de Estadistica y Censo de la Republica Argentina (April 1988).
15. Edward Warzala, *The Politics of Rapprochement: Brazil, Argentina and Peru in Comparative Perspective* (State University of New York at Albany, doctoral dissertation in progress as of 1988).
16. Ruben de Hoyos, 'Malvinas: A Second Gibraltar in the South Atlantic?', in Philip Kelly and Jack Child (eds), *Geopolitics of the Southern Cone and Antarctica* (Boulder, Colorado: Lynne Rienner Publishers, Inc., 1988).
17. '"Fire Focus" in the British press, Negative Impact of Untimely Falklands Maneuvers', *Latin American Regional Reports Southern Cone*, RS-88–03 (21 April 1988) p. 4.
18. Carlos A. Astiz, 'A Post-Mortem of the Institutional Military Regime in Peru', in Constantine P. Danopoulos (ed.), *Military Dictatorships in Retreat: Comparative Perspectives on Post-Military Regimes* (Boulder, Colorado: Westview Press, 1988).
19. Interviews of the author with knowledgeable persons who prefer to remain anonymous.
20. Ruben de Hoyos, 'Islas Malvinas or Falkland Islands: The Negotiation of a Conflict', in Michael A. Morris and Victor Millan (eds), *Controlling Latin American Conflicts: Ten Approaches* (Boulder, Colorado: Westview Press, 1984).
21. See a ten-chapter review by Soviet Latin Americanists, A. Gonchard (ed.), *La Crisis de las Malvinas (Falkland): Origenes y Consecuencias* (Moscow, USSR: America Latina, Estudios de Cientificos Sovieticos, Coleccion 'Ciencias Sociales Contemporaneas', Academia de Ciencias de la URSS, n.d.).
22. Edy Kaufman, *The Superpowers and Their Spheres of Influence* (New York: St Martin's Press, 1976) pp. 195–203, *passim*.

6 Chile and the Great Powers*

Joaquin Fermandois

HISTORICAL BACKGROUND

Chile was able to consolidate and organise its domestic institutional system very early on, which made it an exceptional case during the nineteenth century among the former Spanish colonies. This also allowed the country to pursue a foreign policy of power balance and territorial consolidation relatively free from intervention of the United States or Britain in its affairs. Chile's geographical distance relegated it to a relatively restricted geopolitical value, but also allowed foreign policy to be active and fairly autonomous.[1]

Relative Chilean foreign policy autonomy was compatible with close ties with the great powers. Since the first days of the struggle for independence (1810–1818), semi-official contacts were established with agents of London and Washington although relationships only became official in 1831 and 1832, respectively. Moreover, those who formed the state as well as the Chilean political class at large admired Anglo-Saxon political institutions.

From the very beginnings of its life as a state, Chile had commercial and financial ties foremost with Britain. This is how this remote, southerly country was incorporated into the international economy, once its constraints within the Spanish Empire were broken. Britain maintained this influential position in the Chilean economy until the First World War. However, this position did not give Britain any coercive leverage over Chilean domestic or foreign policy, and in any event Britain only intended to defend its own economic interests. As a result, the relationship with Britain did not prevent Chile from seeking a balance which would be favourable to its interests in South America.

Relations with the United States would be quite different. In spite of longstanding Chilean admiration of the United States, the bilateral relationship has always been burdened by a certain tension, to the

* Translated by Michael A. Morris.

extent that in a recent book it was described as 'an elusive friendship'.[2] Moreover, by the time of the War of the Pacific (1879–1883), the United States was somewhat alarmed by the emergence of Chile as an apparent regional power and one which, up to then, it could not control. Various subsequent events and the attitude of the United States itself towards Latin America have perpetuated this mutual mistrust, although except for certain specific periods this has not escalated to mutual hostility.

Britain's prudent and efficient policy has been rewarded with significant influence over Chile up to the present, without the problems inherent in the more complex presence of the United States. This is quite evident in some institutions, particularly the navy. Similarly, Chile relied on Britain as an arbitrator in its serious disputes with Argentina, and it was under the aegis of the British sovereign that an Argentine–Chilean agreement was reached in 1902, thus emphasising London's prestige in the Southern Cone.

However, as a consequence of the First World War, a process was hastened of replacing British economic leadership with that of the United States.[3] This shift took place not only in the field of trade but also in finance and investment. This extra-regional change coincided with an alteration in Chile's regional position. As a result of the enormous growth in power achieved by Argentina, Chile lost the previous basis for regional equilibrium.[4] The emphasis of Chilean diplomacy on maintaining the status quo continued while beginning to regard the Inter-American system as an eventual substitute for lost regional equilibrium.

The Great Depression of the 1930s marked a new turning point in the relationship between Chile and the United States. The abrupt fall of Chilean foreign trade, the sudden inability to meet payments, and the dizzying decline in the price of Chile's main raw materials clearly highlighted how the Chilean economy was dependent on the global economy and especially the United States. The United States, at this time, emphasised reinvigoration of bilateral trade, and, less helpfully, regularisation of Chile's foreign debt payments.

A new factor emerged in a moderate way as Washington began to pay attention to the domestic situation in Chile and its possible repercussions on US economic interests. This tendency was particularly evident during the political turmoil early in the 1930s, which paradoxically would clear a way for a relatively stable and successful Chilean democratic system until the beginning of the 1970s. A strong leftist current also emerged within Chilean political life, which sometimes involved a radical criticism of the US position in Latin America and Chile.

Although this anti-Americanism is evident in the Chilean Left and is also present in different degrees across the whole political spectrum, in having a strong rhetorical bent it may be misleading. For the masses, the United States represents the paradigm of modernity, and in general it is admired as a social and political model. Furthermore, this dichotomy between hostile rhetoric and admiration is present in a great part of Latin America.

During the 1920s and 1930s, bilateral relations were generally amicable, in spite of Washington's frustration when acting as mediator between Chile and Peru. The 'Good Neighbor' policy and the Pan American Conferences further contributed to this positive atmosphere, especially inasmuch as they reinforced the territorial status quo. The Second World War again placed strains on US–Chilean relations.[5] The majority of the Chilean people sympathised with the Allies, and the Chilean government collaborated economically and diplomatically with Washington. Chile none the less refused to break its diplomatic relations with the Axis until early in 1943, in accordance with its diplomatic traditions. Definite tension resulted between both countries during 1942, which was later dissipated but not without implications for the future.

In Chile, as in Latin America as a whole, the US interest in recruiting allies to oppose 'totalitarian' ideologies and their agents – then identified as members of the Axis – established a precedent, so that after 1945 this joint strategy would be transferred to the USSR in a Cold War context. The Cold War eclipsed, for about twenty years, the influence previously exerted by European powers in the southerly country while tightening US–Chilean relations.

FROM THE COLD WAR TO DIVERSE FORMULAS FOR AUTONOMY, 1945–1973

During the postwar period, Chile generally supported US policy in those aspects relating to the Cold War. Although this alignment would never be as tight as that of other nations located further north in South America, it was the first time such a complete convergence of interests had occurred.

Chile's belated alignment with the victorious powers during the Second World War (including the Soviet Union) did lead to the establishment of diplomatic relations with the USSR in 1945. The Chilean presidential elections of 1946 also were won by Gabriel Gonzalez Videla, the candidate of a centre-leftist coalition which included the Communist Party. Difficulties would arise quite soon within the coalition, including problems with the communists, and national political life became tense.

Pressure exerted by the United States was important in obtaining the expulsion of the communists from the government and the rupture of relations with the USSR and other, new Eastern European 'popular democracies'. This pressure implied a strong economic component, because Santiago continued to need economic assistance from abroad. In fact, official US assistance to Chile was started after the Second World War and in the Latin American context favoured the southerly country.

After a cycle of strikes, the government broke up with the Communist Party in 1947 and suspended relations with the USSR. Later, in 1948, the Chilean Congress approved new legislation whereby legal activity of the communists was prohibited.[6] This event marked the height of US influence on Chilean foreign affairs.

In 1952, a US–Chilean Military Assistance Pact was signed following a more or less common pattern prevailing in the Inter-American system. This was strongly supported by the Chilean armed forces, which at the time were markedly lagging behind in Latin America with regard to military technology. Indeed, the Chilean armed forces saw their support for US Cold War strategy as a means of upgrading Chilean power *vis-à-vis* that of neighbours, mainly Argentina. A privileged relationship between the Chilean military and their US counterpart lasted until the early 1970s.

During the 1950s, Chile remained aligned within the US orbit, although it did not hold a particularly prominent position therein. For the United States, Chile in fact began to lose importance. This country was located far from conflictive regions, lacked an explosive internal situation and did not even qualify as an unconditional ally.

Within the relatively calm Chilean political system, a resentful, anti-US vision of the Inter-American system began to grow. This criticism of the role of the United States particularly related to the field of economics, and occurred both in the form of a radical alternative (mostly Marxist) and in a type of structuralist formulation. In spite of differences in emphasis, a consensus of opinion emerged from such views that some type of nationalisation of the copper industry was required. The United States was always seen as responsible for the allegedly insufficient benefit from copper exports, the country's main source of foreign exchange.[7]

In the early 1960s, the outlook changed again. In the wake of Vice-President Nixon's ill-starred visit to Latin America in 1958 and particularly the 1959 Cuban Revolution, the United States felt compelled to reshape its policy for the region. The so-called Alliance for Progress attempted to support democratic, reformist regimes as a means of maintaining an anticommunist front under altered conditions. Chile soon became a model for implementing Washington's new policy, first with the grudging assent of the conservative government of Jorge Alessandri (1958–1964) and then, with marked enthusiasm and commitment, from the centrist government of Eduardo Frei (1964–1970). However, it was not only positive aspects of Chile that attracted Washington's attention. For the 1958 presidential elections a Marxist-related movement was formed, which espoused an increasingly radical programme including an anti-US thrust, and sooner or later appeared likely to secure power through legal means. US interest in Chile centred on preventing this possibility and included clandestine support of non-Marxist political actors.[8]

This situation contributed towards the delineation of an autonomous, distinctive Chilean international policy, at least as regards the great powers. Occasionally, a certain degree of confrontation with Washington resulted. This first took place during Jorge Alessandri's administration when Santiago refused to play a determined role in a movement to isolate Cuba.[9] This clash became more evident during the centrist administration of Eduardo Frei (1964–1970), but did not prevent important areas of US–Chilean co-operation.[10] At first, this government was favoured by funds and support for reforms from Washington, mainly by Kennedy supporters who remained influential in determining State Department policies for Latin America under the Johnson Administration. US backing also included financial support for the gradual 'Chileanisation' (or nationalisation with compensation) of the major copper mines owned by US companies.

The Chilean government still diverged from Washington in various spheres. Perhaps the same special relationship between the two countries at the time allowed Chilean autonomy and criticism of US policies. Chile launched a campaign to review relationships with Europe, especially with the countries of the Common Market (EC) and Britain (not then a member of the EC). A symbol of this campaign was President Frei's trip to Europe in 1965, including his visit with Queen Elizabeth II as well as the Queen's subsequent trip to Chile in 1967. Santiago also tried to get Britain to accept the role of arbitrator in its border disputes with Argentina, which were then being revived and which would constitute a serious problem in the future.

More spectacular, though involving less real impact, was Frei's decision to resume relations with the USSR and other nations of the Soviet bloc (relations with Yugoslavia already existed). This also played a role in internal politics, as it provided arguments for countering left-wing criticism. On the Soviet side, relations with Chile constituted part of its 'gradualist' strategy that emphasised state-to-state relationships with Latin America, in sharp contrast to Cuban support of the 'armed way'.

As of 1967, the Frei administration developed a type of relationship with the United States that further emphasised difference and contradiction rather than similarity of interests. It sponsored forms of Latin American integration (the Andean Pact) which appeared to be distant from Washington's preferences, as did a kind of continental 'Third Worldism' which culminated in the 'Consensus of Vina del Mar' (1969). But essentially this policy did not reflect a posture of confrontation with the United States. It rather tried to express a type of autonomy which would give more weight and creativeness to Latin America in the international system. In contrast, Nixon's presidency showed a marked lack of interest in regional problems until a Marxist alliance assumed power in Chile as a result of the 1970 presidential election.

The government programme of Salvador Allende and particularly of the Marxist-inspired parties accompanying him was hostile to the US position in Latin America and Chile, and assumed that the Soviet bloc offered a fairer and more promising type of international relationship. Some kind of eradication of Washington's continental influence was envisaged, but the democratic nature of the Allende government and the need for coexistence with the states of the region called for a cautious policy which ultimately asserted itself.

To a certain extent, Washington had a similar reaction of official caution, although it also fashioned a clandestine policy of intervention. At first, the United States tried to organise a military coup to prevent Allende's accession to power after the elections. Having failed, it chose low profile interventionism by gradually terminating economic aid, maintaining military aid to encourage friendly elements with the armed forces and financing opposition to the regime.[11]

Chile did not promote a direct confrontation with Washington nor did it threaten US strategic interests, at least from a military point of view.[12] Allende's government instead sponsored a critical position in the region towards the United States without taking things as far as a real confrontation, since an openly hostile attitude would have led to the country's isolation within the region. Thus the Chilean government performed a balancing act, between nationalism of the Third World type, on the one hand, and more ideological admiration of the Soviet bloc as a pattern of fair international behaviour, on the other. Selective reliance on the first position gathered support not only within the region and in the Third World in general but also from Western Europe (mainly from France and Sweden but also to some extent from Britain and West Germany). Despite the fact that Chile maintained privileged relationships with Cuba during these years – which would strongly influence the development of internal policies – such relationships did not define the character of Chilean foreign policy.

While Chilean diplomacy acted pragmatically with the Western powers, its ideological outlook was reflected in the hope of securing considerable Soviet economic aid as had occurred in the case of Cuba. But the USSR–Cuban pattern was not replicated. Although the USSR welcomed Allende's election and gave some aid to Chile, it was far short of what the Chilean Left had expected. Moscow was not ready or able to give substantial economic support to a 'new Cuba', regardless of its approval of the Chilean model as an example for Latin America. For the USSR, the governing coalition, the *Unidad Popular* (United Peoples' Party), mirrored its own strategy for Latin America, which emphasised prudence and measured support to 'progressive' regimes of the area.

While only having modestly backed up the new left-wing government in Chile, the violent overthrow of the *Unidad Popular* did come as a severe shock for Moscow. From the point of view of the Chilean people, they became aware of the fact that there was no substitute for a preferential economic relationship with the industrial powers of the West.

While the Allende government's 'anti-imperialistic' strategy did not involve confrontation with the US government on the plane of interstate relations, there was to be a test of strength with 'capitalism' on the domestic front. The copper mines owned by US companies, in addition to the prominent case of ITT, were to be expropriated (in practice, confiscation without compensation). Oddly enough

Washington's policy also consisted in isolating the issue of expropriation from overall diplomatic relations by considering it as a specifically Chilean state-multinational corporation affair. The US was not indifferent to virtual confiscations, but this constituted part of its strategy of minimising the damage that Chile represented to its own interests.

The US support given to the domestic Chilean opposition was more intrusive. Although the importance of this assistance generally has been exaggerated, it undoubtedly played an indirect role in the final fall of the *Unidad Popular* in September 1973. The funding disbursed was relatively modest (about 7 million US dollars), but it still played a role in keeping the opposition alive. (Cuban intervention was also present, but it will not be dealt with here.)

The violent outcome, represented by the military coup that followed the virtual rebellion of broad civil and institutional sectors, had a global impact. In fact, under Allende's government Chile already had become a focal point of worldwide attention, and not only from leftist sectors. For many of different persuasions, it constituted a sort of modern Utopia. Whatever followed would most probably have become an 'anti-Utopia' and all the more so considering the violence accompanying the establishment of the military government. Furthermore, when the military government did not return power to civilians or develop towards a democratic regime but rather slipped into a personalist praetorianism, the measures taken by international actors during the *Unidad Popular* government were subjected to a severe scrutiny. At the forefront was the policy of the Nixon White House, especially as designed by Kissinger. But the new Chilean rulers and political actors that would reappear or emerge in the following years had their own ideas about relationships with the great powers.

MILITARY GOVERNMENT AND ISOLATION, 1973–1981.

The drama of the *Unidad Popular* and its end, coupled with the permanent nature which from its beginnings has characterised the subsequent military government, have maintained Chile in the forefront of world debate. As happened with Spain in the 1930s and with Vietnam in the 1960s, Chile has become a symbol or paradigm (almost unfailingly negative) before which contemporary individuals are measured, sometimes just for the sake of argument. The attitude of the great powers in their relations with Chile could not ignore this powerful and persistent reality. Furthermore, within the Western circle of nations, the influence of public opinion has often been the determining factor in forging this attitude, which on most occasions has been extremely critical of Chile. This is the case particularly with the United States, but also to a certain extent, with Britain.

The new Chilean rulers construed their position in the world as an extension of their internal legitimacy, that is, as an anti-Marxist struggle. Full endorsement of the Western perspective of the Cold War, it was expected, would involve a close alliance with the United States. Likewise, the traditional relationship with Britain would remain unaltered. This avowedly pro-Western position would also be reflected in a new 'open market' policy. Compensation was paid to the US companies which previously owned the copper mines that were nationalised in 1971. Lastly, a generous policy of opening the country to foreign investment was established.

However, the US domestic and foreign policy setting had evolved, and US–Chilean relations had acquired great political sensitivity. The years of Washington's political turmoil and confusion commenced with Vietnam and Watergate, with a concomitant decline in executive power. Nixon's policy regarding Chile was the object of increasing and often uninformed criticism. Although Washington was pleased with Allende's fall and initially supported the new government with economic loans and military assistance, this posture could not be sustained because of the attacks of Congress and US public opinion. For the latter, Chile often would become a symbol of immoral behaviour in Washington's foreign policy. Furthermore, the politics of the military government headed by Augusto Pinochet, including preparations for a prolonged period in power, represented an embarrassment for the White House.

By 1975–1976 strains with Santiago would commence and, at an OAS assembly held in the Chilean capital city in 1976, Kissinger would publicly criticise the human rights situation in Chile. For the first time Chile was named in a 1976 televised presidential debate between Gerald Ford and Jimmy Carter, with Carter's criticism of Chile gaining the upper hand. Also in 1976 the Senate approved the Humphrey–Kennedy Amendment, which made it practically impossible to sell military material to Chile. Then the assassination of Orlando Letelier, a former Minister of Foreign Affairs of Allende's

Government, on a Washington, DC street provoked a wave of indignation in US political circles complicating relationships between both countries up to the present.

Washington had been successful in the sense that a Marxist regime was not established in Chile, although this was primarily due to endogenous causes. The new situation led to other problems, so that Chile continued to pose policy dilemmas for the United States yet without the urgency perceived in 1970.

In the case of London, a cooling off in the relationship with Chile also became evident. As a result of a specific human rights problem at the end of 1974, Great Britain's ambassador in Santiago was recalled for several years. With the Labour party heading the government, London even disavowed pending military contracts, which it only agreed to execute when Chile appealed to British courts. Here as elsewhere, there was a combination of altruistic motives alongside a crusading human rights policy, which led to a double standard in judging foreign countries.

While the Chilean military regime's international anti-Marxist strategy was expected to attract Western support, instead it soon found itself irremediably isolated in the region and in the whole world. The deterioration of Chile's relations with the US and Western Europe produced a deep frustration, and led the military regime to transform its international anti-Marxist strategy into a vehicle for promoting internal legitimacy. While this strategy has performed a real political function at home, abroad it has failed and in fact has stirred up considerable hostility.[13]

From its inception, the Chilean military regime was faced with determined hostility from the USSR and the Soviet bloc, with the rupture of diplomatic relations occurring in September 1973. Even though Moscow had not backed the *Unidad Popular* with unqualified enthusiasm, its fall apparently had a great impact on Soviet policy-makers even though similar situations had not provoked a similar reaction (for example, Indonesia). By condemning the military overthrow of an elected left-wing government, Moscow probably sensed that it could obtain a widespread and continuing propagandistic triumph in the West and the Third World. In January 1980 Brezhnev in fact justified the Soviet military occupation of Afghanistan by arguing that the country should not be left 'at the mercy of imperialism (as) for example, Chile'.[14]

In this way, Soviet policy towards Chile gradually became a distinctive case in contrast to overall USSR behaviour towards Latin

America emphasising gradual change and state-to-state relationships. Moscow subsequently carried out a destabilisation policy towards the Chilean military regime, but in a low profile version and sometimes indistinguishable from rhetoric.

The Argentine military government (1976–1983) was as strongly anti-communist as the Chilean one but somewhat more acceptable at the international level. Moscow's systematic refusal to endorse accusations of violation of human rights in Argentina at the time makes the singularity of the Chilean case even more dramatic.

For Chile, Soviet hostility has certainly been troublesome because of Moscow's influence on some Third World nations, though this very hostility has reinforced the self-image of the military government. Thus Pinochet has been able to appear before his supporters as a legitimate and necessary defender of an anti-communist cause. At the same time, the People's Republic of China not only has continued the diplomatic relations with Santiago established by Allende, but has even shown a certain degree of cordiality.[15]

The election of Jimmy Carter as President of the United States in 1976 complicated the threatening panorama which was already facing the Chilean government. The military government was soon ostracised by Washington, particularly as a result of the assassination of the former Chilean minister. Since Carter could not apply his activist human rights policy world-wide, Chile was the most propitious target. Towards the end of the Carter administration practically all types of military collaboration with Chile had come to an end, including the UNITAS exercises between the navies of both countries. Future loans by the US Export-Import Bank (Eximbank) and OPIC (Overseas Private Investment Corporation) guaranties were prohibited. Santiago blamed 'Western decadence' or 'Marxist infiltration' for the criticisms made by Western democracies, headed by the US, thereby revealing a profound lack of knowledge of the US political system by President Pinochet's entourage.

As long as the cycle of military governments in the region lasted (with the exception of Colombia and Venezuela), Santiago had a sort of defensive shield. However, towards the end of the 1970s, Chile began to be isolated in this sense as well as democratic regimes spread.[16]

It would none the less seem that the Carter administration obtained few successes in dealing with Chile. Pinochet did have to agree to the announcement of a constitutional schedule, but only with the purpose of extending his own rule. He also had to reorganise the secret police (which did not report to the armed forces but rather to him directly) and to drastically restrict certain practices that were unanimously considered dreadful and unnecessary. But in these matters, it is not clear to what extent internal factors intervened and how much was due to external pressures.

The US government did intervene on another occasion which was beneficial for Chile. At the end of 1978, it actively helped prevent a war between Argentina and Chile over the Beagle Channel issue. Chile was notoriously weaker in military terms, although its position was based on the binding award of an arbitrator. Furthermore, it was apparent in 1974–5 that the United States, using the restricted means at its disposal, had helped Chile avoid an armed skirmish with Peru, a country that received substantial military support in armaments from the Soviet Union.

Termination of economic assistance did not present a serious threat for Chile. The situation could be remedied through loans from private US and Western banks, even though scant direct investment was received. The cut in aid and military links, coupled with economic sanctions, left Washington without any elements of pressure when dealing with Santiago. Pinochet's government, in surviving US sanctions, proved its ability to achieve relative autonomy.

Carter and the US government did not resort to the extreme measure of imposing a commercial embargo on Chile. The latter would have had devastating consequences for Chile, yet also very possibly would have led to an entirely uncontrollable situation opposed to Washington's own interests. The utility of US intervention influenced that country's attitude towards Chile, while the essential instability of authoritarian regimes called Washington's attention to the limits of US intervention. This dilemma for the White House remains virtually unchanged up to the present, and does not refer exclusively to Chile.

For Chile, alignment under a global leader was not easy, and in fact the military government claimed that the leader had lost its way. Chile, likewise, learned to its dismay that positive relationships with 'capitalism' (private economic agents) in no way insured a good relationship with the US government.

Some other transnational factors also began to complicate US–Chilean relations. Quite a few Chilean exiles chose the United States for shelter, and Washington came to support democratic opposition forces inside Chile. Sustained exchange between the Chilean political class, the US government and to a certain extent the broader US society has resulted. Groups close to the Chilean government and above all those belonging to the opposition (moderate left and centre) started to perceive a more differentiated picture of the US political system. At the same time, certain conservative sectors – long admirers of the United States who advocated an active US role in Latin America – came to incorporate criticism of 'imperialism' into their own discourse. On the other hand, sectors traditionally critical of such an active US role now began to promote Washington's interventionism to obtain either a peaceful transition to democracy in Chile or simply the collapse of the military regime.

In sum, by the end of the 1970s, Chile had reached a high level of autonomy, measured according to its capacity to resist pressures that it had never felt in the past. However, this autonomy could not be used to achieve regional influence or to win space for negotiation with the great powers. It has been an autonomy earned at the cost of isolation. It is a remarkable capacity, although fruitless as regards Chile's international relationships.

THE OPTIONS OF THE EIGHTIES

In 1979, the conservatives came into power in Britain under the leadership of Margaret Thatcher, which for Santiago was a favourable development. Ambassadors were again assigned to each country and military relations attained the level reached prior to their rupture in 1974. With the conservative wave of the early 1980s, the economic policies sustained by Chilean technocrats seemed to receive unquestionable legitimacy, at least from their own point of view. Chilean policy-makers emphasised close economic and financial relationships with the Western world to mitigate the effects of the lack of economic assistance originated by Chile's isolation. 'Thatcherism' thereby played a significant role in surmounting some of the adverse effects of Chile's isolation, even if the British Prime Minister had never had that intention.

The election of Ronald Reagan as President of the United States in November 1980 further heightened expectations of Chilean leaders. It seemed as if at last Chile were to achieve its desire of forming part of a worldwide anticommunist alliance, as a recognised member with full rights, for the purpose of fighting Soviet 'imperialism'. In effusive electoral congratulations sent to Reagan, Pinochet stressed that 'in the critical moments currently being lived by mankind . . . your designation represents a hope for (those who) wish that the United States strengthen its leadership role in world affairs'.[17]

For its part, the new Republican administration announced that it would not treat anti-communist authoritarian governments as harshly as the Carter administration had. Inspired by Jeane Kirkpatrick's ideas, a distinction was made between 'authoritarian' and 'totalitarian' regimes, with the latter having no hope of evolution towards democracy while the former offered the opportunity of a convergence with US ideals and certainly with its strategic interests. It was expected that 'quiet diplomacy' would be more efficient than public threats in obtaining, from authoritarian governments that were on friendly terms with the United States, submission to Western norms concerning human rights. Clashes with US political culture over human rights issues would thereby be avoided and a strategic alliance could be fashioned. Forms of pressure used by the Carter administration would no longer be allowed to complicate relations.

Relationships between Chile and the United States did show improvement. Washington lifted many of the sanctions against Chile, particularly within the field of finance. There were to be no vetoes of guaranties or loans from the Eximbank, the OPIC, the IDB and the World Bank. The UNITAS naval manoeuvres, which for Chile had both practical and symbolic importance, were also resumed. Official US visitors, with words of praise for the functioning of the Chilean economy, started arriving in Santiago. The US banking system spearheaded the policy of *rapprochement*, in the hope of stimulating spectacular and permanent economic growth in Chile through credit availability in the world market.

However, the Reagan administration also wanted to improve its relationship with the Argentine military government, and this posed certain problems for US–Chilean relations. During the Carter period, relations between Washington and Buenos Aires had been particularly conflictive. With improved US relations with both Argentina and Chile under Reagan, certain basic power relationships came to the fore. Since Argentina was considerably stronger than Chile, it promised to contribute much more to a strategic understanding with the United States. Despite Chile's improved relationship with the United States, US–Argentine relations improved even more. Because of the hostility existing between both neighbours of the Southern Cone, this only made Chile's position more vulnerable.

The prominent features of Chile's recent political history also forced the White House to observe well established constraints on bilateral relations. Thus, not even in the best of times was there any possibility of the United States resuming its military assistance or sale of arms to Chile. US officials continuously reiterated that the principal obstacles in the path of normal diplomatic relations were Chile's lack of co-operation in the Letelier case and failure to democratise. Official US visitors travelling to Buenos Aires occasionally stopped off in Santiago, but more as a way of maintaining a formal balance than because of genuine interest in the relationship. In addition, official representatives of the economic and military sectors of the US government were much more flattering in public than those who planned US foreign policy.[18]

Several events intervened to make this picture still more complex. Beginning in the second half of 1981, the Chilean economy was affected by a recession followed by a severe depression, which undermined the hopes and illusions that only recently had appeared to be based on solid projections. The fall in the gross national product, the dramatic rise in unemployment and the conspicuous increase of the foreign debt all pointed to the fragility of the economy – one of the bases upon which the regime had relied to offset Chile's external isolation. However, the whole region soon had to face similar economic problems, which made their impact on Chile's international situation somewhat ambiguous.

The Falklands/Malvinas War (April–June 1982) affected the entire region, and with regard to Chile it further accentuated the country's feeling of isolation in spite of some positive aspects. Chilean diplomacy had to play a delicate game fluctuating between the necessary rhetoric of Latin American solidarity in support of Argentina and defence of the national interest against Argentina. The seizure of the Falklands by the Argentine military government had troubling implications for Santiago. Buenos Aires had virtually rejected a December 1980 proposal by Pope John Paul II for peaceful settlement of the Beagle Channel conflict, a proposal that Chile had accepted immediately. The declarations of some Argentine leaders and certain troop movements at the time clearly envisaged a forceful solution to the Beagle Channel crisis. In this context, the 1982 Argentine defeat in the Falklands not only meant an acceleration of democratisation in Argentina but also possibly spared Chile from a subsequent confrontation over the Beagle Channel. Chile appeared to be vulnerable when confronting Argentina, and it was only Argentine involvement in a war with Britain, which the United States finally supported, that allowed Chile to emerge from the situation unharmed. Chile's divergent role within the region, including limited military co-operation with Britain, was thereby highlighted. The Chilean military, and above all the navy, wished to emphasise this co-operation, but Chilean diplomacy managed to keep a low profile. Chile did come to share some interests at least temporarily with a European power, but without breaking out from its overall external isolation.[19]

The regional democratisation process has had various domestic and international effects for Chile. In at least one major respect, Argentine democratisation had a positive impact on Chile. Under the civilian government of President Alfonsin, Buenos Aires finally accepted a modified version of the Pope's proposal regarding the Beagle Channel area. A 1984 treaty and improved relations with Argentina resulted.

By April 1983 a broad opposition movement began to develop within Chile, which was peaceful in many aspects although involving scattered violence that was not easy to control. The initial government response only produced an increase in the level of violence and, at the same time, the notoriety of the Chilean case. Urban guerrilla warfare or simple terrorism, as the case might be, emerged with the Communist Party as the principal actor. This could be extremely serious for the United States inasmuch as a collapse of authoritarian rule could be accompanied by a rise of communist influence associated with the USSR. President Alfonsin has discretely expressed his concern in Washington and possibly in Havana about the reappearance of terrorism in the Southern Cone.

As part of the complex political game in Washington, changes were made among those responsible for Chile-related policies within the State Department. The 'pragmatists' now acquired greater importance *vis-à-vis* the 'ideologues', even if this distinction is somewhat arbitrary. The former designed a more critical, remote posture towards Pinochet's government, aimed at encouraging a peaceful, consensual evolution towards democracy. Contacts with the opposition were multiplied while an attempt was made to point out to the armed forces the need for negotiation with the democratic opposition. The problem of Central America influenced this change of direction, as it forced Washington to be consistent in encouraging democracy abroad in order to obtain the support of Congress. This implied a necessary distance with regard to Pinochet.

Therefore, in December 1984, Reagan referred to the 'lack of progress towards a democratic government in Chile and Paraguay'.[20] An officer of the State Department subsequently explained that 'we go public when our quiet entreaties are not responded to'.[21] The US policy change was fundamentally a reaction to the fear that an unresponsive military regime would allow an explosive and uncontrollable situation to develop, yet this spectre in turn constrained whatever impetus Washington's policy of encouraging the democratic opposition might have attained. Washington's longstanding dilemma of feeling compelled to intervene in Latin America but being constrained by the limits of external manipulation thereby continued to plague US policy towards Chile.

Severe economic pressures could have been brought to bear on Santiago, but an economic collapse resulting from these pressures would have been dangerous for Washington. In 1984, the White House accordingly refused to impose any restrictions on Chilean copper imports as requested by some domestic protectionist groups. On the other hand, in June 1985 the White House used voting on a World Bank loan to pressure Chile to end martial law.

Stronger US economic coercion was also constrained by the laudatory official opinion prevailing in the United States about the Chilean economy. In 1985 the Treasury Undersecretary stated that Chile 'was ahead of the Baker Plan'.[22] Official US discourse has singled out Chile because of the way in which it coupled interest payments on its foreign debt with economic growth, while at the same time condemning political aspects of the country. The problem as perceived by the US government is therefore how to punish the government of Chile without damaging what in their view is a macroeconomic programme placed 'among the best in the hemisphere and perhaps one of the models for the Third World'.[23] This dilemma is posed not only in light of threats of unilateral action on the part of Congress, but also occurs annually on the occasion of the renegotiation of Chile's foreign debt, mainly with the US banking system. A document, the Structural Adjustment Loan (SAL), is required, which must be approved by the World Bank and in 1986 was for 250 million US dollars. The amount is not important for Chile, but it is a prior requirement demanded by the banking system. In both 1986 and 1987 the US abstained from voting, while on both occasions Britain voted favourably for the granting of this loan.

This would have been a crucial moment in which to cause serious damage to Chile, and yet Washington preferred to rely on more modest sanctions. Precisely in December 1987, a few days after the SAL was approved, the United States imposed another type of economic sanction on Chile. The country was excluded from the GSP

Table 6.1   Origin and destination of Chilean trade, 1982–84

	Exports (%)	Imports (%)
USA	25.5	24.0
European Community	31.3	16.1
Japan	10.8	7.1
Canada	1.1	1.9
Middle East	2.3	1.3
Latin America	15.5	25.2
Others	13.5	24.4

Source: Inter-American Development Bank, *Annual Report 1986*.

Program (Generalized System of Tariff Preferences) and from the OPIC which insures US investments abroad. Although the effect of these measures will not be great, they constitute a bothersome warning both to the Chilean government and to foreign investors. Apparently this is the type of limited sanction Washington prefers to continue imposing if the military regime does not come to an end.

US economic levers for influencing Chilean policy have declined in importance. Economic assistance has been at a low level since 1976, and the United States now only participates in about a quarter of overall trade with Chile (Tables 6.1 and 6.2). Washington could only exert overwhelming pressure through a commercial embargo to which Western Europe would adhere. However, this measure would be difficult for the White House to achieve and contradictory to its own interest in guaranteeing stability in the Southern Cone. A similarly drastic measure would involve preventing reprogramming of the foreign debt, but this would punish one of the few countries doing what Washington feels should be done in this field. If as a consequence of economic coercion there were to be a recession or a political upheaval in Chile, this would perhaps cause irreparable damage to one of the essential actors in the reestablishment of democracy, the entrepreneurs.

The possibility of exerting pressure on the military front seems even more remote. Severance of US military assistance caused enormous resentment among the Chilean military, a condition that will surely not disappear when Pinochet leaves the political scene (Table 6.2). The Chilean armed forces were able to surmount the Humphrey–Kennedy Amendment by obtaining access to the inter-

Table 6.2   US economic and military assistance to Chile under five US
Presidents (millions of US dollars)

	Economic Assistance	Military Assistance	Total
Johnson, 1964–1968	457.2	42.4	499.6
Nixon, 1969–1973	97.6	45.6	143.2
Ford, 1974–1976	183.6	16.7	200.3
Carter, 1977–1980	68.9	—	68.9
Reagan, 1981–1984	23.4	—	23.4

Note: The figures aggregate loans and grants for both economic and military
assistance. Export-Import Bank credits are not included.

Source: *U.S. Overseas Loans and Grants and Assistance from International
Organizations* (Washington, DC: US Government Printing Office, Office of
Public Affairs, Agency for International Development, various years).

national arms market, in spite of the existence of similar types of
sanctions in Western Europe. Although the Chilean military has had
difficulties in obtaining sophisticated weapons, improved relations
with Britain have made it possible to equip the navy reasonably well.

Frustration has been evident in US policy, whether on the economic, political or military fronts. This may be seen in the declaration
of Elliot Abrams, Deputy Secretary of State for Latin America, when
he acknowledged that 'although so many pro- and anti-government
Chileans assign great importance to what the US does or does not do
with regard to Chile, we have, in fact, very limited real influence. We
have few carrots and few sticks available'.[24]

Santiago's policy has been fundamentally reactive, since its most
potent weapon has been the fear in Washington (and in Chile) of
what might happen if Pinochet's eventual departure were destabilising. Pinochet has relied on the resentment existing within the armed
forces and in some conservative sectors to query 'just how intelligent
is an alliance with the US'.[25] Each step that has apparently closed the
gap between the strategic interests of both nations (like an agreement
in 1985 to enlarge the Eastern Island airport for its use by NASA) has
been followed by disillusion, at least in the eyes of Chilean public
opinion. Also, Chilean officials complain, and not without reason,
about the contradictory 'signals' which Washington has sent them in
the last 25 years.

Obliged by circumstances and spurred on by its own doctrine, the

Chilean military regime has promoted an economic programme
which has imposed great sacrifices on the population but which has
been successful in getting the country out of the 1982–1983 depression. Interest payments have been made on the foreign debt
(after reprogramming), while being compatible with modest economic
growth and some improvement of the internal situation. A country
that maintains such a balance cannot be severely sanctioned, since if
Washington punished those who were 'behaving well' on the economic front it would remove all incentive for others to follow what is
considered to be the correct road. Therefore, although Santiago has
paid a great deal of attention to and has worried about what is
happening in Washington, the Pinochet government's capacity to
resist has given it great confidence.

As matters stand, relatively successful Chilean resistance to recurring external pressure has accentuated the country's capacity for
autonomy. This proves the potential capacity for regional influence
which Chile would have within a different institutional context.
Chile, in its isolation, none the less lacks a creative policy for dealing
with the great powers, in contrast to the approach that seemed to be
emerging in the 1960s. If the reestablishment of democracy were to
take place without too much upheaval, the Chilean political class
would have a chance to develop a coherent approach to the great
powers relying on the influence and autonomy that would apparently
be at its disposal.

Notes

1. Robert N. Burr, *By Reason or Force. Chile and the Balance of Power in
   South America, 1830–1905* (Berkeley and Los Angeles: University of
   California Press, 1967); Mario Barros, *Historia Diplomatica de Chile
   (1591–1938)* (Barcelona, Spain: Ariel, 1970).
2. Heraldo Munoz and Carlos Portales, *Una Amistad Esquiva. Las Relaciones de Estados Unidos y Chile* (Santiago: Pehuen, 1987).
3. Juan Ricardo Couyoumdjian, *Chile y Gran Bretana durante la Primera
   Guerra Mundial, 1914–1921* (Santiago: Andres Bello and Ediciones
   Universidad Catolica de Chile, 1987).
4. Emilio Meneses, 'Los limites del equilibrio de poder: la politica externa
   chilena a fines del siglo pasado, 1891–1902', *Opciones*, Vol. 9 (May–September 1986).
5. Michael J. Francis, *The Limits of Hegemony, United States Relations*

with Argentina and Chile during World War II (Notre Dame and London: University of Notre Dame Press, 1977).

6. Andrew Barnard, 'Chilean Communists, Radical Presidents and Chilean Relations with the United States, 1940–1947', *Journal of Latin American Studies*, Vol. 13, No. 2 (November 1981), pp. 347–74.

7. Theodore H. Moran, *Multinational Corporations and the Politics of Dependency. Copper in Chile* (Princeton, NJ: Princeton University Press, 1974).

8. *Covert Action in Chile, 1963–1973*, Staff Report of the Select Committee to study Governmental Operations with respect to Intelligence Activities, United States Senate (Washington, DC: US Government Printing Office, 1975).

9. Joaquin Fermandois, 'Chile y la "cuestion cubana" 1959–1964', *Historia*, Vol. 17 (1982), pp. 113–200.

10. Manfred Wilhelmy, 'Christian Democrat Ideology and Inter-American Politics: The Case of Chile, 1964–1970', in Morris Blachman and Ronald Hellman (eds), *Terms or Conflict: Ideology in Latin American Politics* (Philadelphia: Institute for the Study of Human Issues, 1979), pp. 129–60.

11. Among other sources: *United States and Chile during the Allende Years*, Hearings before the Subcommittee on Inter-American Affairs of the Committee on Foreign Affairs, House of Representatives (Washington, DC: US Government Printing Office, 1975).

12. Joaquin Fermandois, *Chile y el Mundo 1970–1973. La Politica Exterior del Gobierno de la Unidad Popular y el Sistema Internacional* (Santiago: Ediciones Universidad Catolica de Chile, 1985).

13. For the entire Pinochet period, see Heraldo Munoz, *Las Relaciones Exteriores del Gobierno Militar Chileno* (Santiago: Las Ediciones del Ornitorrinco, 1986).

14. *El Mercurio* newspaper, 16 January 1980.

15. Augusto Varas, 'The Soviet Union in the Foreign Relations of the Southern Cone', in Heraldo Munoz and Joseph S. Tulchin (eds), *Latin American Nations in World Politics* (Boulder, Colorado: Westview Press, 1984), pp. 243–59.

16. Juan Somavia and Juan Gabriel Valdes, 'Las Relaciones entre los Gobiernos de EE.UU. y Chile en el marco de la politica de los derechos humanos', *Cuadernos Semestrales*, *Estados Unidos: Perspectiva Latinoamericana*, Vol. 6 (Second Semester 1979, CIDE), pp. 255–77.

17. *El Mercurio*, 6 November 1980.

18. Juan Gabriel Valdes, 'Vision Neo-conservadora y Relaciones EE.UU.–Chile', *Cono-Sur*, Vol. 1, No. 3 (October 1982).

19. Wayne Selcher, 'Recent Strategic Developments in South America's Southern Cone', in Heraldo Munoz and Joseph S. Tulchin, pp. 101–18.

20. Servicio de Cultura y Prensa de la Embajada de Estados Unidos en Santiago, 18 December 1984.

21. Richard Shifter (Assistant Secretary of State for Human Rights), *New York Times*, 13 March 1986.

22. *El Mercurio*, 31 October 1985.
23. Robert Gelbard (Joint Undersecretary of State for Latin America), *El Mercurio*, 17 August 1987.
24. *Cono Sur* (December–March 1987–1988); also Mark Falcoff, 'Chile: The Dilemma for US Policy', *Foreign Affairs* (Spring 1986), pp. 838–48.
25. *Cono Sur*, Vol. 4, No. 3 (July–August 1985).

Part III
Issues

7 International Relations in Antarctica: Argentina, Chile and the Great Powers
Peter J. Beck

A FRONTIER REGION

Antarctica covers an area of some 14 million sq.km (5.5 million sq.miles) – this constitutes about 10 per cent of the world's land surface – and exceeds the combined extent of either Argentina, Brazil, Chile, Peru and Uruguay or the USA and Mexico. Normally, Antarctica is perceived as the world's last great wilderness, whose mysteries have yet to be fully unveiled.

> The adventure is on . . . . It is exciting to be here. There are indefinable things which make it very special. . . . We got the real feel of exploration and frontier. . . . Research in Antarctica is still mainstream science on the frontiers of knowledge. . . . And all of it is international. . . . Standing at the Pole one is [able] to feel the emptiness of the snowfield all round . . . 'Great God, this is an awful place' my father had said. . . . Yet the Pole still has a magic and majesty which can be felt . . . Cold and inhospitable it may be, but oh the exquisite beauty of it – and the challenge that is still there.[1]

Peter Scott, visiting Antarctica for the first time over fifty years after the tragic death of Captain Robert Scott, responded in this manner to a cold and ice-covered continent, whose inhospitable features have been accentuated by distance and remoteness, including its apparent status as an unique, marginal and insignificant 'Pole apart' ignored by not only politicians, diplomats and others but also such academic disciplines as history, international law and international relations. Therefore, it is often depicted as 'a continent for science' valued basically for fundamental research in such spheres as the alleged depletion of the atmosphere's ozone layer (the 'greenhouse effect') or the ice sheet's future impact upon world sea levels. According to this view, Antarctica, while continuing to 'export' scientific data, will remain of peripheral political, strategic and economic importance.

However, the international political situation is changing, for the 1980s have witnessed an escalation of interest by those who, treating it previously as 'remote, obscure and forbidding', have identified Antarctica as a new focus of international concern. Recently, one Australian academic asserted that 'the Antarctic is likely to become a major crisis zone in the 1980s', while a former British minister, writing in *Foreign Affairs*, pointed out that 'there are disturbing indications that a major international dispute may be about to emerge over an important but little known area of the world's surface: the Antarctic'.[2] For example, since 1983 the UN has conducted annual debates and produced three reports (1984, 1986, 1987) on the topic, while the Non-Aligned Movement (NAM) has assumed a special interest in the continent's future, which has been discussed also in a range of other international forums (e.g. League of Arab States, Organization of African Unity).

Within this context, many governments were compelled for the first time to consider 'the Question of Antarctica', whose advent as an international issue was fostered by a growing awareness of the region's perceived resource potential; the desire of developing countries to share in the management and exploitation of any resources in the light of changing legal and political attitudes related to the New International Economic Order, the common heritage principle and the 1982 UN Convention on the Law of the Sea (UNCLOS); the attempt to remove South Africa from a management role in Antarctica as part of the anti-apartheid campaign; and the pressure of non-governmental environmental organizations (NGOs) for the transformation of Antarctica into a world park. The infamous 'Falklands factor' should not be forgotten, since the Falklands War of 1982 drew attention to the wider South Atlantic region, including nearby Antarctica, wherein Argentina and Britain were rivals for the same piece of territory. Some might point also to a 'Beagle factor', at least as far as Argentina and Chile were concerned, on account of the Antarctic implications of the Beagle Channel dispute. These trends both caused and reflected the emerging debate about Antarctica's political, strategic and economic utility. Indeed, this enhanced visibility means that – to quote from the report of a study group chaired by Sir Anthony Parsons (formerly Britain's UN representative, 1979–82 – 'as a factor in international relations, it [Antarctica] cannot be ignored any longer'.[3]

However, certain countries, including Argentina, Britain, Chile, the Soviet Union and the USA, possess a long history of involvement in the region, dating back several centuries and culminating in their joint participation in the Antarctic Treaty System (ATS) for over the past quarter of a century. Traditionally, the continent has proved a significant policy interest for Latin American governments located in the Southern Cone, and South America and Antarctica are often considered together on account of not only their relative proximity – they are separated by only about 1000 km of seas and ice – but also the fact that both Argentina and Chile, considering *Antartida Argentina* and *Territorio Chileno Antartico* as an integral part of their respective national territories, treat their Antarctic claims in a possessive manner as prime policy interests (Figure 7.1).

Argentina and Chile, glossing over their own conflicting claims, including previous failures (e.g. 1906–8) to resolve their differences, and seeking wider hemispheric support against rival British claims, performed the key role in the formulation of the concept of a 'South American Antarctic' through the Rio Treaty of 1947 (the Inter-American Treaty of Reciprocal Assistance) – the area of coverage was defined to extend south of South America to the South Pole – and the Argentine–Chilean Donoso–La Rosa Declaration of March 1948. The latter states:

> Both Governments will act in mutual agreement in the protection and legal defence of their rights in the South American Antarctic, lying between the meridians of 25°W and 90°W, within the territories of which the Argentine Republic and Chile are recognised as having unquestionable sovereign rights.

This concept, reaffirmed in February 1978 by the Argentine–Chilean Act of Puerto Montt, has been both reinforced and complicated by the more recent Antarctic involvement of Brazil, Ecuador, Peru and Uruguay. Their support for South American rights in the sector has been qualified by the possibility of alternative legal approaches – for instance, the Brazilian-influenced frontage concept relates Antarctic rights to Latin American mainland boundaries (Figure 7.2) – being advanced to the area staked out already by Argentina and Chile (and Britain).

In general, Latin American interest and activity in Antarctica has been confined to the South American quadrant, although involvement in the ATS and international scientific programmes, in conjunction with anxiety about the consequences of the region's potential militarisation and nuclearisation, has fostered concern about wider

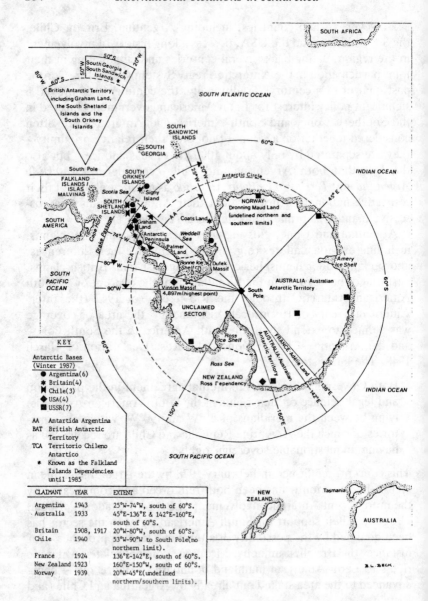

Figure 7.1   Antarctic territorial claims

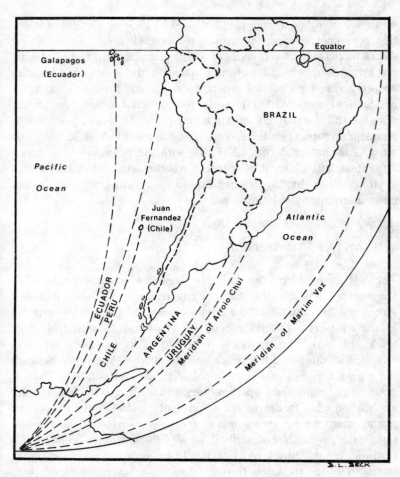

Figure 7.2 The frontage concept

continental issues. By contrast, American, British and Soviet interest has proved traditionally to be wide-ranging, covering the whole Antarctic region as merely one aspect of their world-wide roles, even if currently British territory, entitled British Antarctic Territory (BAT), is confined to the South American sector, wherein its relations with Latin American governments have assumed both a confrontational and co-operative character. Neither the American nor Soviet governments have made sovereignty claims – they have merely reserved their 'rights' to make a claim – but their determination to retain a leading polar role is established by their predominant scientific presences, such as measured by expenditure, base numbers, Antarctic personnel, and levels of logistical support. In fact, Antarctic research resembles that in outer space in the sense that logistics absorb a very high part of expenditure, thereby favouring the USA and Soviet Union. Within the wider international context, Antarctica remains still a relatively minor issue, particularly as compared to mainstream topics like East–West relations and the Middle East. For most Consultative Parties (ATCPs), with the possible exception of Argentina and Chile, it is arguable whether Antarctica constitutes anything other than a peripheral question exerting minimal impact upon international relationships.

THE ANTARCTIC REGIME

The ATS derived from the Antarctic Treaty, which was concluded in December 1959 by the twelve governments – these included Argentina, Britain, Chile, the Soviet Union and the USA – involved in the Antarctic programme of International Geophysical Year (IGY: 1957–8). The treaty, coming into effect in June 1961, was intended to safeguard the peace and stability of Antarctica through the encouragement of international scientific co-operation, the imposition of prohibitions upon military and nuclear activities, and the application of a freeze to the sovereignty question. In effect, the management of the area south of 60° S was vested in the original signatories, which are described as ATCPs and meet biennially at Consultative Meetings (ATCMs) held by rotation within member states in order to agree through consensus on recommendations designed to further ATS purposes. The most recent sessions assembled at Buenos Aires, Canberra, Brussels and Rio de Janeiro in 1981, 1983, 1985 and 1987 respectively. Significantly, the 1989 ATCM is scheduled for France rather than either Chile or China – the latter follow Brazil in the ATCPs' alphabetical order – presumably because of the political difficulties of securing the attendance of all parties in these countries. The Antarctic Treaty, lacking any time limit, may last indefinitely, although there exist provisions for a review conference during and after 1991; in fact, this feature has prompted the mistaken belief that the treaty ends in 1991.

During its period of life the ATS has been characterised by increased international participation, since a further eight governments (e.g. Brazil, India: 1983; China, Uruguay: 1985) have been admitted to ATCP status because of their performance of 'substantial' Antarctic research activity. By June 1988 a further 18 governments – these include Cuba, Ecuador, Peru, Spain – had acceded as non-ATCPs to the Antarctic Treaty, thereby accepting its principles and securing observer status at ATCMs; in fact, accession is often interpreted as a transitional stage towards acceptance as an ATCP, as demonstrated by both the recent examples of Brazil and Uruguay and the current quest of Peru and Spain for this status. The pace of participation has tended to accelerate during the 1980s, and the existing ATS membership of 38 parties (ATPs) seems likely to increase; for example, Colombia has been mentioned as another potential Latin American participant. In addition, the ATS framework has evolved to accommodate new situations and needs, such as through the adoption of relevant ATCM recommendations (164 were agreed between 1961–87) and the conclusion of conventions on Sealing Conservation, Marine Living Resources Conservation (CCAMLR) and Minerals Resource Activities in 1972, 1980 and 1988 respectively. In this manner, the ATS has filled the gaps left by the limited-purpose Antarctic Treaty.

The international politics of Antarctica embrace a range of inter-related elements centred upon legal, strategic, economic, scientific, environmental, diplomatic and other considerations. These policy factors will be examined with reference to Argentina, Chile and the great powers under the following headings:

(a) A question of ownership;
(b) A continent for peace;
(c) The gold rush for South Pole wealth;
(d) A continent for science;
(e) The protection of the last great wilderness;
(f) The 'Antarctic factor' in international relations.

Inevitably, it proves difficult in practice to treat these points as mutually exclusive, as demonstrated by the next section's stress on sovereignty and resources.

A QUESTION OF OWNERSHIP

Resource questions have proved central in the international politics of Antarctica during the 1980s, when the attention of both the ATPs and the wider international community has been focused upon the search for an agreed minerals regime designed to parallel the CCAMLR regime. This resource focus represented a significant cause of international interest in the affairs of the southern continent, especially upon the part of developing countries anxious not only to share in the management and exploitation of any oil and natural gas but also to apply UNCLOS-type principles to another topic. Since 1985 this aspect has preoccupied the UN, which adopted resolutions in 1986 (res.41/88C) and 1987 (res.42/46B) calling upon the ATPs 'to impose a moratorium on the negotiations to establish a minerals regime until such time as all members of the international community can participate fully in such negotiations'. In this manner the minerals issue embodied all the elements raised during recent UN/NAM debates concerning the most appropriate method of management of Antarctica.

However, the principal cause of the delays and difficulties in the Antarctic minerals regime negotiations conducted between 1982–1988 was the ownership issue.

> On the one hand, those States asserting sovereignty in Antarctica start from the position that there can be no exploitation of minerals in their areas which is not wholly regulated by them. On the other hand, those States that do not recognise such assertions of sovereignty start from the position that their nationals are free to go to Antarctica to search for and exploit minerals and that no other State has the right to regulate, in any sense, the activities of their nationals. . . . For all practical purposes, there could be virtually no mineral activity, even prospecting, which would not give rise to the high probability of a dispute.[4]

The CCAMLR negotiations of the late 1970s nearly foundered upon this issue, which was resolved eventually through an imaginative bifocal formula enabling the ATPs, whether or not claimants, to interpret the same wording according to their divergent legal approaches. The sovereignty problem was raised in a more acute form by the minerals negotiations, given the greater political significance attached to oil and natural gas matters and their finite nature as resources. Obviously, it would have been impossible to secure an agreed regime if these rival legal positions had been pressed to the limit, while the situation was exacerbated by the anxiety of the American and Soviet governments to secure recognition for their special 'rights' and large-scale involvement throughout Antarctica.

As a result, for Argentina, Chile and the great powers, the minerals discussions raised significant points liable to have both cooperative and confrontational consequences. At one level they drew attention to Anglo-Argentine–Chilean rivalry for sovereignty, including mining rights, concerning the sector of Antarctica between 20° W–90° W (Figure 7.1), whereas at another level these three claimants were ranged against those ATPs, led by the Soviet Union and the USA but also including Brazil and Uruguay, and non-ATPs, which neither advanced nor recognised Antarctic territorial claims. In fact, this shared Anglo-Argentine–Chilean interest was reflected by their participation in the special meetings held by the claimant nations in order to discuss a collective position for each negotiating session. Nevertheless, the ATPs moved slowly towards consensus, and a convention was concluded in Wellington on 2 June 1988. Regulatory Committees, composed of representatives drawn from claimants and non-claimants as well as from the USA and Soviet Union, will become responsible for mining within 'each area identified' for exploration and exploitation. Any committee(s) established for bloc(s) within the so-called 'South American sector' will include Argentina, Britain and Chile, if involving the area of their respective claims, as well as both the Soviet Union and the USA, thereby providing scope for the pursuit of both shared interests and points of difference on legal, mining, environmental and other matters.

Several question marks remain, especially as it is difficult to know how the Antarctic Minerals regime will operate in practice. According to some commentators the South American Antarctic's relative accessibility is enhanced by the significant mineral potential of the Dufek complex and the Weddell Sea. For instance, Maarten de Wit, a geologist, having noted their location within the area of Anglo-Argentine–Chilean dispute, articulated the fear that:

> The exploitation of these deposits could put the Antarctic sovereignty issue to severe test and undermine the most delicate pivot of the present *modus operandi* of the Antarctic Treaty.[5]

Similarly, Christopher Joyner, writing against the background of the 1982 Falklands War, reflected this uncertainty:

> Should exploitation of Antarctica's living or nonliving resources become commercially profitable, the stakes of Anglo-Argentine rivalry in the region could arise [*sic*] accordingly. . . . If past national behaviour is a prologue to future international relations,

the unravelling of Anglo-Argentine rivalry over Antarctic natural resources would not come as a great surprise. Indeed, given the protracted, highly sensitive territorial dispute over South Atlantic and Antarctic territories, patently exacerbated by the recent Falklands military conflict, some observers might regard such a British–Argentine confrontation as logically inevitable in the near future. Yet, for the foreseeable term such a resource war between Great Britain and Argentina seems unlikely to occur.[6]

In future the Anglo-Argentine problem is accentuated by the involvement of Chile, while there is also the matter of whether Soviet and American participation in any Regulatory Committee will encourage concord rather than division. A further complication derives from Francis Auburn's prediction that 'the regime would be likely to mark the practical end to claims to sovereignty':

Even the most rudimentary form of licensing and decision-making must be regarded as having a considerable impact on sovereignty . . . once this has been achieved in a stable form continuing indefinitely, there will be no apparent difference in Antarctic system entitlements between claimants and non-claimants.[7]

In this manner, the question of 'Who owns Antarctica?' continues to excite controversy as an integral element of the Antarctic scene. Such claimants as Argentina, Britain and Chile refer frequently to their countries' 'long Antarctic histories' and the consolidation of title through 'occupation' in the present century. Argentina, citing its close links 'by reasons of sovereignty, history and geography', points to the fact that since 1904 a meteorological/magnetic observatory has been maintained in the South Orkneys; thus, 'the Argentine Republic has for more than 80 years continuously and effectively occupied its Antarctic territory'.[8] According to Argentina and Chile, their Antarctic claims, albeit undefined until the early 1940s, pre-dated those advanced by other governments.

By 1906, Chile's titles to Antarctica had been effectively established by effective occupation, administration, regulation and political and diplomatic activity.[9]

The *Territorio Chileno Antartico* was defined in November 1940 to cover the sector to the South Pole between 53° W–90° W and comprises about 0.5 million sq.miles. A variety of justifications for national sovereignty have been advanced:

The boundaries of Chile in said polar region . . . constitute a natural prolongation of the national soil . . . (and are based on) historical data [i.e. discoveries by Spain], . . . geographic continuity of the Chilean Antarctic as regards the southern end of the American Continent, . . . geographic contiguity [i.e. geological links], . . . scientific factors [i.e. climatic and glaciological influences], . . . sector theory, . . . different manifestations of sovereignty represented by the acts of occupation realised throughout our history, . . . diplomatic facts, [and] . . . administrative antecedents.[10]

The Chilean declaration prompted Argentina in 1943 to clarify the extent of its polar claim, which embraced an area of about 0.55 million sq.miles between 25° W–74° W south of 60° S. Argentine sovereignty has been supported on a range of grounds:

Argentine sovereignty over the territory is based on deep-rooted historical rights – maintained firmly in every circumstance by the Argentine governments – which are spiritually identified with the feelings of the entire people of the nation; on the superior geographical position of the Republic; on the geological contiguity of its land with the Antarctic territories; on the climatological influence which the neighbouring polar zones exercise on its territories; on the rights of first occupation; on the necessary diplomatic action and finally on its uninterrupted activities in the Antarctic territory itself.[11]

In practice, the announcement of these formal claims merely exacerbated the existing sovereignty problem, since most of the continent had been partitioned already by five governments (Australia, Britain, France, New Zealand, Norway). Only one sector (90° W–150° W) remained unclaimed, while Argentine and Chilean claims fell substantially within the area defined already by Britain in 1908 and 1917 as the Falkland Islands Dependencies (FID). In 1962 the BAT, located between 20° W and 80° W to the south of 60° S and with an area of 0.7 million sq.miles, was formed from the FID.

The root of the United Kingdom's title . . . lies in British acts of discovery between 1819 and 1843, accompanied by formal claims in the name of the British Crown [and] . . . formally confirmed and defined by the Crown in Letters Patent in 1908 (as amended in 1917). Since then there has been . . . a continuous display of British sovereignty and activity appropriate to the circumstances.[12]

Like its Latin American rivals in justifying a claim, the British government has emphasised the relevance of the historical dimension, such as in recalling the voyages of Captain Cook to stress that 'the United Kingdom has been active in Antarctica since 1775', thereby acquiring a polar tradition derived from Bransfield's alleged prior discovery of Antarctica (1820) – there are rival American and Soviet claims for this honour – and the prime role of British explorers in the unveiling of Antarctica.[13]

During the early decades of the present century Britain, building upon its existing foothold in the FID, adopted a somewhat acquisitive attitude towards the Antarctic region. In 1920 the government concluded that 'the whole of the Antarctic should ultimately be included within the British Empire' through the pursuit of a gradualist annexationist strategy intended – to quote one British diplomat in the 1920s – 'to paint the whole Antarctic red'.[14] This was followed by the announcement of British control, albeit through the agency of New Zealand and Australia, over the Ross Dependency (1923) and Australian Antarctic Territory (1933) respectively, and by 1933 the British Empire laid claim to some two-thirds of the region. However, during the 1930s the initial objective to annex the whole continent was scaled down in the face of international realities, since other governments either emerged as claimants (e.g. France and Norway) or refused to recognise Antarctic claims (e.g. the USA). The early years of the Second World War witnessed an even more serious challenge to Britain's position in Antarctica from the revival of Argentine and Chilean interest, so that an Antarctic dimension now supplemented the long-standing Anglo-Argentine dispute over the Falkland Islands.

The unstable Anglo-Argentine–Chilean relationship proved central in the international politics of Antarctica during the 1940s and 1950s, as reflected by the acrimonious tone of the diplomatic exchanges on the subject between London, Buenos Aires and Santiago and the occurrence of occasional incidents, such as the Hope Bay and Deception Island clashes during 1952–3. For instance, in February 1952 Argentine personnel fired shots over the heads of a group of British scientists in an attempt to prevent the reconstruction of the British base at Hope Bay within 'an integral part of the Argentine nation'. This evoked British fears regarding the initiation of 'a miniature Antarctic armaments race' and the dangers implicit in the presence of well-armed and – to quote one British diplomat – 'trigger happy South Americans' in Antarctica.[15] The attention devoted to either the Anglo-Argentine or the Anglo-Chilean relationship tended to obscure the disagreement existing between the two South American countries about the sector between 53° W–74° W. Indeed, Argentina and Chile employed Britain's 'illegal' presence in the FID as a source of unity enabling the development of the South American Antarctic concept. By contrast, Britain, maintaining its Antarctic rights, has responded that 'both claims could not be valid even if either were'.[16]

In general, the three disputants, eschewing force, preferred to rely upon diplomacy to maintain, support and protect their claims. During the late 1950s a fear of chaos over rival claims, in conjunction with an appreciation of the possible consequences of growing American and Soviet involvement in the region, provided the impetus for the negotiation of the Antarctic Treaty. The twelve signatories, perceiving that they were – to cite Roberto Guyer, an Argentine negotiator – 'on the threshold of a conflict which could have had serious political consequences', welcomed the opportunity for a political and legal accommodation of their Antarctic interests designed to facilitate the stable development of international relations in Antarctica.[17] The US government, having failed to secure an international solution for the Antarctic problem during the late 1940s and early 1950s, proved a key influence in the achievement of the treaty, especially as the unstable Anglo-Argentine–Chilean relationship concerned Washington, such as in terms of being compelled to take sides.

The Antarctic Treaty pushed the sovereignty issue aside by article IV's freeze of the legal status quo, but this expedient conceals a rather uncertain and confused situation. For example, in the case of Britain, the Argentine and Chilean challenge remains just below – it has never been beyond – the horizon, since both governments continue to treat Antarctica as a matter of fundamental importance and to act thereto in a relatively assertive and overt manner. In 1982 the British *Shackleton Report* mentioned 'the need for awareness of possible threats to the Antarctic Treaty' and BAT consequent upon Argentine activities, which have included the erection of name plates proclaiming '*Antartida Argentina*', the issue of postage stamps depicting the nature and extent of the claim, periodic presidential visits (1961: President Frondizi; 1973: President Lastiri), and the establishment of an Antarctic settlement (1977), including 'schools', banks and family groups.[18] The first of Argentina's Antarctic citizens, Emilio de Palma, was born at Esperanza base in January 1978. Thus, Argentine governments interpret *Antartida Argentina* as an integral part of national territory, wherein the country possesses a natural right to perform such activities. Chile has assumed a similar approach, such as symbolised by presidential visits during 1968–9, 1977 and 1984; in fact, on the latter occasion President Pinochet inaugurated a family settlement at Teniente Marsh base.

According to the Antarctic Treaty, these post-1961 activities cannot affect the relative strength of title – sovereignty can be neither improved nor weakened by activities and omissions – but it has been suggested that, in the event of the treaty's demise, Argentina and Chile would demand some return for such 'investments'. In the meantime, the British government, when confronted by such fears as those articulated by the 1982 *Shackleton Report*, has stressed 'the protection given by the Treaty to the United Kingdom's position in the British Antarctic Territory'.[19] However, these reassurances failed to prevent the expression of anxieties about BAT's security at the time of the 1982 Falklands War, which represented perhaps the chief perceived threat to *Pax Antarctica* in the recent period. Although the Falklands and Antarctic questions are separate historically, politically and legally, Argentina interprets the Falklands, South Georgia, the South Sandwich Islands and *Antartida Argentina* as part of a single territorial claim.[20] Against this background, certain British parliamentary and media commentators speculated about the Antarctic conflict potential of the Falklands War. Early in April 1982 Lord Shackleton asserted that:

> What is at stake and what understandably is in the minds of the Argentinians is not just the Falkland Islands but their claim to Antarctic territory.[21]

Naturally, President Galtieri's statement that the *Malvinas'* recapture proved 'merely the beginning of the reaffirmation of Argentina's right to assert territories' fuelled such speculation.[22]

In the event, fears about the southwards extension of the conflict proved groundless partly because they reflected an underestimation, even ignorance, of the protective qualities of the Antarctic Treaty. Indeed, subsequently the latter became interpreted as a possible way out of the continuing Anglo-Argentine impasse over the Falklands/Malvinas, but the surface attractions of this proposal conceal a range of difficulties, including the risk of introducing a destabilising element into the ATS and the fact that a legal freeze fails to meet the basic Argentine demand for sovereignty over the islands.[23]

More recently, the Antarctic minerals regime negotiations drew attention to the sovereignty problem, as noted above, while added difficulties have arisen from the emergence of alternative legal approaches to the region. The common heritage concept, advanced by several governments at the UN in favour of the treatment of Antarctica as *terra communis* for the purpose of the management and benefits of resource exploitation, challenges both national sovereignty claims and ATS credibility. In September 1985 Sir Geoffrey Howe, the British foreign minister, informed the UN General Assembly that his government 'firmly' opposed any attempt to apply a common heritage regime to Antarctica basically because the area was subject already to legal claims as well as to an international legal regime based upon the ATS, a view endorsed strongly by both Argentina and Chile. Thus, the Argentine delegate asserted that 'we could never accept the application of other formulas that run counter to our sovereign rights'.[24] Significantly, the Soviet and American governments, albeit non-claimants, have seconded such opposition to the common heritage approach because of their view that the ATS represented an acceptable legal regime for the region. In any case, both governments remain anxious to avoid any infringement of their hitherto undefined Antarctic 'rights'.[25] In this way, the common heritage campaign has tended to unite Argentina, Chile and the great powers in support of the existing system in spite of their fundamental legal differences.

Although the USA has been involved in Antarctica for a long period – Nathaniel Palmer is another claimant for the prior discovery of Antarctica – and often considered announcing a claim, it has merely reserved its 'rights'. To some extent, this position was taken because of the difficulty of deciding which sector to claim – the unclaimed sector was relatively unattractive and inaccessible. Other policy considerations derived from a reluctance either to restrict US access to the whole continent or to compound an already difficult legal situation. In 1984 the US government synthesised its key interests:

The United States for many years has had, and at the present time continues to have, direct and substantial rights and interests in Antarctica. Throughout a period of many years, commencing in the early 1800s, many areas of the Antarctic region have been discovered, sighted, explored and claimed on behalf of the United States. During this period, the Government of the United States and its nationals have engaged in well-known and extensive activities in Antarctica. In view of the activities . . . referred to above, my Government reserves all of the rights of the United States with respect to the Antarctic region, including the right to assert a territorial claim or claims.[26]

For the past sixty years US policy has remained constant:

The United States does not recognise any claims to territorial sovereignty in Antarctica and does not assert any claims of its own, although it reserves the basis of claim.[27]

The Soviet Union, which possesses through von Bellingshausen perhaps the strongest claim to prior discovery, has adopted a similar attitude:

The Soviet Union reserves for itself all of the rights based on the discoveries and explorations of Russian navigators and scientists, including the right to make corresponding territorial claims in Antarctica.[28]

Therefore, existing claims, being 'without basis in international law', were dismissed as 'imperialist devices'.[29]

Although Antarctica's peaceful nature encourages one to forget the pre-treaty scenario, the ATS has kept the lid closed on a veritable Pandora's box of discord centred upon the seemingly insoluble sovereignty problem. In 1984 the Soviet delegate reminded the UN:

Turning back the pages of history, we find that there was indeed a time when Antarctica was the scene of bitter international conflict, dispute and claims . . . the conclusion of the Antarctic Treaty was an important and effective means of preventing disputes, friction and conflict among States . . . its effectiveness and practicality has been verified and proved by its history of almost a quarter of a century.[30]

Recently, it has become fashionable to describe Antarctic claims as anachronistic, colonial remainders, but Argentina, Britain and Chile maintain their positions. Significantly, the British government has assumed a more assertive and visible Antarctic role in the wake of the Falklands War, such as through the post-1982 enhancement of British Antarctic Survey (BAS) research and funding. This trend was reinforced by the emphasis placed upon sovereignty since mid-1982 by the Antarctic minerals regime negotiations; indeed, the British government argued that national sovereignty was capable of making a constructive contribution to the regime.

Therefore, sovereignty considerations have never disappeared from the perceptions of Antarctic policy-makers. In fact, John Heap, head of the Polar Regions section of the British Foreign Office, has observed:

> Where sovereignty has been claimed, it is unlikely that any State, having claimed it, will give it up. And, indeed, the more it is attacked, the less likely it is to be given up.[31]

In particular, the vested interests accruing from claimant status have been reinforced by the manner in which Antarctic sovereignty imparts an added, albeit unquantifiable, bargaining factor within the ATS, such as evidenced by the marine and mineral regime negotiations. It is questionable whether Argentina, Britain and Chile as non-claimants would exert as much influence in Antarctic discussions, especially as compared to the American and Soviet governments. Thus, sovereignty offers one instrument for Argentina and Chile, like Britain, to counter the scientific and logistical weight of the superpowers in Antarctic matters.

In the meantime, Argentina, Britain and Chile continue to assert sovereignty in Antarctica, but there are uncertainties. Are their respective national interests in Antarctica satisfied best by the maintenance of allegedly divisive, unrealistic and anachronistic claims which are not recognised by either most ATPs, including the Soviet Union and the USA, or the international community? Does the 1984 Beagle Channel settlement facilitate a resolution of Argentine–Chilean differences over Antarctica? Was Jack Child correct in detecting a recent moderation of Argentine attitudes towards sovereignty?[32] If the treaty ended, will the claimants prove capable of upholding their respective rights against not only each other but also the Soviet Union and the USA, which refuse to recognise sovereignty, maintain continent-wide Antarctic presences – they have bases located within the South American sector, while the USA's Amundsen–Scott station is strategically-positioned at the South Pole itself – and might emerge as territorial rivals? Will the operation of the Antarctic minerals regime either bring latent legal points of tension to the surface or undermine the force of sovereignty? Will the challenges emanating from the common heritage and frontage concepts be accommodated by the ATS? As usual, it is easier to pose the questions rather than to provide clear-cut answers, although the preservation of the ATS will serve to contain most points of difficulty.

A CONTINENT FOR PEACE

Whenever HMS *Endurance*, the British navy's Antarctic patrol ship, crosses into the Antarctic Treaty area (south of 60° S) its two guns are covered with tarpaulins and no firing practice is allowed. According to the 1959 treaty, Antarctica became a zone of peace characterised by demilitarisation, denuclearisation and inspection provisions, thereby causing it to be described increasingly as a strategic irrelevance. The significance of these developments was accentuated by Antarctica's perceived strategic importance during the 1950s; for instance, this represented a period when American 'defense considerations require that control of the area be exercised by friendly powers and be denied to our most probable enemies'.[33] Naturally, the Soviet Union appeared as the major problem, and in October 1959 the *New York Times* asserted that 'our interest is to insure that this vast region should never be turned by the Russians into a kind of Antarctic Albania', which might be employed as a base for missiles or submarines. Whether or not such suspicions were well-founded remains questionable, but a tendency to perceive Antarctica through Cold War spectacles meant that the US government, having failed to exclude the Soviet Union from a voice in the area's affairs, welcomed the Antarctic Treaty as an instrument to defuse any problems.

In this sense, Antarctica's insulation from external tensions enhanced international stability in general, and proved beneficial to all countries, especially to those, like Britain, the Soviet Union and the USA, with global interests. Thus, the altered strategic value of Antarctica derived less from a concern to use it for military or nuclear purposes but rather from a desire to deny an advantage to a rival. For governments either located in the southern hemisphere, like Argentina and Chile, or possessing territory therein, like Britain, specific strategic concerns derived from Antarctica's character as their 'Near South', as evidenced by pre-1959 fears that the continent might offer the USSR a 'back door' through which to threaten their territory and sea lanes. Roberto Guyer, an Argentine participant in the Antarctic treaty negotiations, has referred to the benefits of the denuclearisation provisions to his country:

> We are less than a thousand kilometres from Antarctica and if, for instance, an atomic explosion occurred, it could have very concrete effects for us.[34]

The ATPs, most notably, the USA and USSR, have articulated the

Antarctic Treaty's precedent-setting qualities, such as in the sphere of regional zone of peace/arms control schemes, while the periodic exercise of its inspection rights is 'an important element of US Antarctic policy' for both global and regional reasons.[35] In addition, the Antarctic Treaty has become interpreted as a southern boundary-point for subsequent projects, including the Latin American Tlatelolco Treaty (1967), the South Pacific Zone of Peace (1985), and the 1986 proposals for a South Atlantic Zone of Peace (SAZOP).

Antarctica's peaceful status has survived controversies dividing ATPs in other parts of the world. For example, Soviet–American co-operation over Antarctica has developed in spite of various crises (e.g. Berlin, Afghanistan), while this feature was highlighted recently by the 1982 Falklands War. In spite of fears that this conflict might acquire an Antarctic dimension, Argentina and Britain continued to co-operate within the ATS framework, as evidenced by their participation in minerals and marine resources discussions at Canberra, Hobart and Wellington *during* the war. Although Britain has withdrawn since 1959 into a NATO/European role, it retains a territorial interest in Antarctica and the South Atlantic, including an associated concern to deny the military use of the region to an adversary. Nevertheless, the Eurocentric nature of British policy has evoked discussion about the realism of a South Atlantic role, and these questions were raised in an acute form during and after the 1982 War, which enhanced Britain's stake in the region and encouraged an appreciation of the Falkland Islands as an alleged polar gateway. Mount Pleasant Airport, opened in 1985, means that Britain, like Argentina, Chile, the USSR and the USA, now possesses a capability to project power in Antarctica, even if military, political, geographical, climatic and other factors indicate that Antarctica is beyond an effective military effort.

> Continuous combat is virtually unimaginable . . . neither Argentina, Chile nor the United Kingdom could effectively defend their overlapping claims. . . . All governments must come to realise that only by compromise and accommodation can any one of them retain any hold in Antarctica, because each could effectively deny the others the precarious toe-holds needed to maintain claims in a very severe climate.[36]

Thus, it remains their mutual interest to preserve the neutralisation of the continent, wherein problems are resolved through diplomacy within the ATS.

However, this has not prevented assessments seeking to identify Antarctica's strategic value, a point demonstrated by the influence of geopolitical thinking upon military elites in Argentina and Chile, including President Pinochet of Chile, who has published a geopolitical study (1968) and visited Antarctica twice (1977, 1984). Jack Child has identified the manner in which Argentine and Chilean geopolitical thinking has stressed the importance of national security, space, the projection of power in the maritime, aerospace and resource dimensions, and the significance of such 'choke points' like Drake Passage.[37] For example, the concept of *Atlantartida* typified the maritime thrust of Argentine geopolitics in terms of establishing not only the Falklands and Antarctica as part of one claim but also the 'geopolitical aggression' committed by Britain against Argentina. Similarly, Chile interprets Antarctica as a significant part of the tri-continental vision of itself as a mainland, Antarctic and Southern insular nation. Within this context, Child asserted that:

> A frequently overlooked source of Antarctic tension is the geopolitical thinking which has been the legacy of military regimes in southern South America over the past quarter century.

It proves difficult to assess the present-day influence of geopolitics in democratic Argentina, although some observers have detected a more realistic and moderate stance on sovereignty.[38] Also controversy continues concerning the contemporary strategic value, if any, of the Drake Passage as an alternative to the Panama Canal and the precise nature of the alleged Soviet threat in the South Atlantic. Does the Soviet 'ring of bases' around Antarctica have a strategic intent or is the threat merely in the minds of those motivated by a ritual deference to the containment of the USSR? Conversely, it is worth noting that Soviet commentators, pointing to the ambitions of 'aggressive imperialist circles, especially of American circles', have presented the ATS as a 'strategic barrier' preventing Antarctica's 'inclusion within the sphere of military strategic interests of the imperialist states'.[39]

Few clear answers have emerged from such speculation about Antarctica's future military and nuclear potential, but the general view has tended to argue that most military/nuclear functions could be performed better elsewhere, especially as technological developments have reinforced Antarctica's strategic irrelevance.[40] For instance, satellites have reduced the need for ground-tracking stations in Antarctica. Parsons' study group concluded recently that 'it is therefore hard indeed to sustain the alarmist assertions' articulated in certain quarters, perhaps encouraging one to observe that Argentina, Chile and the great powers, albeit characterised by varying policy perceptions, benefit from Antarctica's status as a zone of peace, and particularly from the behavioural norms encouraged by this framework.[41]

THE GOLD RUSH FOR SOUTH POLE WEALTH

At present, Antarctica's perceived resource potential explains much of the contemporary interest therein. Historically, Antarctic waters were valued by Argentina, Chile and the great powers for whaling and sealing. At present, a limited amount of krill and fish are caught within the CCAMLR area – the annual catch amounts to about 0.5 million tons – principally by the Soviet Union, whose 80–90 per cent share creates a strong fishing interest. Chile accounts for less than 1 per cent of the catch, while neither Argentina, Britain nor the USA figure in the annual statistics, thereby providing scope for CCAMLR-centred disagreements based upon exploitation versus conservation interests. Environmental groups, pointing to its inadequacies in respect to scientific data and conservation measures, have proved critical of both the CCAMLR regime and member governments:

> Then, there are the fishing countries, whose approach thus far seems to fight all conservation measures . . . they are more interested in short term gain than in the future of the resource they are harvesting.[42]

Naturally, this scenario places 'fishing countries', principally the Soviet Union but possibly also Chile, against Argentina, Britain and the USA. Although Parsons' study group believed that 'current harvesting levels are unlikely to present significant conservation problems', potential over-fishing offers cause for concern, such as in the event of economic pressures prompting the USSR to enhance its activities in the light of speculation that Antarctica's krill potential might total between 4–170 million tons.[43]

However, most interest has been devoted to minerals, as suggested by a 1983 *Sunday Times'* headline regarding the 'Gold Rush for South Pole wealth'. Hitherto, geological research has failed to provide evidence substantiating such notions of Antarctica's riches, and expert comment concludes that neither oil, natural gas nor precious metals of economic value are known to exist in the region. Mining prospects are diminished further by the problem of ice as well as the impact of a series of climatic, economic, technological and other factors. Nevertheless, Argentina, Chile and the great powers, though pessimistic about exploitation possibilities, have supported the minerals regime negotiations in order to avoid an unregulated scramble for resources and sovereignty problems, to establish a management scheme promoting rational use and environmental protection, and to reinforce the ATS.

At present, there are few grounds for optimism regarding short-term exploitation, but should mining occur both the environment and international relations might suffer, especially if any government is tempted to exploit for strategic, non-economic reasons. In the meantime, there exists a clear desire upon the part of Argentina, Chile and the great powers to exert a significant role in the management of resources as well as to secure an appropriate share of any benefits. For example, the post-1982 period has been characterised by numerous British references to Falklands–Antarctic interconnections, including the view that the islands represent a 'latchkey to open the front door of a palace filled with riches beyond calculation' in Antarctica.[44] This polar 'gateway' argument has often been exploited in order to provide an Antarctic rationale for the large-scale post-war expenditure on the Falklands (£3 billion plus).

In general, commercial mining in Antarctica is deemed unlikely until the twenty-first century. However, one needs to allow for changing circumstances and levels of technology, so that any government's interpretation of such aspects as 'appropriate share' might vary over time. A further complication relates to the influence of the developed/developing countries divide upon the relationship between Argentina, Chile and the great powers. This section's emphasis upon marine and mineral resources obscures the fact that future economic possibilities include tourism and the exploitation of icebergs for fresh water; in fact, a limited amount of American, Argentine and Chilean tourism occurs already, and over 7000 tourists are expected in 1988.

A CONTINENT FOR SCIENCE

During 1957–8 the IGY offered a multilateral framework for Antarctic science, and the 1959 Treaty, representing a means of perpetuating international scientific co-operation, enabled the transformation of Antarctica into a continent for science valued as a laboratory for both fundamental and applied research. Each of the five governments dealt with in this chapter undertake scientific research in Antarctica; indeed, they perform a predominant role therein, as evidenced by the fact that they operated 24 out of 38 bases operational in Winter 1987 (Argentina: 6; Britain: 4; Chile: 3; USA: 4; USSR: 7). But this national emphasis has been qualified by the collaborative elements fostered by the ATS through the exchange of scientists and information, participation in international research programmes (e.g. the BIOMASS project on krill), and membership in SCAR (Scientific Committee on Antarctic Research). Richard Laws, BAS' Director (1973–87), has identified 'the extremely good' nature of international scientific co-operation in Antarctica, and current examples include BAS/Chilean co-operation on South Shetlands geology, American, Argentine, British, Chilean and Soviet collaboration in the multilateral BIOMASS project, and American, Argentine, British and Chilean involvement in NASA's 1987 Airborne Antarctic Ozone Experiment.[45] In this manner Antarctic science has provided, and continues to provide, a practical framework for co-operation between the ATPs. Naturally, it is difficult to assess how far such contacts possess political consequences, but even the existing modest level of scientific co-operation offers an added and meaningful dimension to, say, British relations with Latin American nations capable of further development. However, David Drewry, writing prior to his recent appointment as Director of BAS, detected evidence of decreased scientific co-ordination in certain quarters, including the USA and Latin America: 'One may liken the process to the Antarctic nations with their hands linked moving back progressively into their own corners', as evidenced by the 'distinctive South American axis' developing around Argentina, Brazil, Chile and Uruguay.[46]

Although individual governments have often stated the 'highly important' nature of Antarctic research, in reality it is difficult to ignore the interconnection of politics and science, including the fact that science proves the currency of Antarctic law and politics. Antarctic research, providing an on-the-spot presence, means that claimant governments, like Argentina, Britain and Chile, have viewed science as a means of exercising their sovereignty – for example, BAS scientists are appointed to various administrative posts in BAT – and giving domestic and international visibility to their claims. The post-1982 period has been characterised by a considerable enhancement of British Antarctic policy, as reflected by a 60 per cent increase in BAS funding and research. In fact, during 1987–8 BAS was allocated extra funding into the early 1990s in order to facilitate expensive logistical improvements in spite of the contemporary fiscal constraints imposed upon other British research bodies. In turn, Argentina and Chile, while operating significant research programmes, have often been accused of being more concerned to record a sovereignty presence rather than to perform science *per se*. Similarly, the anxiety of the USA and USSR to perform leading Antarctic roles is interpreted to demand a prime research commitment, thereby explaining the contemporary 'international rivalry in science as the various Antarctic nations strive to demonstrate their scientific competence and technical prowess in the various fields of Antarctic research'.[47] As a result, scientific research, albeit apparently non-controversial, continues to prove a political instrument reflecting and influencing international relations in Antarctica in both positive and negative directions.

THE PROTECTION OF THE LAST GREAT WILDERNESS

The recent resource-related discussions have focused attention upon the alleged threat posed to the fragile Antarctic environment by exploitation. The ATS has devoted considerable attention to conservation, as evidenced by numerous ATCM recommendations and the ecosystem approach adopted for CCAMLR, even if NGOs, advocating a world park approach, have proved somewhat critical of the ATPs' record. Argentina, Chile and the great powers have all stressed the importance of environmental protection partly because of a sense of responsibility for the sound management of the continent and partly because of the global significance of treating Antarctica as a specially protected conservation region. In any case, geographical proximity renders Argentina and Chile extremely aware of this aspect. Obviously, there are varying degrees of response to environmental priorities and pressure groups; for example, the USA's inclusion of a NGO representative on its ATCM delegations contrasts with the relative unimportance of NGOs as an influence upon Argentine, Chilean and Soviet policy. Already the CCAMLR regime has shown evidence of polarisation centred upon the exploitation/conservation divide, and the operation of the minerals regime may raise this problem in a more acute form. As a result, it is difficult to make any definite pronouncements regarding the impact of Antarctic environmental questions on international relationships, although any assessments need to appreciate the manner in which conservation, like science, is perceived by governments within the broader geopolitical milieu, that is, as a less important policy interest than political, legal and related considerations.

THE 'ANTARCTIC FACTOR' IN INTERNATIONAL RELATIONS

During the 1980s the UN/NAM-based critique has fostered an enhanced awareness on the part of the ATPs of the ATS' benefits, thereby causing them not only to deny the existence of any fundamental Antarctic management problem but also to appreciate the regime's delicate balance of interests, such as between claimants and non-claimants, developed and developing nations, or exploitation and conservation interests. Basically, Argentina, Chile and the great powers have expressed satisfaction with the operations of the ATS, which is perceived to offer the most appropriate framework within which to pursue and maximise specific national Antarctic interests. In particular, it provides a means of avoiding the unmanageable escalation of national policies at variance with each other; thus, the ATS, having ensured the peace and stability of Antarctica for over 27 years, may continue to perform this role into the indefinite future. Significantly, at the UN Argentine and Chilean delegates have argued that the ATS 'must be maintained and strengthened' for 'we do not believe it would be possible to create a better system'.[48] Indeed, both governments 'could never accept the application of other formulas that run counter to our sovereignty rights' – this attacked the common heritage principle – and 'cannot participate in or support any kind of parallel mechanism'. American, British and Soviet spokesmen echoed such sentiments in respect to advocating the maintenance of the ATS and the dangers implicit in any effort to upset this proven system.

Naturally, the ATS' future prospects will prove a function of the extent to which it succeeds in securing an external accommodation with the wider international community, but this should not obscure the continuing need also for an internal accommodation of divergent interests within the system itself, such as of the nature identified in previous sections. Any evaluation of the manner in which the ATS has united Argentina, Britain, Chile, the USA and the USSR should be qualified by an awareness of points of difference consequent upon varying legal, strategic, scientific, environmental and other approaches towards Antarctica. More recently, the question of South African participation within the ATS has caused complications, and at the UN during 1986 and 1987 Argentina and the Soviet Union voted for the exclusion of South Africa, an original ATCP, from ATCMs, whereas Britain, Chile and the USA, like most ATPs, expressed opposition to UN interference in Antarctic matters by non-participation (as distinct from abstention) in the vote. The practical implications of these developments remain uncertain, even if the 1987 ATCM held at Rio de Janeiro was seemingly unaffected by the problem, for South Africa sat down at the same table as Argentina and the Soviet Union.

Roberto Guyer, an Argentine diplomat, has identified the importance of the 'Antarctic spirit' – this has been fostered through the ATS' consensus and collaborative procedures – as a factor serving not only to facilitate the regime's smooth operations but also to exert a series of incalculable effects upon bilateral relationships, especially between governments having either little else in common or clear points of dispute. Against this background, the ATS provides Argentina, Britain, Chile, the USA and the USSR with an additional instrument for meaningful, practical bilateral/multilateral contacts with each other. For example, Argentina, Britain and Chile, having assumed a somewhat distant relationship within the ATS for the regulated management of their territorial dispute, have been forced increasingly to talk to each other in order to seek consensus on a range of questions, including those raising sovereignty issues. Even during the 1982 War Argentine and British delegates sat down together on three occasions on ATS business, and subsequently Antarctic questions have offered an invaluable Anglo-Argentine point of contact unaffected by the 'Falklands factor'. Similarly, Chile has found that the ATS provides a regular channel for dialogue with both Britain and the USSR unencumbered by human rights problems.

It proves difficult to quantify the wider diplomatic impact of such practical contacts, but clearly the pursuit of common Antarctic goals, in conjunction with the accommodation of points of difference, represent a factor of some significance. Clearly, the Argentine, British and Chilean governments have come to value the extra foreign policy dimension offered by the ATS; for example, it allows Argentina and Chile an extra channel of access to most European governments, Australia, China and India, while Antarctica proves a shared interest with fellow Latin American governments in Brazil, Cuba, Ecuador, Peru and Uruguay. In future, more governments seem likely to join the ATS, a trend posing the question of whether 'the Antarctic factor' will survive any further enlargement of the membership.

CONCLUSION: A POLE APART?

Although the ATS is confronted by various uncertainties, including the UN challenge, the South African question and a possible treaty review in 1991, it represents a well-established fact of international life, whose success and durability will prove an important influence upon the Antarctic future of Argentina, Chile and the great powers. The 38 parties, though constituting only a low proportion of the international community, include the most significant governments and account also for over 70 per cent of the world's population.

Antarctica is far from being a mainstream global issue, but the polar dimension represents a significant co-operative and confrontational element affecting current and future international relationships both within and outside Latin America, particularly for Argentina, Brazil and Chile. The apparent simplicity of Antarctica's international politics disguises a rather complicated reality of bilateral and multilateral linkages between Argentina, Britain, Chile, the USA and the USSR, which constitute five of the continent's leading actors. Within this five-cornered relationship, one can point to the manner in which Argentina and Chile, united as local actors and claimants as well as through Latin American solidarity and support for the South American Antarctic concept, are divided by historical and geopolitical perceptions, sovereignty over the 53° W–74° W sector, South African participation in the ATS, and possibly over fishing exploitation. In fact, this point serves to remind one about the absence of a Latin American consensus over Antarctica, a feature reinforced by the more recent involvement of other regional governments, including Brazil, Cuba, Ecuador, Peru and Uruguay. For instance, Brazil, while co-operating with Argentina on various political and scientific questions, has not only refused to recognise existing claims but also has been associated with an alternative legal approach centred upon the frontage concept. Similarly, Chile and Uruguay have adopted a contrasting strategy at the UN to that of Argentina and Brazil on

South African participation in ATCMs. In the sphere of scientific co-operation the Latin American nations come together in various combinations as well as with other ATPs, especially Britain and the USA because of their interest in the same part of the continent; for instance, the recent period has been characterised by a range of British scientific/logistical links with Brazil, Chile, Ecuador and Uruguay.

Significantly, Antarctic affairs possess an ability to bring together in a meaningful grouping such governments as the USA and the USSR, while since the 1982 War the ATS has provided one of the few areas of Anglo-Argentine dialogue. Indeed, the operations of the ATS have provided the foundation for the formation of a co-operative American–Argentine–British–Chilean–Soviet relationship, which has been developed for positive and negative reasons and has exerted varying and incalculable impacts upon international politics.[49] In turn, the ATS' enduring qualities suggest that in future this five-cornered linkage may qualify gradually the force of the existing two, three or four-cornered relationships deriving from both Antarctic (e.g. claims, science) and external (e.g. the Falklands dispute, East –West and North–South relations) causes. Nevertheless, this five-power relationship will need still to be viewed within the parameters of the ATS, such as in terms of the various linkages formed with other ATPs. Although Antarctic questions have proved capable of qualifying, even countering, the impact of external factors, this 'Pole Apart' theme should not be allowed to obscure either the manner in which the polar scene both reflects and influences international relations in general or the fact that the region's issues concerning ownership, resource management and conservation are merely Antarctic manifestations of global problems.

Notes

1. Miranda Weston-Smith (ed.), *Peter Scott. Travel Diaries of a Naturalist: I* (London: Collins, 1983) pp. 233–46.
2. Peter J. Beck, *The International Politics of Antarctica* (London: Croom Helm, 1986), pp. 3–16; Peter J. Beck, 'A Continent Surrounded by Advice: Recent Reports on Antarctica', *Polar Record*, Vol. 24, No. 151 (1988).
3. Sir Anthony Parsons (ed.), *Antarctica: the Next Decade* (Cambridge: Cambridge University Press, 1987) p. 3.
4. British Foreign Office, *Foreign Policy Document no. 98: Antarctica – an*

Overview (London: FCO, 1983), p. 6; Peter J. Beck, 'The Antarctic Minerals Regime Negotiations', *Polar Record*, Vol. 24, No. 148 (1988) pp. 59–61.

5. Maarten J. de Wit, *Minerals and Mining in Antarctica: Science and Technology, Economics and Politics* (Oxford: Oxford University Press, 1985) p. 68.

6. Christopher Joyner, 'Anglo-Argentine Rivalry after the Falklands: On the Road to Antarctica?', in A.R. Coll and A.C. Arend (eds), *The Falklands War: Lessons for Strategy, Diplomacy and International Law* (London: Allen & Unwin, 1985) pp. 206–7.

7. F.M. Auburn, 'The Antarctic minerals regime: sovereignty, exploration, institutions and environment', in S. Harris (ed.), *Australia's Antarctic Policy Options* (Canberra: CRES, 1984) pp. 273–4.

8. United Nations General Assembly Records (UNGA) A/39/583 Part II, Vol. 1, pp. 10–11, Argentina to UN, June 1984; UNGA A/C 1/39/PV53, p. 7, 29 Nov. 1984.

9. UNGA A/39/583 Part II, Vol. 2, p. 34, Chile to UN, 27 June 1984.

10. Quoted Beck, *International Politics of Antarctica*, p. 121.

11. Ibid., p. 119.

12. Ibid., p. 122.

13. UNGA A/C 1/38/PV44, pp. 16–18, 29 Nov. 1983.

14. Beck, *International Politics of Antarctica*, pp. 26–30.

15. Peter J. Beck, 'A Cold War: Argentina, Britain and Antarctica', *History Today* (June 1987) pp. 16–17.

16. F.M. Auburn, *Antarctic Law and Politics* (London: Hurst, 1982) p. 57.

17. Roberto E. Guyer, 'Antarctica's Role in International Relations', in F.O. Vicuna (ed.), *Antarctic Resources Policy: Scientific, Legal and Political Issues* (Cambridge: Cambridge University Press, 1983) p. 270.

18. Lord Shackleton, *Falkland Islands: Economic Study 1982* (Cmnd 8653, London: HMSO, 1982) p. 3.

19. Quoted Beck, *International Politics of Antarctica*, p. 133.

20. Jack Child, *Geopolitics and Conflict in South America: Quarrels among Neighbors* (New York: Praeger, 1985) pp. 71–4. See Jorge A. Fraga, *Introduccion a la Geopolitica Antartica* (Buenos Aires: Direccion Nacional del Antartico, 1983).

21. *Hansard (Lords)*, Vol. 428, Col. 1585, 3 April 1982.

22. Quoted Child, *Geopolitics in South America*, p. 81.

23. Peter J. Beck, *The Falkland Islands as an International Problem* (London: Routledge, 1988) pp. 148–9.

24. UNGA A/40/PV9, p. 62, 25 Sept. 1985; UNGA A/39/583 Pt.II, Vol. 1, pp. 22–4, June 1984; UNGA A/C 1/38/PV46, p. 2, 30 Nov. 1983; UNGA A/C 1/39/PV53, p. 11, 29 Nov. 1984; UNGA A/C 1/40/PV50, pp. 22–3, 26 Nov. 1985.

25. UNGA A/C 1/39/PV53, p. 44, 29 Nov. 1984; UNGA A/39/583 Pt.II, Vol. 3, pp. 125–8, 29 May 1984.

26. Quoted Beck, *International Politics of Antarctica*, p. 124.

27. Ibid.

28. *Pravda*, 4 June 1958.

29. Peter Toma, 'Soviet Attitude towards the Acquisition of Territorial

Sovereignty in the Antarctic', *American Journal of International Law*, Vol. 50 (1956), pp. 619–22.

30. UNGA A/C 1/39/PV53, pp. 41–5, 29 Nov. 1984.
31. Quoted Rüdiger Wolfrum (ed.), *Antarctic Challenge* (Berlin: Duncker & Humblot, 1984) p. 58.
32. Jack Child, 'Antarctica: Arena for South American Cooperation or Conflict', paper presented at International Congress of Latin American Studies, New Orleans, March 1988, p. 9.
33. US Position Paper, 15 July 1952, 702.022/7-1552, State Department Records, US National Archives.
34. Quoted Beck, *International Politics of Antarctica*, p. 87.
35. UNGA A/39/583 Pt.II, Vol. 3, pp. 110–11, 29 May 1984.
36. Parsons, *Antarctica: Next Decade*, p. 104.
37. Child, *Geopolitics in South America*, p. vii, p. 33, pp. 42–7. Note Jack Child's *Antarctica and South American Geopolitics* (New York: Praeger, 1988).
38. Child, *Antarctica: Arena for South American Cooperation or Conflict*, p. 9.
39. Y. Deporov, 'Antarctica: A Zone of Peace and Cooperation', *International Affairs* (Moscow), No. 11 (1983), p. 37.
40. Peter J. Beck, 'Antarctica as a Strategic Irrelevance?', *Contexto Internacional* [Brazil], (1988).
41. Parsons, *Antarctica: Next Decade*, pp. 98–107.
42. *Eco*, Vol. 37, No. 2 (1986) pp. 1–2.
43. Parsons, *Antarctica: Next Decade*, pp. 66.
44. *Daily Telegraph*, 25 Sept. 1984; *Hansard (Commons)*, Vol. 25, col. 740, 15 June 1982, Thatcher.
45. Beck, *The International Politics of Antarctica*, p. 99.
46. David Drewry, 'International Scientific Coordination in Antarctica', in T.B. Millar (ed.), *Australia, Britain and Antarctica* (London: Australian Studies Centre, 1986) pp. 32–3.
47. Phillip Law, *Antarctic Odyssey* (Melbourne: Heinemann, 1983) p. 272.
48. UNGA A/C 1/39/PV53, p. 16, 29 Nov. 1984; UNGA A/C 1/40/PV50, p. 23, 26 Nov. 1985.
49. See also Carlos Moneta, 'America Latina, la Antartida y el Atlantico Sur', *Flacso: América Latina*, Vol. 3, No. 10 (1986) pp. 76–9; Christopher Joyner and Ethel Theis, 'The United States and Antarctica: Rethinking the Interplay of Law and Interests', *Cornell International Law Journal*, Vol. 20, No. 1 (1987) pp. 101–2.

8 The External Debt*
Ricardo Alagia

INTRODUCTION

The so-called external debt crisis involves those developing countries
with a chronic imbalance in their external sector or with fundamental
shortcomings in their system for generating productive capital. Besides the social and political problems caused directly or indirectly by
the external debt, so too a vicious circle of domestic economic
problems is generated including inflation, insufficiency of internal
savings for investment in productive facilities and resulting obsol-
escence of these facilities. The set of financial demands which capital-
exporting creditor countries are able to impose on the chronic debtors
in the developing world constitute a modern, efficient and insidious
tool for domination and dependency.

The external debt crisis threatens social peace, economic development and political stability of the Third World debtors, and at the
same time draws in governments of both debtor and creditor countries even when loans were made by the private sector. When
developing countries have not been able to pay the principal and/or
the interest of the external debt, governments of developed states
have had to become involved as well to forge at least temporary
solutions. This impasse did not occur simply through greed or impru-
dence of developing states in incurring massive loans. Capital-
exporting countries competed with one another to loan to developing
countries with pressing needs and often offered enticing, easy loan
conditions but with the potential for high interest rates. The expectation was of course that money could be easily recycled from North to
South and that lucrative profits could be made.

General guidelines governing debtors have included recipes for
financial stability associated more or less closely with the International Monetary Fund (IMF). These guidelines embody economic
common sense as formulated in Western developed countries, but
they are often inappropriate for developing countries if inflexibly
applied. In order to achieve short-term financial goals, debtors are to

* Translated by Michael A. Morris.

apply recessive policies including reining in inflation, restricting internal consumption, and cutting public spending and subsidies. Such measures raise the cost of living and impose often harsh conditions on long-suffering populations without necessarily remedying the economic dilemmas of a wide variety of debtors. The domestic market is to be liberalised for international competition with exports to be encouraged through a variety of measures, although debtor states are faced with increasing protectionism for their products especially when competitive with those of developed states. Reserves are to be accumulated for maintaining a tranquil monetary system, regardless of the constraints this may place on underprivileged classes. Finally, the political system is to be stable, which all too often has masked an affinity for right-wing and/or military governments.

For supporters of such an approach, problems of the internal economic structures of Third World debtor countries block satisfactory adjustment measures and lasting stabilisation. It follows from such a view that debtors should orient their economies towards new forms of production, consumption and trade at the domestic, regional and global levels. In effect, this is the modern version of the international division of labour decreed several centuries ago by the classical economists, although this time the governing formulas assign a dominant role to developed states while relegating developing ones to a subordinate, dependent one.

On political as well as economic grounds, these solutions and preferences usually associated with the North have not been appropriate for the South. Self-interest and misunderstanding have fused in the formulas conceived by and for the North. The debt crisis is instead a North–South problem and not just one which can be resolved by developed countries disciplining allegedly wayward developing ones. Politicisation of the ostensibly economic external debt crisis has resulted. High political stakes, domestic and international, can lead to confrontation, but politics also can help generate and sustain the will for imaginative solutions. Since the stability of the international financial system and not just of debtors is threatened, it is of great importance to find at least the outline of a solution to the debt crisis that is mutually acceptable while addressing the real needs and problems of the South.

THE LATIN AMERICAN EXTERNAL DEBT

Flows of financial capital are an integral part of the world economy, although specific rules and characteristics of these flows vary. Latin America was frequently affected by foreign loans in the last century, which when unpaid occasioned financial crisis and even led to intervention by creditors.

During the nineteenth century and first part of the twentieth century, the European role in international capital flows was especially prominent. Debtors were more subject to coercion by creditors to settle accounts than in the contemporary world. For example, Britain, Germany and Italy intervened on the Venezuelan coast in 1902 to demand payment of outstanding debts. Inasmuch as the United States was also a creditor of Venezuela, it approved of this European intervention. In contrast, the position of the Argentine government reflected Latin American views. As expounded by Luis Maria Drago, the doctrine of Carlos Calvo set forth the opposition of the Argentine government to the coercive collection of the Venezuelan public debt. The International Court of the Hague determined that the demands of creditors were just in principle, but reduced the British claim to 6 per cent of that demanded, that of Germany to 28 per cent, France to 14 per cent, Italy to 7 per cent and the United States to 2 per cent.

The rise of the United States as the leading Western power during this century also made an impact in the international financial sphere and on creditor–debtor relationships. US interventions in Central America and the Caribbean between the first and third decades of this century often had a financial element, including alleged financial irresponsibility as a trigger for intervention or US control of financial management once intervention occurred.

During the period of the gold standard, there generally was a certain balance in relationships between debtors and creditors in which markets regulated credit needs. Latin American fitted into the system as a provider of basic products with little value added. The rough balance between supply and demand lasted until the financial crisis of 1929, which drastically affected the region while impacting differently on individual countries.

During the 1930s, the Great Depression created new problems for the management of the Latin American external debt. The region suffered particularly from the decline in foreign trade, the drastic decline in international prices of primary products, aggressive protectionist policies of consuming countries towards Latin American products, and the lack of monetary liquidity. An economic crisis resulted throughout the region, with the partial exception of Argentina, as countries fell in arrears and then became wholly unable to service international financial obligations. A solution to the debt crisis was hammered out in several ways. Accords were reached which lowered interest rates and substantially reduced the global percentage of the debt of each debtor country (i.e., 60 per cent in the case of Brazil and 80 per cent in the case of Mexico). Since the debt was represented by public bonds issued by each debtor, bond holders organised themselves into the Council of Foreign Bond Holders to take charge of negotiating debt arrears. The Council only succeeded in negotiating 10 per cent of the total debt, and the rest was negotiated in highly favourable conditions for the debtors during the Second World War.

Profound changes in the international economy during the 1970s provided a new context for international capital flows and external debt. In addition to the petroleum crisis, international inflation and the inconvertibility of the dollar to gold, excess international liquidity helped spur international lending. Capital flows tended to go from North to South, especially to Latin America because of its apparent developmental potential, and the external debt increased rapidly.

Creditor–debtor relationships have been shaped by this new context, although the United States and Latin America are again principal protagonists, and, all too often, antagonists. The Latin American debt is primarily in US currency, even though the US share of trade and foreign investment with the region has declined. Since the debt is mostly in dollars and carries variable interest rates, Latin American debtors have been vulnerable to decisions of US domestic monetary authorities. High interest rates were passed on to the debtors, and a lowering of interest rates has been rejected by major creditor states as a solution to the current debt crisis. More drastic solutions are not given serious consideration as the demands of Latin American states are systematically ignored.

The Latin American foreign debt rose rapidly from $10 billion (thousand million) in 1965 to $100 billion in 1980. By 1987, Brazil alone had surpassed the $100 billion foreign debt level. Table 8.1 shows the large portion of the Latin American debt in Third World terms and the largest debtors within the region. Of the fifteen leading Third World debtors listed, ten are in Latin America and nine are in South America. All of the Southern Cone countries are included

Table 8.1   Size of the external debt of the 'Baker Plan' countries (end of
1986, billions of US dollars)

Brazil	$109.2
Mexico	$100.4
Argentina	$53.0
Venezuela	$34.1
Philippines	$28.3
Nigeria	$25.2
Chile	$21.6
Yugoslavia	$21.1
Morocco	$15.9
Colombia	$15.0
Peru	$14.6
Ecuador	$9.0
Ivory Coast	$7.6
Uruguay	$5.2
Bolivia	$4.5
Total	$464.8

Note: Figures are rounded.

Source: *Perspectivas Economicas* (United States Information Agency), Vol. 4,
No. 60 (1987).

(Argentina, Chile and Uruguay). Table 8.2 documents the burden of
the external debt on selected Latin American debtors again including
the Southern Cone states. While the absolute level of indebtedness of
Chile and Uruguay is considerably lower than that of Argentina,
their burden is nevertheless comparable because of smaller national
economies. Chile has had some success recently in restoring national
and international confidence in the economy, but the external debt
remains a heavy burden and grave socio-economic problems continue.

The escalating debt has cast an ever larger shadow over the entire
national economy of the three largest Latin American debtors
(Argentina, Brazil and Mexico). These three countries also have the
largest and most diversified economies in the region, which places
them in the strategic position of serving as engines of progress
benefiting all countries in the area. However, if the external debt
continues to burden their economies and hinder overall development, adverse results will be region-wide.

While the debt crisis assumed global proportions by 1982, the

Table 8.2   Debt burden of selected Latin American countries (1985)

	Debt service actually paid (millions of US dollars)	Interest payments/export of goods and NFS (non–factor services) (percentages)
Argentina	8 269.0	50.9
Brazil	13 581.1	40.3
Chile	2 525	41.8
Mexico	12 423.0	37.7
Uruguay	406.0	34.2

Source: *Economic and Social Progress in Latin America: 1987 Report* (Washington, DC: Inter-American Development Bank, 1988) pp. 214, 246, 254, 342 and 400.

situation of Latin American debtors was especially pressing. As new credits dried up, the expedient of refinancing debts in arrears was offered. A vicious circle was set in motion – new debts continued to pile up to service the previous debt and subsequent refinancing would become necessary since the circle of deepening debt could not be broken. Accumulated debt became increasingly burdensome as rising interest payments and new loans were added to the principal. For example, Brazil's debt rose from $60 billion in 1980 to $90 billion in 1982 and then to nearly $110 billion in 1986. (This does not count the added accumulation since the unilateral Brazilian debt moratorium decreed in February 1987 and subsequently suspended.)

During the initial period of easy credit for Latin American debtors, private lenders had dispensed with the IMF. But when it became necessary to refinance massive loans in arrears, they relied on this institution. Belated reliance on the IMF by private bankers was intended to assure fulfillment of debt obligations through enforcement of the standard policies of stabilisation and adjustment of the national economies of debtors. At the same time, the bankers increased their reserves to cover for potential default by debtors. They still know that the IMF with the backing of their home governments is an efficient negotiator disposed to defend the interests of the existing international financial order.

While the IMF has somewhat moderated its financial orthodoxy, it has been able to insist on case-by-case negotiations with debtors thereby keeping the interests of the latter fragmented. Latin American disunity on the debt question has weakened its negotiating position. In contrast, the creditors are ensconced behind the IMF and their home governments, they hold meetings and plan joint strategies and with an eye towards control they monitor policies of high-risk debtors. Brazil's unilateral debt moratorium was short-lived and chain reaction unilateral moratoria were prevented. Finally, conditions for refinancing external debts have been imposed involving readjustments in the domestic economies of debtors, whereby the international financial system has been assured almost certain control of key decisions in national economic policy.

This is not to deny that high inflation in a number of Latin American countries is fed by inappropriate domestic measures including protectionism, subsidies and budget deficits. President Alfonsin recognised that through official subsidies Argentina lost \$12 billion between 1980 and 1987 in the international agricultural market. Regional economic structures are often backward and goods and services tend to be expensive and inefficient. While the creditors have been guilty of offering easy money for frequently unsound projects, Latin American debtors have been addicted to borrowing as a temporary expedient to fend off deeply-rooted problems requiring more imaginative, vigorous action. There is a resulting need to fit domestic socio-economic actors into more dynamic models of growth and development capable of projecting a Latin American presence more actively into the international economy.

While recognising a whole series of problems of domestic origin, the critical problem of the debt has an obvious external dimension which has tended to impact unfavourably on a highly constructive regional development, democratisation. Especially since 1983 in the Southern Cone of South America, the debt crisis has coincided with elected democratic regimes (Argentina, Brazil, Peru and Uruguay). Latin American debtor countries have highlighted, through statements and declarations, the danger for political stability in the region posed by the problem of the external debt as it is currently constituted.[1] For example, the Declaration of Quito reaffirmed the regional desire to sustain democratic principles in spite of the debt crisis. Both internal and external factors combined to produce the debt crisis, it was acknowledged, but the vulnerability and dependency of the Latin American economies have made it necessary for developed states to play a leading role in helping establish conditions for regional economic and political stability.

THE ARGENTINE EXTERNAL DEBT

The origins and subsequent evolution of the escalating Argentine debt are closely associated with recent political history of the country. However, the problem has become so politicised that dispassionate analysis is difficult. Self-interested observers have tried to justify the debt with economic and financial arguments, but it is hard to deny the crucial responsibility of Argentine military governments, 1976–1983, in allowing the external debt to get out of control. In fact, prior military governments added disproportionately to the external debt as well.

The Peronist government was overthrown violently by the military in 1976, and left an external debt of $7.5 billion dollars. The preceding Illia government also had been overthrown by the military, and had left an external debt of $3.5 billion. The military interregnum between the two civilian governments therefore had increased the foreign debt by over 100 per cent. When the democratic Alfonsin government took over the government in late 1983, it inherited an external debt of $43 billion from its military predecessor. By 1988, the Alfonsin government had paid over $20 billion in interest payments and refinancing charges, well over 50 per cent of receipts from exports were destined to servicing the debt and the total debt was creeping upwards towards $55 billion.

A policy of indebtedness began with the economic plan of Martinez de Hoz of 2 April 1976, which tended to sustain and even strengthen mechanisms underpinning an unequal and unjust international economic order. Foreign credits on advantageous terms allegedly would be channelled to innovative producers and sectors to modernise and renew the national economy. Competition would be encouraged through imports and governmental incentives. In fact, marginal national producers dropped out of production, and imports rose without being offset by a proliferation of innovative entrepreneurs invading both domestic and international markets. The national electronics industry is a case in point. The automobile industry was less tractable to governmental manipulation because of its very complexity, although some increase in competition was promoted.

The only sectors that teemed with activity were the state industries and foreign lenders. Easy credit was available to the state industries, whose loans were guaranteed and eventually assumed by the Argentine state. By the end of 1985, Argentina was faced with the formidable task of servicing debt obligations to 300 US private banks.

Massive arms buying by the successive military governments un-deniably contributed to the external debt. A recent study quantified the relationship between the Latin American external debt and weaponry imports.[2] In the case of Argentina, $4450 million was paid for arms imports plus interest from 1970–83; interest paid in 1984 for arms acquired up to that time was $550 million; and this debt incurred for arms was 18 per cent of the overall public debt.

As matters now stand, since late 1983 democratic politicians have had the tremendous responsibility of developing some kind of sol-ution to the debt problem which unavoidably would have profound effects on national life. As for military affairs, military expenditure was cut and arms imports were curbed. Joint action was not under-taken with other Latin American debtor states, and a programme of adjustment and stabilisation in accord with IMF guidelines was being followed. Stages in this process have included: a rigid adjustment plan of 15 June 1985, the Austral plan; the policy of freezing prices and salaries in the second half of 1987; and negotiation of successive agreements with the IMF. Still, the Argentine external debt has continued to mount, inflation has worsened and the foreign trade balance has become less favourable. The failure to meet targets agreed with the IMF (including targets for cutting the domestic budget deficit) has triggered another cycle of pressure on Argentina to take more vigorous measures to achieve goals.

These rather grim trends place the findings of a recent study about Argentina's bargaining with the IMF in perspective. The study con-cluded that Argentina had significant influence in negotiating suc-cessive agreements with the IMF, although 'this influence seems to be slowly eroding' as IMF 'methods of influence naturally make it more difficult for a debtor to deal effectively with the institution'.[3] This conclusion of continuing Argentine influence is seriously hedged. Argentina managed to retain influence in determining specific debt repayment conditions even as its overall economic and external debt situation was deteriorating. However, Argentine influence regarding the external debt situation has had narrow parameters and decreased over time. At most, Argentina was influential in postponing its agony.

Concrete, reciprocal measures by creditors, which would make the Argentine effort to shoulder the external debt more tolerable, have not been forthcoming. For example, Argentine products could be allowed easier, more equitable access to international markets. The European Economic Community subsidises its meat exports by as much as 100 per cent with respect to the cost of production, and the United States subsidises its grain sales by some $2 billion dollars annually. It has been estimated that these and other protectionist measures have accentuated the fall in international prices of Argentine raw materials, representing a loss to the country of over $1 billion annually. Similarly, for each increase in the interest rate of a single point (at times because of US pressure), servicing of the Argentine external debt rises by more than $400 million.[4]

In the initial months of the Alfonsin government between December 1983 and July 1984, Argentina did practice a *de facto* unilateral moratorium. This made it possible to accumulate $2 billion to stimulate the economy. The creditor countries and the IMF feared that a common front might be forged with Brazil, and they successfully insisted on negotiations with individual states. One reason for Brazil's subsequent inability to sustain its declared unilateral debt moratorium was the lack of Argentine interest and support. While a joint debtor strategy including the two major South American states and perhaps others would have caused problems of its own, it certainly would have tended to enhance Argentine bargaining power.

Argentina still has no viable strategy for long-term refinancing of the debt or for achieving a substantial reduction in interest rates. Creditors essentially impose higher interest rates on Argentina and other debtors, just as they shape a discriminatory context for foreign trade from which the debtors are compelled to try to generate substantial foreign exchange. The opposition Peronist (*Justicialista*) party has promised a debt-interest moratorium, which, while popular with voters, would aggravate relations with creditors.

What is certain is that the return of democracy has unleashed popular resentment across the political spectrum about the external debt. In part, this resentment has been directed at preceding military regimes and in part at the creditors. As the social costs of shouldering a mounting external debt rise, any democratic government in Argentina will be the object of growing popular pressure to take dramatic action to resolve the crisis. At the same time, options are narrowly defined for democratic governments. Generally moderate responses by the Alfonsin government have not prevented the debt problem from worsening. Radical responses would likely fail because of opposition by the creditors. Continuing inability to handle the ongoing crisis will likely threaten the very foundations of Argentine democracy. Paradoxically, a great strength of Argentine democracy is to have released pent-up emotions about social justice and foreign manipulation, but constraints in resolving the crisis turn this strength into a potential lethal weakness.

CONCLUSIONS

The Latin American external debt, in the context posed by the creditor states and the IMB, is unpayable without severe hardship for the region. Dangers include social upheaval and the overthrow of the democratic governments in the region including those in the Southern Cone.

There is no shortage of proposed solutions. Drastic measures proposed or threatened by some debtor states include temporary or permanent suspension of debt payments, fixing debt payment to a set percentage of exports, and cancellation by creditors of part of the debt. Such proposed measures are attractive to debtors, and they might involve co-operation between debtors or even a joint debtor strategy. However, they inevitably convey a hostile message to creditors and all the more so when associated with joint action by debtors. Other proposed solutions have a technical overlay but are also replete with political implications. A Mexican proposal involves partial purchase of the debt with monetary reserves of debtor countries represented by bonds backed by the US Treasury. Alternatively, the World Bank might assume part of the debts. Capitalisation of the debt would involve paying the debt with assets of the debtor country such as state-owned enterprises, which allegedly would reduce the role of the state as well as the need for foreign exchange.

All of these potential solutions and combinations thereof deserve careful examination because of the gravity of the problem. Distinctive characteristics of individual countries and specific creditor–debtor relationships will require and should help generate multi-faceted approaches. But at root the obstacles to resolving the external debt crisis are political rather than technical. Mutual comprehension of both creditor and debtor problems as well as flexibility and goodwill are required to forge satisfactory solutions.

While at this stage in the international debt crisis it is not particularly productive to blame one party or the other, the debtor states obviously played a key role in giving rise to unmanageable debts and subsequently have often not pursued appropriate economic policies. However, the Southern Cone democracies have been responding prudently and responsibly to the external debt crisis and all the more so when contrasted with previous military governments. Their national polities and economies are none the less fragile and they are under great pressure to distribute wealth more equitably among the masses which elected them. Consequently, they dispose of little leeway, their options have been closing still further over time, and they are vulnerable to demands of external creditors whether reasonable or not.

It follows that the creditor states must play the central role in shaping mutually acceptable solutions to the external debt crisis. They dispose of relative freedom of action and are capable of sustaining imaginative initiatives on multiple fronts including foreign trade and investment measures to supplement an external debt strategy. However, the analysis of the Latin American debt in general and that of Argentina in particular has indicated that the leverage enjoyed by creditor states has generally been used to entrench longstanding dependency relationships with debtors.

While the debt crisis has dramatised the continuing dependency of Latin American states at least in financial affairs, a long-term policy subjugating Latin American states and especially the larger ones is no longer viable. Over the past decades, numerous Latin American states have managed to achieve middle-income status and relatively diversified economies, so that fundamental pillars of economic strength remain. Regional foreign policies have also tended to become more assertive and autonomous, even if constraints are especially prominent on the external debt issue. Consequently, Latin American states will continue to forge their destiny, even though severe problems have been posed by the external debt crisis. If mutually acceptable solutions to the debt crisis cannot be developed, a major casualty will be relationships between the creditor and debtor states and most especially between the United States and the larger Latin American debtors. Harsh austerity measures will surely be accompanied sooner or later by harsh authoritarian regimes harbouring grudges against the United States and other major creditor states.

Notes

1. Latin American debtor countries have joined in endorsing this theme of the danger posed by the external debt to regional democratisation at a

series of meetings and resulting declarations. These have included the Contadora Group and its Support Group, meetings of the Group of Six, and the Latin American Economic Conference at Quito, 9–13 January 1984, which produced the famous Declaration of Quito.

2. Carlos Portales, 'Seguridad Regional en Sudamerica. Escenarios prospectivos', in Augusto Varas (ed.), *Paz, Desarme y Desarrollo en America Latina* (Buenos Aires, Argentina: Grupo Editor Latinoamericano, 1987) p. 362.

3. Kendall W. Stiles, 'Argentina's Bargaining with the IMF', *Journal of Interamerican Studies and World Affairs*, Vol. 30 (1988) pp. 82, 81.

4. Paper presented by Professor Alejandro Serra Quiroga, 'El FMI, la Republica Argentina, la deuda externa y la banca privada multinacional', at the IX Congress of the Argentine Association of International Law, Tucuman, Argentina, August 1987.

9 Great Power Military Relations
Michael A. Morris

PROMINENT CHARACTERISTICS OF SOUTHERN CONE MILITARY POWER

There are both positive and negative aspects of military power in South America in general and the Southern Cone in particular. On the negative side, considerable military weaponry possessed by neighbouring countries often aggravates mistrust just as this mistrust in turn fuels arms expansion. In a word, arms tend to contribute to interstate tension and tension spurs arms build-ups. Ongoing disputes accentuate the international action–reaction process connecting hostile relations and weaponry growth. This circular process dragging countries into militarisation and conflict is as threatening for South America and the Southern Cone as other parts of the developing world.

Argentine and Chilean military power is particularly relevant for disputes in the Southern Cone of South America, but other regional states have importance there and outside powers bring formidable military capabilities to bear as well. For example, during the 1982 Anglo-Argentine Falklands war, possible military responses of non-belligerent South American states were of great concern to the two contending parties, one of the contending parties was an extra-regional great power (Great Britain), and the politico-military response of the traditional regional hegemon (the United States) influenced the course of the conflict but not to the complete satisfaction of either party.

Military modernisation and weaponry renewal have tended to occur in cycles in South America, and historical swings between civilian and military governments have helped trigger these cycles of military expansion. Military governments presided over the latest cycle of arms expansion and modernisation for over a decade up to the early 1980s. New patterns of civil–military relations are emerging under democratic governments, although the armed forces remain powerful actors promoting the interests of the military institution.

While pressure continues to build in Chile for a rapid transition from military to civilian rule, as elsewhere in the region the military would almost certainly remain influential under an eventual democratic government.

On the other hand, arms can have a positive or at least a stabilising impact. Military power may help deter an aggressor, enforce rights entrenched in law or provide the means for pursuing highly valued national interests. While military power can reward an aggressor and contribute to instability, so too can balanced military capabilities of adversaries help prevent conflict and create time for political solutions to be explored.

Weaponry expansion has been less pronounced in South America than in conflict-prone Third World regions such as the Middle East. Relatively less South American emphasis has been placed on quality and quantity of modern weaponry, and levels of military expenditure generally have been lower both in absolute terms and with relation to the size of national economies. South America has also been relatively free from major armed conflicts in recent decades.

While most South American military governments sustained weaponry expansion into the 1980s, the successive civilian governments generally have tried to brake and in some cases even reverse arms build-ups. An adverse economic climate in the 1980s, to which arms build-ups of previous military governments contributed, has tended to constrain further military expansion as well. Sharp cuts in military spending will still be difficult for civilian governments to implement and sustain, but stabilisation of military spending and arms procurement may be achieved through a civil–military consensus.

While there are both positive and negative facets of military power in the Southern Cone of South America, the dividing line between them is not clear-cut. In spite of relatively low levels of regional militarisation, each adversary regards its own side as righteous and tends to blame the other for intransigence and military provocation. The recurring nature of South American arms build-ups also makes it hard to distinguish between cause and effect and positive and negative expressions of military power. Prediction of conflict prospects is complicated accordingly.

Even though causes and effects of military expansion are complex and often unclear, some indicators portray prominent characteristics of South Cone economic and military power (Table 9.1). Brazil's profile is clearly that of the economic giant of South America, but

Table 9.1 Economic and military power of selected South American
states (1984)

	GNP	POP	ME	ME/GNP	AF	AF per 1000
Argentina	61 190	30.2	2 250	3.7	174	5.8
Brazil	205 200	136.3	1 719	0.8	459	3.4
Chile	18 870	11.8	790	4.2	123	10.4
Peru	19 600	19.2	1 402E	7.1	135	7.0
Uruguay	4 866	2.9	139	2.9	30	10.3

Abbreviations. GNP: Gross National Product in millions of constant 1983
dollars. POP: Population in millions. ME: Military Expenditures in millions
of constant 1983 dollars. ME/GNP: Military Expenditure divided by Gross
National Product expressed in percentage. AF: Armed Forces size. AF per
1000: Armed Forces per 1000 people. E: Estimate based on partial or
uncertain data.

Source: *World Military Expenditures and Arms Transfers 1986* (Washington,
DC: US Arms Control and Disarmament Agency, US Government Printing
Office, 1987). Data were derived from Table I, pp. 59–100.

modernisation and expansion of the armed forces have been quite
moderate in comparison to the size of the national economic base.
When the Brazilian military occupied the government it did modernise and expand all the armed forces, while military spending remained rather restrained throughout.

While Argentine economic power is substantially below that of
Brazil, the Argentine military has tried to maintain qualitative
weaponry parity with Brazil. As a result, the economic burden of
military spending has been substantially heavier for Argentina than
Brazil (Table 9.1). A quantitative balance has not been attainable for
Argentina especially in numbers of troops.

Table 9.2 indicates the great uncertainty about the level of Argentine
military spending. Estimates of the level of Argentine military expenditure are especially difficult and sensitive. Politically-charged questions involving the level of Argentine military spending relate to the
1982 Falklands war, relations with neighbours and the great powers,
and civil-military relations. Argentine military spending was certainly
large before and during the Falklands war, but there is a debate over
how soon the military government in Argentina may have replaced
and even increased weaponry after the war. The subsequent civilian
government in Argentina as well as neighbouring states and Britain

Table 9.2   Alternate estimates of Argentine military expenditure

Year	ACDA	SIPRI
1974	1 049	
1975	1 357	
1976	1 989	
1977	2 155	3 952
1978	1 952	4 019
1979	2 237	3 975
1980	2 463	3 936
1981	2 374	4 178
1982	3 620	<8 784>
1983	2 745	(6 536)
1984	2 250	5 633
1985		6 647
1986		6 315

Abbreviations. ACDA: *World Military Expenditures and Arms Transfers 1986*. SIPRI: *SIPRI Yearbook 1987: World Armaments and Disarmament*. < >   Estimates with a high degree of uncertainty. ( )   Uncertain data.

Sources: *World Military Expenditures and Arms Transfers 1986* (Washington, DC: US Arms Control and Disarmament Agency, US Government Printing Office, 1987). ACDA data were derived from Table I, p. 65. ACDA figures are in constant 1983 US million dollars. *SIPRI Yearbook 1987: World Armaments and Disarmament* (Oxford, England: Oxford University Press, 1987). SIPRI data were derived from Table 6A.2, p. 172. SIPRI figures are in US $m, at 1980 prices and exchange rates.

have all tended to associate high levels of military expenditure with a militaristic impulse of the Argentine military. Inclusion or exclusion of ambiguous areas of military spending such as national military industries affect the ongoing debates about the military burden and threat one way or the other. The higher spending estimates would signify a substantially heavier Argentine military burden with attendant greater risks for Argentina's neighbours including Britain in the Falklands.

The civilian Alfonsin government in Argentina has been committed to cutting national military expenditure while negotiating a settlement with Great Britain over the Malvinas/Falklands dispute. The democratic government was able to negotiate a settlement with Chile over the Beagle Channel dispute in 1984, but has blamed British intransigence for the failure to achieve a counterpart negotiated settlement over the Falklands issue. Britain is faulted on political

Table 9.3   Arms transfers of selected South American states

Year	Argentina AI	AE	Brazil AI	AE	Chile AI	AE	Peru AI	AE	Uruguay AI	AE
1975	52	0	174	104	35	0	208	0	9	0
1976	82	0	229	114	212	0	425	0	8	0
1977	62	8	139	123	93	0	663	0	31	0
1978	528	0	285	143	86	0	442	0	7	0
1979	660	13	317	145	251	0	145	0	7	0
1980	254	6	157	169	303	0	315	0	48	0
1981	560	11	67	190	347	6	325	0	67	0
1982	303	0	31	335	293	0	387	63	21	0
1983	975	20	40	130	90	0	190	0	10	0
1984	435	77	135	483	155	19	203	0	0	0
1985	140	0	19	56	19	19	75	0	0	0

Abbreviations. AI, Arms imports. AE, Arms exports.

Source: *World Military Expenditures and Arms Transfers 1986* (Washington, DC: US Arms Control and Disarmament Agency, US Government Printing Office, 1987). Data were derived from Table II, pp. 101–42.

grounds for a lack of willingness to compromise about the future of the islands. On the military front, Britain's establishment of a strong military presence through the Fortress Falklands policy and its exclusion of Argentine military and merchant vessels from a 150-mile zone around the islands have been regarded by Argentina as provocative.

ARMS TRANSFERS AND SUPPLIERS

High levels of arms imports have been sustained by Argentina *vis-à-vis* other prominent South American states, as shown in Tables 9.3 and 9.4. The highest level of arms imports roughly correlates with the years of military government, 1976–1983.

The budgetary squeeze on the Argentine military since the advent of civilian government is evident in new arms transfers. Table 9.3 indicates that since the military government exited in late 1983 there has been a pronounced drop in arms imports. Both Chile and Peru have depended heavily on arms imports, while those of Brazil have been moderate.

Diversification of sources of arms imports tends to mirror the diversification of South American foreign policies (Table 9.4). Up to

Table 9.4 Major arms suppliers to selected South American states
(cumulative, 1981–1985, millions current dollars)

| | Suppliers | | | | | | |
	Soviet Union	United States	United Kingdom	France	West Germany	Italy	Others	Total
Recipients								
Argentina	0	40	90	230	1400	110	530	2400
Brazil	0	90	10	60	0	70	50	280
Chile	0	0	60	460	130	0	220	870
Peru	390	110	0	210	230	100	110	1150
Uruguay	0	5	0	50	5	0	40	100

Source: *World Military Expenditures and Arms Transfers 1986* (Washington, DC: US Arms Control and Disarmament Agency, US Government Printing Office, 1987). Data were derived from Table III, pp. 143–6.

the mid-1960s, the United States was still holding undisputed sway in South America and Cold War rhetoric still carried conviction, which allowed it to maintain a near-monopoly of arms supply to the area in the form of second-hand or outdated equipment. In 1967, the US Congress imposed restrictions on military assistance and the export of arms to Latin America, in part because of the renewed cycle of military coups in the region. The new restrictions in US policy contributed to a shift in regional arms-buying patterns, since pressure by the traditional regional hegemon was resented by countries increasingly anxious to lessen their dependency. Alternate arms suppliers, too, were anxious to increase their market share in the region. The main beneficiaries of this new pattern of trade were Western European suppliers and the Soviet Union. Prior to the 1982 Falklands/ Malvinas war, Great Britain was a significant arms exporter to Argentina, although this link was severed by the war.

After the mid-1960s, owing to the proliferation of sources of arms supplies, South America's armed forces were no longer as dependent on United States supplies as before. More sophisticated armaments also were introduced in plain defiance of the US policy of limiting armaments. Co-production and licensing arrangements spread as well.

In 1982, the United States did conclude a memorandum with Brazil for co-operation with the Brazilian military industry. Problems hampering achievement of the potential of this accord have included Brazilian concern that extensive US involvement in national arms production might allow the United States to exert pressure to control Brazilian arms exports. Political problems have prevented conclusion of counterpart US–Argentine or US–Chilean arms production accords.

Investment in national military production can increase self-sufficiency of national armed forces and may eventually be able to gain foreign exchange through arms exports, thereby helping offset the heavy financial outlay. Argentina and Brazil are the acknowledged leaders in domestic arms production in Latin America.

Although substantial resources have been invested in Argentine military industries, this has led to few arms exports (Table 9.3). Argentine dependence continues on foreign technology and components for national arms production as well as on foreign sources for imports of relatively sophisticated aircraft, tanks and warships.[1]

Brazil has had much more success in developing national military industries, which have helped promote self-sufficiency in basic weaponry for the armed forces as well as generate arms exports. In part, Brazil's relatively low level of arms imports has been compensated through supplies of basic *matériel* for the armed forces from national military production. A recent study concluded that of major Third World arms producers Brazil had the highest rate of national arms production to arms imports (well over 70 per cent) while that of Argentina was relatively low (somewhat over 20 per cent).[2] Of all the Latin American states, only Brazil has had sustained success in exporting arms (Table 9.3).

Political problems involving the major arms suppliers have further complicated the Argentine position, as suggested in Table 9.4. While the United Kingdom had been an arms supplier of some importance to Argentina prior to the 1982 Falklands war, during and after the war Britain has embargoed arms sales and for a time successfully encouraged its Western allies to do likewise. Western European arms suppliers supported the British-instigated arms embargo during the war, but subsequently returned to export arms to Argentina.

In the late 1970s the United States cut military assistance and embargoed its arms sales to Argentina and Chile when both countries were under military governments, primarily because of alleged human rights abuses. (Several other South American countries were targets of US pressure as well at the time.) The US arms sales ban was confirmed in 1982 because of the Argentine invasion of the

Falklands, and in deference to British policy was continued after the Argentine transition to civilian government. As of mid-1988, the United States still embargoed major arms sales to Argentina although discussions were underway to permit transfers of at least some weaponry.

Because of recurring Western arms embargoes, Argentina has had to increase reliance on a variety of minor suppliers especially during the 1982 Falklands war. The embargoes also gave a boost to national military production.

Peru is the only South American state which has relied heavily on the Soviet Union as an arms supplier, although Western and other arms suppliers still remain very important. Argentina has developed a significant commercial relationship with the Soviet Union, but this emerging relationship has not yet come to include arms transfers. In October 1988, Brazil did conclude a treaty, with potential military implications, on space co-operation with the Soviet Union.

Chile has had hostile relations with the Soviet Union since the 1973 coup overthrew the leftist-leaning Allende government, which precluded its following the Peruvian pattern of reliance on Soviet arms. Chilean human rights abuses and delays in returning to democratic government have led some of the major Western suppliers to impose an arms embargo. Chile's failure to make notable progress towards democracy has continued to be an insuperable obstacle to overturning the US arms ban. Political constraints on arms imports have required Chile to place considerable emphasis on minor arms suppliers. Chile has also responded to arms embargoes, as Argentina and Brazil previously did, by building up a small national military industry which has been able to generate some limited exports.

In 1980, Britain's Thatcher government lifted an arms embargo of the previous Labour government against Chile. This contrasts with continuing British policy to deter arms from any source which might enhance Argentine military capabilities for the Falklands dispute. While arms embargoes originally spurred development of an arms industry in Chile, the lifting of the British embargo helped sustain the initial momentum achieved by national arms production. For example, the president of Cardoen, Chile's leading non-government defence contractor, noted that the British policy change 'meant the chance to do what we would eventually like to do with the US – openly to trade in arms components'. He added that 'We've been able to integrate things from both countries [Britain and Chile], and save a lot of time by not reinventing the wheel'.[3]

The continuation of the US arms embargoes of both Argentina and

Table 9.5   Comparative naval power of selected South American states (1987)

	Major surface warships and submarines					
	Carrier	Cruiser	Destroyer	Frigate	Corvette	Submarine
Argentina	1	0	6	6(4)	0	4(3)
Brazil	1	0	10	6	0	7
Chile	0	1	8	2	0	4
Peru	0	2	6	4	0	12
Uruguay	0	0	0	3	1	0

Note: Warship numbers indicated in parentheses are building, while all others are active.

Source: *Jane's Fighting Ships 1988–89* (London: Jane's Publishing Co., Ltd, 1988) pp. 9, 49, 88, 414, 789.

Chile up to present (mid-1988) has reinforced the region-wide trend of diversification of foreign arms suppliers. By that time, US and UK arms supply policies nevertheless began to diverge. Britain favoured continuing an arms embargo against Argentina and urged the United States to maintain its counterpart embargo, while US policy-makers were becoming increasingly inclined to supply arms to the moderate, civilian Alfonsin government. In contrast, US policy-makers were becoming increasingly exasperated with the reluctance of the Pinochet government in Chile to move towards democracy, and urged Britain to reduce its military ties with Chile including arms sales. In 1987, the United States was able to block a British sale of Sea King helicopters to the Chilean military because of their US-made components.

SOUTHERN CONE NAVAL POWER

The various debates regarding Argentine military power are mirrored in naval power. The civilian Alfonsin government originally intended to sell over half of the major combatants of the fleet and cancel other outstanding orders. However, the navy has been able to keep its newest and best equipment and sustain a modest programme of renewal (Table 9.5).

In assessing naval power, the number and kind of vessels must be considered along with their age and armament. The extent of national naval production and naval aviation are also relevant for

Table 9.6   Hierarchy of selected South American navies (Argentina, Brazil, Chile, Peru and Uruguay)

---

(1) Regional force projection navies (top of 6 ranks among all Third World navies): *Argentina and Brazil*.
  (a) Naval/naval aviation structure. All Third World naval and naval aviation equipment categories strongly represented. More than 15 major warships and/or submarines.
  (b) Naval capabilities. Impressive territorial defence capabilities and some ability to project force in the adjoining ocean basin.
  (c) Production/supply characteristics. Thriving national military construction industry with some indigenously designed and licensed naval and naval aviation construction; large naval expansion programme including imports.
(2) Adjacent force projection navies (second of six Third World ranks): *Chile and Peru*.
  (a) Naval/naval aviation structure. Most Third World naval and naval aviation equipment categories well represented. More than 15 major warships and/or submarines represented.
  (b) Naval capabilities. Impressive territorial defence capabilities and some ability to project force well offshore (beyond the exclusive economic zone).
  (c) Production/supply characteristics. Some licensed production and limited or no indigenously designed naval and naval aviation construction; considerable naval expansion programme including imports.
(3) Inshore territorial defence navies (fourth of six Third World ranks): *Uruguay*.
  (a) Naval/naval aviation structure. Third World naval and naval aviation equipment categories moderately represented at lower levels and only sparsely represented at upper levels, if at all. 1–5 major warships and/or submarines.
  (b) Naval capabilities. Primarily inshore territorial defence with limited offshore defence capability.
  (c) Production/supply characteristics. Even licensed naval construction very limited; rate of foreign naval acquisitions varies widely.

Source: Michael A. Morris, *Expansion of Third-World Navies* (London: Macmillan Press, 1987 and New York: St Martin's Press, 1987). Data were derived from Chapter 2, 'The Hierarchy of Naval Capability'.

naval power comparisons. Relying on such multiple criteria, Table 9.6 indicates that Argentina has been able to maintain rough naval parity with Brazil in spite of economic and political obstacles to naval expansion. The Chilean and Peruvian navies occupy the same naval rank, but the latter has been rising rapidly in status. Much lower in rank is the Uruguayan navy.

The Argentine navy has none the less felt the budgetary squeeze of the civilian government. Older vessels have been sold, the annual conscript intake and sea time have been reduced, and naval expansion has been slowed. Plans to buy an aircraft-carrier have been blocked as has a project to build a nuclear-powered submarine although several conventional submarines are on order. Nuclear-powered submarines also pose several issues related to nuclear proliferation, which are discussed below.

The Argentine military withdrew from the annual UNITAS naval exercises between the US and various Latin American navies after the 1982 Falklands/Malvinas war because of US support for Britain. In October 1988, for the first time since the war, US–Argentine naval manoeuvres were held although they were still not part of the UNITAS series.

THE REGIONAL BALANCE

From the various tables and related evidence, Chile and Peru emerge as roughly comparable in economic and military power. However, larger Peruvian military spending and arms imports have been leading to a rise in military status.

Chilean–Peruvian relations have long been strained by border problems and competitive military build-ups. More recently, democratically-elected President Alan Garcia of Peru has taken initiatives to defuse tension between the countries and Santiago has responded positively. Both governments have been exploring the possibility of reducing arms expenditure, freezing arms purchases and creating a demilitarised zone on both sides of the border.

Uruguayan economic and military power is the weakest of the Southern Cone states, although Uruguay's position as a buffer between Argentina and Brazil it is not without strategic importance. As Uruguay has become associated with Argentine–Brazilian economic integration, its strategic value as a buffer between two traditional adversaries has declined. National leaders have increasingly come to discount the prospect of any conflict with either of the South American leaders, as witnessed by an increasing amount of Uruguayan weaponry being oriented toward internal security and coming from Argentina and Brazil. The return of democratic government and severe economic problems in Uruguay have also combined to limit arms imports and reduce military expenditure and troops.

With the caveats noted above, there is overall conventional military parity between Argentina and Brazil. However, concern with monitoring and maintaining a rough military balance has receded on each side because of the bilateral *rapprochement* during the 1980s which has extended to military affairs. For example, May 1980 agreements signed by both sides included aeronautics and nuclear co-operation. Both countries also have held joint military exercises.

Less pressing, too, is the need for Argentina and Chile to monitor mutual arms acquisitions and military behaviour following the accommodation inaugurated by the 1984 bilateral treaty over the Beagle Channel. While Chile has been militarily inferior to its larger neighbour, prospects for conflict between the two countries have decreased measurably since their confrontation in the late 1970s over the Beagle Channel.

Britain's military build-up through the Fortress Falklands policy has deterred any potential Argentine military adventurism since the 1982 war, and in any event the Alfonsin government has sought a peaceful settlement to the dispute. The British military presence in the Falklands and environs also compensates for Chilean military inferiority *vis-à-vis* Argentina by drawing Argentine attention away from remaining disputes with Chile. British ties with Chile, including arms sales and arms production, constitute a rare exception to Chile's international isolation.

While the Antarctic Treaty demilitarises and denuclearises the cold continent, the regional military balance has still made an indirect impact there. Argentina, Britain and Chile all maintain a presence with a central military component just to the north of the treaty zone, and this infrastructure supports their Antarctic presence and territorial claims there as well. The military competition generated by the Falklands and Beagle Channel disputes has not been expressed openly in Antarctica, but all the great powers and local contenders have been affected by linkages between these areas. Chapter 7 of this volume documents the political conflict and co-operation involving the parties in the five-cornered relationship in Antarctica.

NUCLEAR PROLIFERATION

The 1967 Treaty of Tlatelolco attempts in part to constrain the freedom of action of the great powers regarding nuclear weaponry in and offshore Latin America. The nuclear weapons states are to observe the statute of military denuclearisation of Latin America, including territories within the treaty area for which they are responsible. This would include Great Britain in and around the Falkland Islands, and Argentina claimed that the presence and military operations of British nuclear-powered submarines offshore the islands during the 1982 war violated the Treaty. At the same time, Argentina has signed the Treaty but has still not ratified it. Brazil and Chile have signed and ratified but have not availed themselves of the waiver provided for in Article 28, paragraph 2 for the entry into force of the Treaty in their territories, so that the Treaty is not in effect for them.

The great powers, for their part, have sought to curb the nuclear ambitions of Argentina and Brazil, especially in so far as their national nuclear energy programmes might contain the potential for the development of nuclear weapons. Great power attention has focused on Argentina and Brazil, since their nuclear energy programmes stand out in Latin America and Argentina is generally recognised as the regional leader.

The methods used to deter nuclear proliferation have included a global non-proliferation regime, the nuclear powers' restrictive or punitive national legislation and specific measures targeted at suspected violators. Coercion or pressure is intrinsic to this general strategy of non-proliferation, and both Argentina and Brazil have objected to it on these grounds.

On a global level, the 1968 Nuclear Non-Proliferation Treaty has constituted a key element in deterring the emergence of new nuclear weapons states, although neither Argentina nor Brazil is a party to the treaty. Full-scope IAEA (International Atomic Energy Agency) safeguards cover all peaceful nuclear facilities (both indigenous and imported), which Argentina and Brazil have also refused to accept.

A number of more specific measures have been designed to deter or discourage Argentina and Brazil from developing a nuclear weaponry potential. In a prominent case of external interference the United States in 1974 cut Brazil off from supplies of enriched uranium for reasons of nuclear non-proliferation. In order to achieve a position independent of the United States, Brazil then turned to West Germany for the supply of a complete nuclear fuel cycle. The United States energetically opposed this 1975 Brazilian–West German agreement, which in any event has not kept up with the original ambitious expectations because of increased costs among other reasons.

The Argentine nuclear programme has been less dependent on foreign supplies and hence less vulnerable to external pressure. Great power pressure has none the less been applied on numerous occasions with some effect, since Argentina's nuclear programme, while having made considerable progress towards independence, is likely to remain dependent in some critical areas for some time. A 1984 survey of Argentina's nuclear prospects concluded that 'the nuclear program has been and will remain constrained by technological dependence upon the advanced nations for at least the next dozen years'.[4] The United States and Canada have been the most insistent of the developed states in controlling the transfer of nuclear technology to Argentina. A recent example was in 1988 when the Reagan administration increased pressure on Argentina to halt development and discourage potential export of a medium-range missile, the Condor II, allegedly capable of carrying nuclear warheads. A British diplomat emphasised that 'Our position is every bit as strong as that of the US because of the proliferation of missiles and of course because of the Falklands.'[5]

Argentina and Brazil have pursued an autonomous nuclear technological capability in the face of formidable technological hurdles and foreign constraints. Nuclear technology with potential weaponry implications is gradually proliferating in Latin America.[6] In addition to the efforts of both Argentina and Brazil to develop their own nuclear programmes, a number of developed state suppliers have willingly, and at times enthusiastically, supplied both countries with nuclear technology that has potential military application.

Argentina has committed considerable resources to developing self-sufficiency in nuclear technology, which has been all the more impressive in view of the political instability in the country over the past several decades. Since Argentina has not been able to dispense with reliance on foreign technology, it has attempted to circumvent strict controls through diversifying foreign suppliers. The list of alternative suppliers has come to include West Germany, Switzerland and the Soviet Union.

The May 1980 Argentine–Brazilian agreement on nuclear cooperation also was intended to promote the independence of both countries in the field of nuclear energy. This was complemented in 1986 by an economic integration treaty that included joint nuclear development and exports. With a similar aim, both countries have also looked beyond the developed states for Third World partners in the nuclear field. Argentina aspires to be a major regional supplier of nuclear material and know-how.

The quest of Argentina and Brazil for self-sufficiency in nuclear technology does not commit them to develop nuclear weapons, but in time allow them to do so. Argentina and Brazil have retained the option for so-called peaceful nuclear explosions permitted by the Treaty of Tlatelolco without necessarily committing themselves to taking the additional step of developing nuclear weapons. However, the peaceful and military dimensions of nuclear technology overlap, since peaceful nuclear devices could also be used as weapons.

CONCLUSIONS

While great power military relations in the Southern Cone are closely related with an array of local military developments and trends, several broad conclusions do emerge. As for conventional military affairs, developed states as a group have been keen to sell arms to the area and increasingly they have become associated as well with local arms industries in order to cement their commercial relationship. Two great powers, the United States and Great Britain, while sharing a commercial interest with other developed states as arms suppliers, at times have also had clear political motives in regulating and/or banning outside arms to local states.

While British and US pressure on one or another local state has recurred, the political motives for arms embargoes have varied over time. The British-inspired arms embargo of Argentina during the Falklands war was generally respected by Western suppliers, but other attempts by the US and the UK to exert this type of indirect military pressure have generally not been very effective. Numerous arms suppliers, anxious to establish or maintain a niche in an increasingly competitive global arms market, have been willing to help local states circumvent arms embargoes. Arms embargoes also have played an important role in stimulating local arms industries, which have tended to make the local states less vulnerable to external pressure. The transformation of erstwhile local pariahs into new arms exporters has further congested the international arms market, making it harder for the great powers to manipulate arms sales for political ends.

The Soviet Union, however, has not been able to convert its emergence as an important arms supplier to Peru into a political opening there or even into an entrée as an arms supplier in neighbouring states. It remains to be seen if the Argentine–Soviet economic relationship will be complemented by a military dimension.

At the same time, even major Third World arms producers such as Argentina and Brazil, continue to depend on foreign technology. Argentine and Brazilian arms imports have continued and are likely to continue, especially for relatively sophisticated weaponry.

Both Argentina and Brazil also remain dependent on foreign suppliers for their nuclear programmes, and these suppliers, especially the United States, have used their leverage to deter both states from developing a nuclear weaponry potential. While foreign and especially US pressure has slowed Argentine and Brazilian progress in developing an autonomous nuclear technological capability, it appears to be only a matter of time before both states acquire a complete nuclear fuel cycle with weaponry implications. A number of foreign suppliers have continued to transfer critical materials and technologies to both countries, and Argentina in particular has made considerable progress in developing an autonomous nuclear technological capability.

Restrictive and punitive policies in both conventional military and nuclear affairs by the developed states as a group and the United States in particular have had mixed results. Any effectiveness such policies may have had appears to be a diminishing asset, especially with reference to the largest and most militarily capable South American states, Argentina and Brazil. Local states have greatly resented such an approach, and have responded effectively by diversifying conventional military and nuclear suppliers and emphasising eventual achievement of autonomous national capabilities.

Britain's policies towards Argentina on these issues have had a negative orientation as well and have evoked similar responses, thereby reinforcing the desirability of an early peaceful settlement to the Falklands/Malvinas dispute. The 1982 Falklands/Malvinas war reinforced the commitment of some groups within Argentina to acquire nuclear weaponry or at least nuclear-powered submarines. The British Fortress Falklands policy has been regarded as provocative and requiring in response an ongoing conventional military build-up. Brazil has been drawn indirectly into the Anglo-Argentine conflict as well, since Argentina and Brazil have continued to compete on the conventional military and nuclear fronts as in other areas in spite of the greater emphasis in recent years on the collaborative dimension of the bilateral relationship.

While the Southern Cone states have been moving towards greater harmonisation of their diplomatic and military relations with each other, the great powers have been unable to reach such an accommodation with the local states. Great power military relations have all too often involved pressure and interference. Since all the local states have been vocal supporters of Western interests, it is to be hoped that an accommodation can be reached.

Notes

1. Victor Millan, 'Argentina: schemes for glory', in M. Brzoska and T. Ohlson (eds), *Arms Production in the Third World* (London: Taylor & Francis, 1986) p. 50.
2. M. Brzoska and T. Ohlson, 'Arms Production in the Third World: an overview', in Brzoska and Ohlson, *Arms Production in the Third World*, p. 28.
3. Mary Helen Spooner, 'Chile's arms industry exports worth $100 a year', *Financial Times*, 30 October 1984, p. 5.
4. Daniel Poneman, 'Nuclear Proliferation Prospects for Argentina', *ORBIS*, Vol. 27, No. 4 (Winter 1984) p. 853.
5. Mark Tran, 'Argentine missile raises US and British fears', *Guardian*, 21 September 1988, p. 6.
6. Michael A. Morris and Martin Slann, 'Proliferation of Weaponry and Technology', in Michael A. Morris and Victor Millan (eds), *Controlling Latin American Conflicts: Ten Approaches* (Boulder, Colorado: Westview Press, 1983) pp. 138–9.

Part IV
Comparisons and
Conclusions

10 Brazil and the Great Powers: Gradual Reorientation
Cynthia Watson

The three great powers (Great Britain, the Soviet Union and the United States) are not as central for contemporary Brazilian foreign relations as for Argentina and Chile, although at different times in the past Britain and the United States were able to exert decisive influence. Brazilian relations with the great powers of the international system include those powers of the declining international system as well as those of the emerging global system. An initial discussion will therefore focus on the status of the international system and Brazil's role in that system. Prominent in this constellation is the historical relationship between Brazil and the United States, with emerging bilateral problems in recent years. Brazilian links with the Soviets, the Europeans and the European Economic Community (EEC) have gained importance, and Brazil has also moved to strengthen its position within Latin America and increase ties with Japan and the People's Republic of China. Brazil's success or failure in attempts to alter its role in the international system *vis-à-vis* the great powers will be assessed.

BRAZIL IN THE GLOBAL SYSTEM

Brazil's role in the international system remains more one of a 'delayed candidate to the First World than that of a revisionist opponent to it'.[1] Brazil, long considered a slumbering giant, remains stifled in attempting to cross the threshold into major power status. Yet, its relations with the great powers offer an interesting contrast to those of other Third World states, particularly Argentina and Chile.

The difference between First World and Third World states has been described as protectors of the status quo versus those seeking to change their status in the international system.[2] The Brazilian position is distinctive. Brazil tries to change the status quo, but does not

163

desire to share power with others. Brazil is not a military superpower but a superdebtor. It does not have nuclear weapons, but produces large volumes of conventional arms. It also competes directly with the United States in several product areas. Brazil's role in the international system is not insignificant and is likely to grow, but it has not grown as quickly as anticipated.

The enhanced Brazilian role is tied to the evolving international hierarchy rather than the post-Second World War deteriorating one. Indeed, Brazil's major difference from Argentina and Chile in relations with the great powers is that Brasilia is actively pursuing relations with the newly emerging economic powers in the world system rather than concentrating solely on improving relations with the declining great powers. Brazil has the economic clout to make some inroads into relations with the great powers but not nearly as many as would be expected. The result is that its emerging industries are putting Brazil into competition with the more traditional great powers (the United States and the Soviet Union) and enhancing Brazil's participation in some forms of global decision-making (through greater interaction with emerging economic powers).

Brazil is not yet able to achieve its goals through the unilateral actions with which one associates superpower or great power status. After taking innovative (sometimes labelled extremist) positions on debt repayment, Brasilia's position has become much more pragmatic. Brazil has had to accept the economic and political realities of the international system where it is still a peripheral, albeit growing, player. Brazil still seeks First World status but is not substantially affected by US withdrawal of trade supports as are the so-called Asian economic miracle states (Taiwan, Republic of Korea, Hong Kong and Singapore).

Brazil may have sufficient clout to change its position more rapidly in the near future than might be expected from a superficial evaluation of great power relations. Brazilian action on the debt repayment issue has reflected a change in the balance of power because the international banking community has had to reduce its level of expectation for repayment (in other words, 'write off' some of the loans). This trend, recognised after considerable denial in mid-1987, constitutes an opening for Brazil in its attempts to equalise, or at least improve, its position with the great powers

This change has not yet conveyed great power status on Brazil. Brazil is playing a role as a middle power in contributing to the decline of the post-Second World War international economic system. In so doing, Brazil is pursuing national interest and accepting pragmatic limits on its capabilities. The Republic's goals are to take steps which will aid in Brazilian development and ultimate elevation to a genuine First World status. Brazil is assuming positions of leadership on some controversial issues where it is practical, but it is also backing away where necessary from extremist positions which may affect national interests adversely. Brazil, expecting to lead in the region, has been strengthening co-operative relations.

The states outside of Latin America with which Brazil increasingly is involved are established economic powers as well as those seeking a more powerful position in the developing international regime replacing prior US hegemony. Brazil is developing ties with major economic powers (the People's Republic of China, Japan, and West Germany) and Newly Industrialising Countries, all of which offer competition to the United States. It is expected that economic benefits from these relationships will help balance the traditional great powers, especially the United States.

Brazil's slowly rising status in the international system reflects the changes which are making it unlikely that any state will be able to have true hegemony on the global level, as enjoyed by the United States in the 1945–1965 period. The Brazilian experience of entering into a variety of industrial relationships shows that the world is increasingly interdependent and that established powers will face increasing competition. Brazil has been able to create more favourable conditions for itself through accumulating more partners, sometimes at the cost of the United States and other competitors in various industries. In doing so, the steps which Brazil takes towards a more assertive international role will not be subject to punishment by the great powers. Brazil has become so linked into the major parts of the international system that punitive steps taken against it would rebound. The result of these changing global relations will have an impact on the region as Brazil attempts to strengthen regional links.

BRAZIL'S EUROPEAN TIES: PAST AND PRESENT

With the preponderance of British influence in the Portuguese empire, Brazilian relations with the great powers date back to the period prior to independence.[3] While Britain had significant ties with Brazil, they were never fully colonial in nature, as between London and India, for example. British involvement increased dramatically with Brazilian independence from Portugal in 1821 because Britain provided the direct shipping link to the European continent.[4] Britain already had supplanted Portugal as Brazil's major trading partner by the time of the temporary relocation of the royal court to Rio de Janeiro in 1805.[5] The removal of formal colonial status allowed Britain to exploit the budding relationship more directly.

The strength of the connections between Brazil and Britain waned as the United States became the major trading partner for the newly established republic (as of 1889). The individual credited with this fundamental reorientation of Brazilian policy was Foreign Minister Baron Rio Branco, Jose Maria da Silva Paranhos Junior. Rio Branco cultivated and intensified a growing trend towards relying on the United States to support Brazilian needs as opposed to accepting British and general European preponderance in the international system.[6] The explicit desire of Brazil to cultivate ties with the potential hegemon of the Americas was warmly reciprocated by Washington, which saw this policy shift as a long-awaited opening into a traditionally British area. The Brazilian warming to the United States coincided with US attempts to pursue a hemispheric Pan-Americanism.[7] However, closer Brazilian–US ties actually thwarted Pan-Americanism because the growing bilateral nexus appeared threatening to the remainder of Latin America.

West Germany is now the predominant European country with links to Brazil, including through bilateral ties as well as through its capacity as a leading EEC state.[8] Germany signed extensive agreements with Brazil on nuclear technology (to the consternation of the United States) in 1975, and has provided substantial bank loans for Brazilian industrial growth.

Contemporary European links with Latin America, be they bilateral or through the EEC, are largely economic in nature. The Brazilians are increasingly interested in diversifying foreign relationships here as elsewhere to counterbalance traditional US predominance in the region. European powers do not, however, offer any major political or military balance to the United States and are not likely to offer such in the near future. European arms do offer an alternative to reliance on the United States, European technology broadens Brazil's options, and trade with Europe gives it another outlet.

SOVIET–BRAZILIAN LINKS

Brazil's connections with the Soviet Union have been fairly weak due to the strength of US–Brazilian relations coupled with the vehement anti-Soviet perspective of most Brazilian governments. The strong links between the United States and Brazil until the 1970s largely left no room for Soviet activity.

Soviet interest in Latin America dates to the beginning of the Bolshevik regime. Brazil's obvious importance as a large, populous country with vast natural resources and geostrategic location made it interesting from Moscow's perspective. Formal channels for interaction have been limited, depending on the whim of the particular Brazilian government.[9] Although Brazil has had a major Communist Party throughout the century, long-standing, fierce anti-communism has influenced several governments to reject close ties with the Kremlin for fear that communism might gain ground at home.

With the Brazilian drive to fashion a more diversified, independent foreign policy, the apprehension regarding the Soviets has subsided somewhat. Several Soviet exports, such as petroleum in the 1970s, have had some importance for Brazil.[10] More importantly, Brazil offers a valuable economic connection with associated political benefits for the Soviets. Brazilian raw materials are of interest to the Soviet Union, while Brazil seeks to enter the Soviet market with many exports which it finds difficult to sell in the West. An October 1988 visit by President Sarney to Moscow may boost bilateral relations.

Should Brazil decide to play a more overt balancing game between the United States and the Soviet Union, then Soviet involvement in Brazil might increase substantially. But that is not likely, since Brazil's diversifying relations are just as likely to place greater emphasis on relations with the People's Republic of China. The relationship between the USSR and Brazil is thus largely a commercial one with fairly limited prospects for short-term expansion. The Soviets are aware, however, of Brazil's growing role in multinational forums discussing the North–South division, and this fuels Soviet political interest.

BRAZIL AND THE UNITED STATES: PROTRACTED BONDS

Self-interest long sustained Brazilian support for close relations with the United States, while the majority of Hispanic America has harboured fears that Brazil, in association with the United States, would become militarily and economically predominant in South

America. The long-term Brazilian shift from a British-based international link to a broader, if not US-based, foreign policy gained momentum after the First World War, and accelerated after the 1929 crash. Certainly with the advent of the Depression, substantial US interests extended to the south beyond the Caribbean Basin emphasis of the 1889–1930 era. Britain's economic withdrawal and the accelerating US expansion coincided with the Getulio Vargas era (1930–53).

Partially because of its uniqueness, partially because of Vargas, and partially because of geography, Brazil increasingly became the South American state most closely allied with Washington. The mere 1900-mile oceanic gap between the bulge of northeastern Brazil and west Africa created sufficient US strategic concern for Brazil to receive much of the Lend Lease money going to Latin America during the Second World War. This contributed to widening the gulf between Argentina and Washington while causing South American anxiety about Brazilian goals within the region. As the Second World War ended and the United States assumed the role of external patron in Latin America, resentments similar to those of Argentina surfaced in other regional neighbours.

Getulio Vargas was the pivotal figure in the middle years of the twentieth century for Brazil, in domestic as well as foreign affairs. He transformed Brazil into an industrialising state while also beginning to assert Brazilian interests in world affairs. His leadership laid the foundation upon which Brazil still relies at the close of the twentieth century. Vargas maintained some controversial links with the Axis (particularly Germany) well into the Second World War, but this did not cause the same international consternation as did Argentina's similar actions, particularly under Peron.[11] Brazilian ties with Germany dated back to Bismarck when German immigrants were a major factor in elevating German economic links to a position second only to those of Britain.[12] German expansion into Brazil during the inter-war period allowed Vargas to balance Germany against the United States for the aim of enhancing Brazilian development, thereby marking final British relegation to a lesser role in the Western Hemisphere.

With the conclusion of the war, Vargas relied selectively on the United States while upholding Brazilian nationalist sentiments against US encroachment. Benefits accrued from faithful execution of the anti-Nazi role assigned by the United States during the war included the Volta Redonda power station. The resupply and upgrading of the Brazilian military through US assistance also occurred,[13] and the major Inter-American military agreement of the postwar world was the Rio Treaty of 1947, signed in Brazil.

While the war enhanced US prominence in Brazilian relations, one must not exaggerate the impact of these links. Vargas was not ideologically linked to the United States before or after the war. Instead, he was committed to internal development and advancement of Brazilian national aspirations. Subsequent regimes have manipulated relations with the United States in varying degrees but none – even the infamous military governments of the 1960s – lost sight of Brazilian national interests.[14] At the same time, a decline in US leadership was setting in by the mid-1960s.

TENSION IN CONTEMPORARY US–BRAZILIAN AFFAIRS

The greatest change in Brazilian foreign relations – decay in its links with the United States – resulted from neglect as well as the strains of an increasingly competitive, multipolar order. As part of an emerging multipolar order, Brazil has acquired some economic weight of its own. Brazil's competition with US companies in steel, computer items, conventional arms, shoes, and citrus has strained the bilateral relationship. This competition illustrates distinctive Brazilian constraints and opportunities. Brazil is not yet a major player in the international system (at least in so far as not yet acquiring First World status), but the hegemony of the United States continues to deteriorate because of evolving interdependence within the international system. As a result of this interdependence, Brazil does not have to achieve full First World status to have economic influence.

Brazil's advantage which few other Third World states have (or are likely to acquire) is its diverse, flexible relations with both emerging and established powers. Each relationship can help a pragmatic need. Brazil's trade with the People's Republic of China in nuclear technology lessens dependence on the United States or Western Europe for provision of nuclear parts and fuel. The lack of fresh loans to Brazil save for maintaining debt service payments has created economic hardship within the Republic and spawned greater feelings of nationalism. Brazil is able, however, to look to sources outside the traditional great powers for commerce and trade.

THE DEBT QUAGMIRE

The debt question is central to Brazil's relations with the great powers. The external debt owed by the Republic to banks primarily located in great power states is in excess of 110 billion US dollars. Much of the discussion on the debt occurs in multilateral forums, such as the International Monetary Fund or World Bank, but is significant to Brazilian–great power links.

Brazil's reaction to the debt crisis generally has been pragmatic, although somewhat contradictory in its evolution. The civilian government of Jose Sarney, like the military governments preceding it, has recognised two fundamental facts which both constrict and free Brazil:

(1) The international banking community is no longer in any position to exert overwhelming pressure, such as getting the great powers to exert military pressure on a debtor state to collect money owed, as occurred in the earlier years of this century;
(2) Internal social and political demands require attention and money, which must often come from cultivation of outside sources.

In trying to operate under these constraints, Brasilia attempted a debt repayment moratorium but abandoned that action without getting the banks to guarantee longer-range loans and longer-term rescheduling. At the same time, because of economic diversification and a growing international impact in some critical industries, Brazil has been able to pressure the great powers both on direct debt negotiation and trade policies. Lastly, Brazil is also pursuing multilateral – largely Latin American – approaches to the debt question.

Brazil has largely failed to change the conditions of its indebtedness and its status as a less than First World state. The Brazilian government took actions on the debt problem, as O'Donnell noted, from a position of weakness rather than strength.[15] Rather than making demands at a time when it had new options available, the Brazilian government tried to change the rules of the game at a point when it was weak because of debts and unlikely to gain any concessions from its critics. Yet, the Brazilian approach also created some opening for Brazil in its relations with the traditional great powers. Those states have banks with such a stake in the $110 billion Brazilian debt that their only options are either to write off some of the massive debt or to put pressure on Brazil. Political leaders in Brazil fear that any more outside pressure to cut back on domestic expenditures in order to continue paying the debt as scheduled will contribute to the breakdown of the domestic system. Brazil's precarious domestic situation, as emphasised by national leaders, tends to make creditors more receptive to Brazilian attempts to forge alternatives for debtors.

On 20 February 1987, the Brasilia government announced suspension of its interest payments until a multi-year pact on debt repayment could be agreed upon by Brazil and the creditor banks. The Financial Minister responsible for the moratorium resigned within two months of the action, but Brazil maintained its hard line position through the end of 1987 despite the international perception that personnel changes would create policy changes. The international banking community responded to the moratorium in various ways. Japan urged Brazil to make at least some token payment,[16] and relations deteriorated when it did not. Brazil did not receive any of the new loans issued by the Japanese for Latin America in October.[17] The United States responded with hostility to a Brazilian proposal for converting or altering the debt from dollars, but several US banks did write off part of their Latin American debts. Fears increased that other states might follow suit and declare non-payment of the debt.

Beginning in October 1987, Brazil cautiously indicated that resumption of payment on debts was possible if the banks were willing to write off some loans rather than merely renegotiate with Brazil. Further concessions followed. Brazil initialled agreements with its top seventy creditors on 6 November and 15 December for a bridge loan to end the eleven-month moratorium on debt repayment,[18] and it made two payments after the decision to end the moratorium in late 1987.

Brazil's position reflects several important conditions. Domestic pressure for economic heterodoxy is strong, and a result of the Brazilian moratorium was the first write offs by Western banks. But since US banks still expect to receive payment for the outstanding loans, Brazil must continue promoting exports in order to garner the foreign exchange. Many of the Brazilian export targets are those shared with US industries, thereby adding to strains in Brazil's great power relations.

TRADE PROTECTIONISM

Considerable tension has emerged between the United States and virtually all of its trading partners as US ability to dominate exports of many industrial products has declined. The decay of US–Brazilian ties has been as much based on US attempts to retain control through trade protectionism as on the debt question.

Brazil's largest single trading partner remains the United States, with which it has run a trade surplus. US corporations have protested that unfair Brazilian trading practices cause the surplus, while the Brazilian view is that competitive national goods have gained new markets. Bilateral trade disagreements have included Brazilian exports of steel (alleged government subsidies creating unfair competition for US producers), shoes (competition with small industries in Missouri and Maine), textiles, arms and most recently computers. US demands for protectionist measures do not singularly target Brazil, but illustrate the growing Brazilian role as a capitalist state participating more actively in the international economic system. In several instances, the issues have been purely non-governmental, but each government has been forced into an inflexible stance.

Protectionist sentiment in the US–Brazilian relationship began in 1982 when tariffs were imposed on over a dozen Brazilian exports, thereby decreasing exports markedly in footwear (off $22 million) and textiles (down $44 million, both figures in US dollars).[19] Two years later the United States sought to impose 25 per cent tariffs on Brazilian steel imports. In 1986 as the fervor for protectionism rose in Washington, Brazil's shoe industry again became a target for protectionists in the US Congress. Brazilian pharmaceuticals, orange juice, steel, and aircraft remain under tariff clouds.

Still a further dimension to trade problems is Brazilian arms sales, tenth largest in the world.[20] Brazil's arms sales compete with those of the great powers in export markets in often being cheaper, more adaptable, and easier to use than European or US weaponry. Brazilian arms exports provide not only domestic economic benefits (foreign exchange and bartered goods) but also geopolitical leverage as the Republic attempts to change the international system.

BRAZIL AND LATIN AMERICA

Another aspect of Brazil's changing foreign relationships is with Latin America. Rather than assuming an aloof or adversarial balance-of-power position, Brazil has been taking great pains to co-operate with its neighbours while also asserting leadership. These actions are designed to signal a changing role in the international system as a leader.

Brazil has begun a subregional economic integration scheme with Argentina and Uruguay. Brazil, as the largest Third World external debtor but ninth largest world economy, was concerned about maintaining its position as leader in the Latin American economic sphere. The 1986 General Agreement on Integration and Development was a major step in formally consolidating Brazil's role as a leader while also taking substantive steps toward economically beneficial changes.

The accord, signed by Presidents Alfonsin of Argentina and Sarney of Brazil in late July 1986, was designed to create a customs union between the two states. Brazil would increase its purchases of wheat from Argentina while the two states would greatly increase their joint ventures in industrialised areas. Integration had been long discussed as a possible remedy for the two largest economies in South America, and this agreement by the elected presidents seemed to seal bonds between old-time competitors while also assisting sustained economic growth for this debt-ridden subregion. Brazilian reaction was fairly positive, but some Argentines expressed concern that the Argentine economy would become subsumed into the much larger Brazilian one.

New Brazilian emphasis on regional co-operation does not merely reflect commitment to regional solidarity (rhetorical protestations notwithstanding), but also results from pragmatism again. Brazil benefits from international perceptions that it is not a belligerent state within its region, so that conciliatory moves may ease the way for Brazil eventually to assume a regional leadership role.

CONCLUSIONS

Brazilian foreign policy is pragmatic in the end, even if experiments occasionally appear. Regional goals illustrate the pragmatism woven throughout Brazilian foreign relations. In the region, the desire for greater economic interaction and possible economic integration reflects the goal of enhancing economic growth and establishing the basis for regional leadership, if not hegemony. Brazil's relations with the emerging and established powers in Asia and Europe illustrate pragmatism as well. For example, the People's Republic of China and Brazil have common energy needs and are co-operating in nuclear technology in the face of substantial international pressure. The needs outweigh pressure exerted by the United States, which in any event adds to increasing tension in US–Brazilian relations. As the international bankers and others have found, pragmatism has been compatible with vigorous defence of the national interest.

Brazil's relations with the great powers show that the country has not graduated to a role of protector of the status quo, but it has enhanced its power in the international system somewhat. Part of the reason for the change is the marked decline in US hegemony in the global capitalist economic system, and another reason is the decline in traditional capitalist/non-capitalist bipolarity.

Brazil's foreign policy has traditionally tried to use external states in order to gain greater access to the international system, but it has never had any client relationships such as those which have plagued Argentina and Chile. Argentina, in particular, has been far less autonomous in its relations than self-perception allows. Brazil, with its more diversified economic production, has become somewhat autonomous and has been considered more of an international power than its neighbours. This results partly from demonstrable, measurable factors but also from perceived roles in the world system. Argentina today questions its status in a manner which Brazil does not.

Contrasting international postures carry over into the redemocratisation process, which so far has been somewhat less painful in Brazil than in Argentina or what likely will occur in Chile. Brazil's position in the global system as a significant economic player gives it a more cohesive international approach, which in turn supports domestic cohesion. This is not to imply that the transition to a democratic system in Brazil is either simple or guaranteed. Instead, this is to recognise that Brazilian foreign relations with the great powers have been distinctive and have allowed more flexibility and assertiveness – albeit mixed with caution – since Brazil does have some economic power.

Brazil has taken steps on its own to increase its position from a marginal Third World state to a more active role. Brazil now competes with the United States and Europe in many products while also posing a significant challenge to the international banking community. Brasilia's relations with emerging powers have gained momentum, but any individual state must recognise that its national interests often are thwarted by protectors of the status quo. Part of the Brazilian strategy has involved championing radical plans which can be withdrawn after some consideration, as in the case of the movement to limit debt repayment. Co-operation is also pursued along multiple paths, including relations with regional states and through international organisations. While policy inconsistency

sometimes detracts from pragmatism, Brazil is gradually forging a
role as a state likely to become much more powerful.

Notes

Thanks go to Drs David Nordstrom, Sharon Murphy and Susan Schroder for
their comments.

1. Wayne Selcher, *Brazil's Multilateral Relations* (Boulder, Colorado: Westview Press, 1978) p. 25.
2. Wolf Grabendorff, in *The European Challenge* (London: Latin American
   Bureau, 1982) p. 46.
3. See Peter Flynn, *Brazil: A Political Analysis* (Boulder, Colorado: Westview Press, 1978), Ch. 1.
4. E. Bradford Burns, *A History of Brazil* (New York: Columbia University Press, 1970) p. 111.
5. Ibid., p. 101.
6. Ibid., p. 237.
7. Ibid., p. 238.
8. A. Glenn Mower, Jr., *The European Community and Latin America*
   (Westport, Connecticut: Greenwood Press, 1982) p. 42.
9. Cole Blasier, *The Giant's Rival* (Pittsburgh: University of Pittsburgh
   Press, 1983) p. 32.
10. Ibid., p. 36.
11. Frank McCann, 'Brazilian Foreign Relations in the Twentieth Century',
    in Wayne Selcher (ed.), *Brazil in the International System* (Boulder,
    Colorado: Westview Press, 1981) pp. 10–11.
12. Stanley Hilton, *Brazil and the Great Powers* (Austin: University of
    Texas Press, 1975) p. xviii.
13. McCann, 'Brazilian Foreign Relations in the Twentieth Century', p. 12.
14. Robert Wesson, 'Brazil: Independence Asserted', in *U.S. Influence in
    Latin America in the 1980s* (New York: Praeger, 1982) p. 64.
15. Guillermo O'Donnell, 'Brazil: What Future for Debtors' Cartels?',
    Third World Quarterly, Vol. 9, No. 4 (1987) p. 1157.
16. *Latin American Weekly Report*, 87–37, 24 September 1987, p. 7.
17. Ibid., 87–40, 15 October 1987, p. 7.
18. Ibid., 87–49, 17 December 1987, p. 7.
19. Ibid., 87–42, 29 October 1987, p. 6.
20. Latin American Bureau, *The European Challenge* (London: Latin
    American Bureau, 1982) Table 5, p. 212.

11 South America, the Great Powers and the Global System
Fred Parkinson

South America's position in both regional and world affairs is seen here through the prism of system theory. Great power relations in Argentina, Chile and Antarctica both affect and are affected by these regional and global trends.

THE GENESIS OF THE GLOBAL SYSTEM

Before the opening of the nineteenth century, the global diplomatic and economic system had its epicentre in Europe. It was not until the early 1940s that the infrastructural backbone of that system – the balance of power – ceased to be dominated by European powers. And it was not before 1960, when the bulk of the remaining dependent territories was granted sovereign independence that a fully rounded, though unevenly developed and culturally diverse, as well as increasingly complex global system of international relations came into being.

With Latin American independence from Iberian rule largely accomplished in the early part of the nineteenth century, attempts were made to isolate the Western hemisphere on the ground of its supposedly separate system of values and its alleged affinity of political institutions. The success of those efforts depended in the final analysis on the ability of the United States to promote and to support an internationally autonomous Western hemisphere. In view of the geopolitical limits of United States power this was hardly feasible, and wide margins were consequently left within which a rudimentary South American balance of power could operate on an *inter se* basis to bring about local adjustments which were of little or no relevance to the rest of the Western hemisphere. In this respect South America differed considerably from the Central American-

Caribbean region, which came to feel the weight of United States power quite substantially and quite early.

BOLIVARIANISM: LOWEST STAGE OF SOUTH AMERICAN ORDER

Whereas a regional international order in Europe had been established by multilateral conference (1648, 1815), the furthest that independent Latin America ever got in that respect were attempts to form defensive alliances directed against Europe's great powers. Bolivar's basic conception of a loose confederation of Hispano-American states entertaining a special relationship with Britain while staying clear of the United States was indeed defensive.[1] The principal exponent for well over a century of such an aloof version of Bolivarianism was Argentina whose power position was generally strong, which explains why she consistently showed far less enthusiasm for international co-operation than did other South American states.[2]

The frustrations suffered by Bolivarianism and the simultaneous advent of what ultimately turned out to be an all-South American system of the balance of power have been well chronicled and need only be lightly touched upon here.[3] The system was fragmentary at first, being composed of two foci, one located in the River Plate basin and the other within the inter-state nexus of the west coast. From about 1860 onwards those two components began to merge into a truly continental system, a process completed in the 1870s. Where the balance of power was concerned, Bolivarianism had to yield to South American continentalism. When after 1865 United States power began to be projected over most parts of South America, the peculiarly South American system of the balance of power went 'underground', not to resurface for another century.

MONROVIANISM: HIGHEST STAGE OF THE WESTERN HEMISPHERE IDEA

Originating in the United States, the Monroe Declaration was from the beginning associated with Washington's Farewell Address of 1796 and its notion of diplomatic isolation from Europe, as well as with the idea that Europe and the Western hemisphere had developed on different lines. Basically, President James Monroe's Declaration was intended to prevent the European powers from repossessing their formerly dependent territories or from interfering in any way in the Western hemisphere. The Declaration was therefore extra-hemispheric in intent and unilateral in form. None of the new states of Latin America were consulted while the Declaration was being drawn up, and no effort was made to obtain their support or co-operation in enforcing it. It carried no intra-hemispheric implications, since the United States meant to remain uncommitted to the military defence of the hemisphere, of which task it would in any case have been incapable before 1868 at the earliest, and after that only within the limited radius of the Central American–Caribbean complex.

PAN-AMERICANISM: HIGHEST STAGE OF MONROVIANISM

The logical outgrowth of Monrovianism and at the same time the apotheosis of the Western hemisphere idea, Pan-Americanism added to the Monrovian conception the dimension of inter-American organisation, to be managed directly by the United States. An Inter-American Bureau which was an organ of United States government sent its annual reports directly to the United States Congress, while the Secretary of State appointed the Chairman of its Governing Board, its director and its staff. It seemed in 1885 that the United States was, in the words of Richard Olney, the then Secretary of State, 'practically sovereign on this continent' and that its fiat was 'law upon the subjects to which it confined its interposition'.[4] Only the Southern Cone, composed of Argentina, Chile and Uruguay, in which British economic and diplomatic influence was paramount, was capable of retaining a certain degree of autonomy, which persisted even after British influence had all but vanished.[5]

While advocating in 1916 the association of the Latin American states in the decision-making process of the Pan-American Union on the basis of a formally comprehensive multilateral treaty, President Woodrow Wilson considered it the duty of the United States to continue to intervene in the name of Pan-Americanism.[6] Since Wilson also advocated the creation of a universalist League of Nations, he was caught between the rival conceptions of regionalism and globalism. He solved his dilemma by according preference to the League, while dropping his plans for a reformed Pan-Americanism.[7]

In the 1920s the Latin American states were none the less associated with the Pan-American system on a footing of formal equality, but it was only in the 1930s that the United States was prepared to renounce its right to intervene. That decision had more to do with United States interests in Europe than in Latin America. When the Organisation of American States was established in 1948, the United States had world-wide interests that were very different from those in the Latin American region.[8] It seemed as if regionalism, in whatever form, was to be perennially bedevilled by the pull of global interests.

Simultaneously with the loosening of the tight grip of the United States on Latin American organisation went a deepening of its economic involvement in the region. Nelson Rockefeller's 'cartel' plan of June 1940 – in essence a beneficial endeavour to rationalise Latin America's commodity trade with the help of the United States – was rightly described as 'the most extreme economic expression ever given to the Western hemisphere idea'.[9] Though wholly benevolent in intent, it was to be highly interventionist in economic conception and therefore was never allowed to get off the ground.

The Alliance for Progress, conceived at the tail-end of the Eisenhower administration but put into effect by President John F. Kennedy in 1961, may be seen in retrospect as either as extreme and enlightened an expression of Pan-Americanism as Rockefeller's 'cartel' plan, or – just as convincingly – as a victory for reassertive neo-Bolivarianism by the United Nations Economic Commission for Latin America (ECLA) in which Latin American views prevailed.[10] The latter interpretation would imply the onset of the decline of Monrovianism.

DECLINE OF UNITED STATES POWER – MONROVIANISM DESCENDANT

Experience has shown that direct United States intervention is feasible only in the Central American–Caribbean region. In the remainder of Latin America the Colossus of the North has to be content with exercising its power indirectly, by conventional economic and diplomatic means. It would be apposite, therefore, to distinguish between (1) US 'paramountcy', exercised in the Central American

–Caribbean region – marked by a willingness to intervene, by military means if necessary – and (2) mere US 'hegemony' applied in South America – which excludes direct intervention.[11]

After the formal renunciation by the United States of direct intervention in Latin America in 1936, attempts continued to be made by the former to align Latin America as closely as possible with United States foreign policy on a world scale. Between 1947 and 1965 this was done *inter alia* by manipulating the mechanisms of the Rio Treaty (Treaty of Inter-American Reciprocal Assistance of 1947). The Rio Treaty was, however, to be completely overshadowed from 1949 onwards in global significance by the North Atlantic Treaty Organisation (NATO) of which the United States was the sheet-anchor. It would only be a slight exaggeration to claim that the Rio Treaty was regarded by the latter as little more than an annex to NATO. The global dimension once again proved to be the primary diplomatic consideration in United States foreign policy. When the latter lost its ability to manipulate the Rio Treaty system after 1965, the practice of direct intervention in the Central American–Caribbean region was resumed.

The economic causes for the relative decline of United States power can be traced to the reversal of direction of its external payments from 1958 onwards.[12] And even though the impact of those changes is politically less relevant on account of the fact that at least two of the most dynamic economies – West Germany and Japan – are firmly attached to the United States diplomatically, the ability of the latter to impose its strategic and economic policies on a world scale has diminished considerably, and produced a redistribution and diffusion of power within the global system of international relations. Multiple 'summit' meetings are now the main instrument for agreeing and co-ordinating international economic policies.[13]

In addition to economic causes, the decline of United States power in South America also has psychological roots, which are manifested in a persistent inflexibility of attitudes. Thus, the complementarity of economic interests assumed between the United States and South America could be objectively justified only so long as the southern continent acted as supplier of raw materials. This ceased to be the case after industrialisation had taken off in 1930. Furthermore, the assumption of the geopolitical unity of the Americas could be seen as an objective fact before the mid-1950s, but was altered by the rapid strides made by weapons technology, especially inter-continental missile delivery systems – which also had the effect of revolutionising strategic thought in South America. As Jaguaribe put it succinctly: 'Within Latin America, the United States is still showing a manifest economic, technical and military superiority in relation to any single country or their aggregate . . . but the scale of that superiority and its content have been modified decisively'.[14]

What has accentuated the effect of the relative decline of United States power in South America is its coincidence in time with the rise on that subcontinent of Newly Industrialising Countries (NICs) other than Argentina, the prototype of a Latin American NIC. Industrialisation in the second half of the twentieth century has been taking place in a world economic context in which the 'core' countries are already fully industrialised. Yet, most NICs have demonstrated a capacity to overcome that disadvantage, and their success has affected their political behaviour. Argentina's foreign policy has always reflected that fact through self-confident pursuit of independent policies. In the measure in which other South American countries have followed her in attaining NIC status, their foreign policies have similarly changed, tending to conform to the patterns of Argentina.

The most spectacular rise of a South American NIC is that of Brazil, matched in kind, though not in magnitude, by that of Venezuela.[15] By virtue of Brazil's size and importance, her economic rise has transformed the entire geopolitical map of the subcontinent. So long as Argentine power and influence in the Southern Cone outweighed that of Brazil, the latter tended to range herself behind the United States in order to contain Argentine power.[16] Once risen to NIC status about 1970, Brazil's diplomatic perspectives began to change appreciably. United States' apron-strings were eventually discarded and an active, independent foreign policy pursued. In the process, the traditional Argentine–Brazilian antagonism gave way to a steady *rapprochement* between those two erstwhile rivals.

SOVIET THEORY TOWARDS SOUTH AMERICA AND OTHER DEVELOPING COUNTRIES

While the main limiting factor of United States policy has become relative decline in power – both world-wide and in relation to South America – one of the obstacles to the spread of Soviet influence in that region has been the confused state of Soviet political theory in respect of the role and place of developing countries within Soviet cosmology. Soviet theory in this respect moved awkwardly through several stages of evolution before eventually settling down.

It was not before the 15th Congress of the Soviet Communist Party held in Moscow in 1926 that sophisticated debate on the subject commenced. The conclusion reached then was that under conditions of capitalist encirclement of the Soviet Union, the developing countries – whether under formal colonial rule or informal imperialist dependence – could fulfil a useful 'buffer' function in Soviet policy. Bukharin's thesis that the 'national' (native) bourgeoisie in those countries was weak and needed Soviet support to exercise that buffer function was broadly adopted – though without enthusiasm – as a guide to action.[17]

With the termination of capitalist encirclement in 1945 when the Soviet Union became one of the two dominant world powers, the former theory needed revising. In Stalin's tract on *The Economic Problems of Socialism in the USSR* published in 1952, therefore, the thesis was advanced of a world divided into two camps – one capitalist, which comprised all developing as well as all developed countries, and the other Socialist, covering the Soviet Union and her allies. In this scheme the Socialist camp was considered stable by definition, but the capitalist one was seen as riddled by internal contradictions. In Stalin's thesis the developing countries were given cavalier treatment in being firmly assigned to the capitalist camp.[18]

Some significant modifications in Stalin's binary model were introduced under Khrushchev (1953–1964), when elements of Bukharin's paradigm relating to the developing countries were reintroduced (without attribution). Instead of focusing on the alleged contradictions afflicting the capitalist camp, the focus was shifted to peaceful inter-camp competition (*mirnoye sosovshchustvovaniye*) for the allegiance of the developing countries. Khrushchev was convinced that these could be won over to the Soviet side not only through the demonstration effect of the alleged superiority of the Soviet over the capitalist model of development, but also by generous injections of Soviet aid and credits on easy terms. At the 20th Party Congress in 1956, Soviet academics therefore were enjoined by Mikoyan to engage in serious research on all aspects of those countries.

In the political sphere the tone was set by Professor Ivan I. Potekhin, a noted Africanist, who elaborated the new concept of 'national democracy' which was viewed as a suitable halfway house to Soviet-style socialism. The emphasis here was placed on the 'non-capitalist' path to development, with the state sector in industry and radical reform on the land playing key roles. The national bourgeoisie was to be gently guided politically by local, pro-Soviet Communist parties. Promising 'national democrat' leaders, including military officers, seemed in plentiful supply: Nehru in India, Nasser in Egypt, Sukarno in Indonesia, Nkrumah in Ghana, Keita in Mali, Ben Bella in Algeria, Fidel Castro in Cuba – to name but a few.[19]

Under the subsequent Brezhnev regime (1964–1981) the pace of modification of the Stalin model was maintained. Khrushchev's great faith in aiding developing countries of promise was severely criticised as having been costly in terms of finance and disastrous in terms of political returns.[20] The new leadership began to adopt a markedly detached approach towards developing countries, in which the observation of objective conditions was taking the place of preconceived theory.

In view of the disappointing performance of 'National Democrat' statesmen – Sukarno, Keita, Nkrumah, and Ben Bella had fallen like ninepins – the concept of 'national democracy' was dropped, and no more was heard of Professor Potekhin. Soviet academics meanwhile – and certainly after 1976 – began to use their professional skills to create new content, thereby injecting a growing sense of realism into the current debate about the developing countries. Some startling ideas were thrown up in the process, which may be summarised as follows: the emphasis on heavy industrial development was abandoned; the size of the state sector was no longer exclusively relevant; nationalisation of foreign property was played down; an open debate was encouraged on the role of market forces and centralisation that was conducted in terms of cost–benefit analysis; a positive attitude towards private business was recommended; and large landed estates were not to be broken up lightly in the name of agrarian reform.[21]

Latin America was assigned a place within a new economic typology which was designed to match the existing political typology, as follows: poorest landlocked states; relatively advanced countries (North Africa and Asia); oil-rich states; and Latin American states, through the precise rationale of that typology does not seem to have been spelt out.[22]

Under the present Gorbachev regime (1983–present), few new elements have been added, but past innovations were collated and set out in explicit terms. It would appear that the present Soviet leader is willing to put into practice what many academics have been preaching for years. Thus, there is now a commitment on the part of the

Soviet Union to improve relations with developing countries 'following the path of capitalist development' – a complete negation of Khrushchev's notion of favouring developing countries travelling down the 'non-capitalist' path of development. A warning was sounded to Socialist developing countries not to expect to receive Soviet aid unless that were 'within Soviet means'. Above all, there was a determination to strengthen Soviet relations with the NICs. With Mexico, Argentina and Brazil expressly in mind, such a course has been urged by Karen Brutents, a close adviser to the Soviet leader. Gorbachev himself has described the NICs as 'the moderate capitalist-oriented States with large markets, dynamic economies and regional influence'.[23]

EVOLVING SOVIET STATE PRACTICE

In its diplomatic relations with Latin America since October 1962, the Soviet Union has placed the cultivation of good relations with the United States above any specific Soviet interests in South America. It was only in the wake of the Cuban Revolution that an Institute of Latin American Studies was established in Moscow in 1961, commencing publication of its organ, *America Latina*, in 1969 only. The practical effects of the Cuban missile crisis of 1962 were to reduce Soviet military activities in the Western hemisphere to showing the flag, to naval and air provisioning, to patrols and to intelligence gathering missions.[24]

As for the Southern Cone, the most notable Soviet action has been the abrupt termination of relations with Chile after the military coup of 11 September 1973 and the almost immediate transfer of Soviet favours to Argentina. The latter were not withdrawn after the military coup there of 24 April 1976. Three reasons have been advanced for these Soviet decisions:

(a) That Soviet diplomacy saw Argentina as a counterpoise to Chile on account of the existing tensions between the two countries over the Beagle Channel;

(b) Chile's vastly inferior strategic position when compared with Argentina's;

(c) indifference to the Argentine government's brutal repression directed against left-wing forces.[25]

In 1976 the Soviets offered Argentina credits twice as large as had been offered to Allende's Chile.[26] When faced with a United States-led grain embargo in 1980, Soviet buyers offered huge purchase contracts to Argentine exporters. In the Antarctic the Soviets have introduced their merchant and fishing fleets on a permanent basis, and have shown a mounting interest in offshore and deep-sea resources.

CHANGING SOUTH AMERICAN INTERNATIONAL RELATIONS

The Diplomatic Plane

In terms of the balance of power – still the most reliable overall indicator of any system of international relations – the increasing diffusion of power has resulted in the replacement of the old, predominantly bipolar global system by a new, increasingly complex binary 'bipolar–multipolar' system. The solid Northern tier has remained predominantly bipolar, whilst the amorphous Southern one is exhibiting multipolar configurations of power. Of these, only South America is showing any signs of developing an indigenous system of regional international relations peculiarly its own.

By and large, United States tutelage was tolerated under the Rio Treaty system of 1947 for the duration of the acute stages of the Cold War because of the perceived helplessness of Latin America to cope on its own with Cold War issues.[27] During the prolonged diplomatic crisis provoked by the Cuban Revolution, Latin American concern was such that considerable restraint had to be exercised in the way of criticism of the United States for fear of giving comfort to Soviet or Cuban foreign policy. However, as the sharp edges of the Cold War were getting blunted in the 1960s, the South American states began to review their position while the United States tended to concentrate its energies more and more on the Central American–Caribbean area, which was regarded as a strategic area of primary security interest.[28]

In those new circumstances, the Rio Treaty lost its relevance. The growing irrelevance of the Rio Treaty led to a certain distancing on the part of the South American states from US perceptions of hemispheric security. The relationship of the Big Two of South America (Argentina and Brazil) with the United States cooled remarkably, and only Venezuela remained close to the United States perceptions of security.[29] After 1965 Latin American worries increasingly focused on the diplomatic conduct of the United States itself in the Central American–Caribbean region. Latin American, and in particular South American states became less and less self-conscious about forming diplomatic combinations *inter se* in restraint of United States policy and in pursuit of independent solutions for Latin American crises.

The activities of the Contadora Group from 1983 onwards, subsequently expanded into the present Group of Eight through the inclusion of the so-called Support Group composed of Argentina, Brazil, Peru and Uruguay, is a case in point. The prime objective of that Group may be expressed in President Alfonsin's statement as avoiding 'the tendency to situate the conflict [in Central America] in the context of East–West confrontation'.[30] Whether the Group of Eight can be kept together remains to be seen.

The growing diversification of South American diplomacy is manifesting itself not only in multilateral initiatives, but, above all, on the level of individual states. In these endeavours, one-sided commitments were avoided while world-wide contacts were sought to bring about a balanced distribution of diplomat favours. The Big Two of South America were to be found in the vanguard of these multidirectional developments.

Rapprochement with the Soviet Union and Eastern Europe was one way of balancing. Thus, Argentina from 1973 onwards attempted this, and relations remained cordial even under the Argentine military dictatorship (1976–1983), whilst similar moves in Brazil were initiated under President Geisel in the mid-1970s under the aptly named policy of 'responsible pragmatism' (*pragmatismo responsavel*).

The Military Plane

The Rio Treaty is for all intents and purposes defunct, and the Central American–Caribbean region has been incorporated into the US security system. South America is dealing with its own intra-South American security problems largely by reverting to its own traditional system of the balance of power developed in the mid-nineteenth century and as a subsystem of the inter-American system in the 1930s, 1940s and 1950s. In the present system, the states of the region tend to define their security interests not according to some all-embracing inter-American concept but simply in relation to the interests of their neighbours, as in any classical system of the balance of power. The present, self-contained nature of the system is attested by the fact that 'the inter-State conflicts of South America, unlike those of Central America and the Caribbean, are not tied to extra-regional ones'.[31] The Southern Cone conflicts constitute a partial exception.

The system as at present evolving is showing some marked affinities with the one prevailing in the 1930s, which had to cope with the Chaco War between Bolivia and Paraguay (1932–1935), the Leticia dispute between Colombia and Peru (1932–1935) and the perennially intractable Maranon conflict between Ecuador and Peru, which had its origins in 1829 but is still simmering on. The manner in which the South American subsystem was operating at that time was shown by the fact that the United States, anxious to restore peace and stability on its southern flank by applying techniques short of the use of force, found that these had only a slight effect on states that, though weak, were determined to have their way in disputes with other weak states by using every trick and thrust at their command. As Bryce Wood commented, although all the states involved in those three conflicts were members of the League of Nations 'they behaved toward each other as though they were in a primitive society'.[32] As for post-1945 disputes of an intra-South American kind, both the Rio Treaty and the United Nations systems of collective security were inoperative in the Argentine–Chilean dispute over the Beagle Channel in its critical stage (1978), in the Peruvian–Ecuadorian Maranon conflict (1981) and in the Argentine–British war in the southwest Atlantic (1982).

Theoretically, Jaguaribe is right in noting that, where security is concerned, South America is the only sector of Latin America endowed with an 'operational individuality'.[33] In practice, however, as the late Steven Clissold rightly remarked, Latin Americans have become increasingly aware that they are 'different not only from the Europeans and the North Americans, but also from their neighbours'.[34] Indeed, South American security interests are too diverse to allow for a comprehensive South American system of collective security to emerge. For one thing, Colombia and Venezuela maintain a double orientation, Central American–Caribbean on the one hand, and South American on the other. 'Venezuela is projecting herself economically, politically and militarily . . . trying to provide a counterweight to Cuba'.[35]

The revival of intra-South American disputes has undoubtedly disturbed the intra-South American balance of power and stimulated an arms race in the region which would appear to be developing a dynamic of its own.[36] Although the intra-South American balance adumbrates the entire southern continent, some points in it are of particularly sensitive nature by virtue of their ability to set off disturbances capable of spreading insecurity throughout the rest of the system. The west coast of South America, with Peru as its flashpoint, is an example. Embroiled in a longstanding conflict with Ecuador and constantly nervous about the intentions of Chile, Peru has become the pivot of the balance of power on the west coast. Southern Cone conflicts constitute another example.

The Economic Plane

There has occurred a marked regression in intra-Latin American economic relations from a priori multilateralism to pragmatic bilateralism indicative of the crumbling of most attempts at multilateral economic development. The United Nations Economic Commission for Latin America and the Caribbean, once the powerhouse of neo-Bolivarian ideas, has declined in influence and its formerly distinct profile among United Nations regional Economic Commissions has been lost. Similarly, the all-Latin American economic organisation, SELA (Latin American Economic System), has been a disappointment.

Having lost its original impetus and suppleness, multilateral economic integration in Latin America has had to yield to patterns of spontaneous co-operation based on bilateral contacts. This is to be witnessed in the vital sphere of international trade with the Latin American Integration Association (LAIA), which is tolerant of widespread discriminatory arrangements so long as they are compatible with the so-called 'enabling clauses' decided on by the General Agreement on Tariffs and Trade (GATT) in 1979. (LAIA replaced the rigidly a priorist Latin American Free Trade Association or LAFTA of 1960.) The political prerequisite of an accommodation between Argentina and Brazil is now being effected.

South America, while failing in its efforts at regional economic integration, has asserted itself within the global economic system by taking important initiatives, even if their fruition requires the co-operation of extra-South American agencies. Only a few instances can be cited here. The new regime of the Law of the Sea, as laid down in the Convention of 1982, presents a case in point.[37] The same can be said of the budding Law of International River Basin

Development[38] and of the establishment of the Organisation of Petroleum Exporting Countries (OPEC).[39]

THE DOMINANT GLOBAL SYSTEM: SYSTEM ADAPTATION AND SYSTEM CONVERGENCE

Ironically, South America is feeling the pull of the global system in the measure in which its scope for autonomous foreign policies is widening. As one prominent Chilean author put it as early as 1969, the fate of Latin America is 'more and more affected by what happens in the rest of the world'.[40] Moreover, Latin America has found that it is unable to cope with the lengthening range of technical problems on any other but a global scale. While physical integration is making progress and the interdependence of Latin American economies never ceases to deepen, a priori schemes for the economic integration of the region, however ingeniously plotted and logically coherent, have proved too rigid in practice not to give way to pragmatic co-operation.[41] Even Monrovian-type financial institutions like the Inter-American Development Bank, which by virtue of the relatively high degree of Latin American participation in its administrative cadres has acquired some neo-Bolivarian traits, had to extend its membership beyond its geographical region to ensure an ongoing flow of adequate funds. Antonio Ortiz Mena, for many years its director, had to admit that this was merely acknowledging Latin America's strengthening links worldwide.[42]

In the sphere of international trade, Latin America also was unable to achieve results by acting on its own. It was symptomatic that on the formation of the United Nations Conference on Trade and Development (UNCTAD) in 1964 – at core an instrument of developing countries-directed groups – Latin America tried to stand on its own but, finding itself isolated, swiftly changed its mind by merging with the Asian and African groups in the so-called 'Group of 77' (now swollen to number about 135), one of the most notable pressure groups in post-1960 international economic relations. To achieve their objectives in international commodity trade, the relevant producing countries of Latin America had to enter into inter-continental combinations, whether of a producer or producer-consumer type.[43] In each of these cases, as in many others, the pull of the global system was such as to force Latin America to seek convergence.

The more the present global system is loosening its structure, the greater its attraction for developing subsystems, such as the South American one, and the more apparent the trend towards convergence between it and those subsystems. The origins of that convergence go back to the middle of the last century, but did not start to pick up speed until recently.

CHANGING SOVIET PERCEPTIONS OF THE GLOBAL SYSTEM

Liberalising tendencies in the international system may have received a fillip by some fundamental changes brought about recently in Soviet perceptions of the global system. As late as 1974 an authoritative Soviet source could still proclaim that 'the principal tendencies of sociopolitical development are determined not by the contradictions and relations between individual States but by the development of class antagonism of an epoch – between world socialism and world capitalism'. It was added for good measure that 'the renovated, modernised variant of the "balance of power" . . . is designed to preserve the diplomatic and social status quo'.[44]

That thesis of bloc confrontation has lately been substantially modified, first by the Soviet admission that power has been more widely diffused internationally in recent decades,[45] and then, under the Gorbachev regime, by the notion that 'world interdependence' has taken the place of class as the key concept in the global system.[46] A further significant gloss was put on the new perception by the revival, without attribution, of the Khruschevian notion of 'peaceful coexistence', according to which the world is threatened by both nuclear weapons and ecological disaster to which no country is immune. 'Peaceful coexistence' therefore has to take precedence over the struggle against capitalism. Alexander Yakovlyev, Gorbachev's close collaborator, reinforced the new thinking recently by declaring that Marxism was 'the understanding of common human interests from the viewpoint of history and the perspective of the development of mankind, not just certain of its countries and classes, people and social groups'.[47]

These fundamental changes in Soviet cosmology are only gradually seeping down into Soviet specialist writings. A comparative reading of the two most recent expert publications on Latin America, while as yet revealing no basic change of approach, do exhibit differences.[48] One looks forward with eager expectation to forthcoming volumes to ascertain whether further easing of South America's passage into the global system can be expected.

FINAL THOUGHTS

Neither Monrovian nor Bolivarian attempts to introduce a measure of regional order into South America have had lasting success. On the one hand it proved impossible to muster the political unity that alone could have guaranteed Bolivarian solutions, while on the other United States power has never been wielded as energetically as would have been required to produce a firmly grounded Monrovian-type regional order.

The considerable power at the elbow of successive United States administrations in their dealings with Latin America has been used by way of 'paramount' domination in Central America and in the Caribbean but only through 'hegemonial' predominance in South America. It was in the latter rather than in the former region that the relative decline of US power was most noticeable. During the tense stages of the Cold War that decline was disguised as most South American governments felt they were unable to cope with Cold War issues, but with the abatement of those tensions their inhibitions were seen not to have any further point. South America's governments subsequently began to diversify their foreign relations to decrease the impact of United States hegemony. Several of them, especially the leading NICs, have pursued notably activist independent foreign policies, and have even emerged as important actors not only within the region but as acknowledged middle-rank powers on the world scene.

By virtue of being one of the two principals in the Cold War, the Soviet Union has been a constant factor, both directly and indirectly, in South America. However, for a long time it was hampered in the formulation of its policies towards the region by conceptual confusion in regard to the status and function of developing countries in general.

During the acute stages of the Cold War, the high degree of tension prevailing between the two superpowers precluded a convergence between South America and the global system. To the extent that a *rapprochement* between them has since materialised, the states of South America have been able to resurrect their autonomous subsystem of the balance of power of mid-nineteenth-century vintage in order to cope with intra-South American problems. At the same time South America, realising that it was increasingly on its own, has had to forge inter-continental links in search of solutions for many of its most pressing economic problems. The fact that this could not be accomplished through either Monrovian or Bolivarian formulas has cast doubt on the utility of regional economic institutions. Pragmatic approaches are now being favoured, while a priori ones are being shunned.

It would seem that beyond operating a rudimentary balance of power, South America may be in the process of forming a Concert of South America roughly analogous to that of Europe in the nineteenth century, which managed to keep the continent free from entangling alliances between 1815 and 1879. What is lending some substance to those expectations are the activities displayed by the Group of Eight on the political, and the Cartagena Group on the economic level to deal with practical problems as they arise. If these trends persist, perhaps not in the too distant future the world might witness in South America the emergence of a highly flexible system of multilateral diplomacy capable of adopting increasingly sophisticated problem-solving procedures for dealing with intra-South American crises.

While it would be rash to be too specific about the mode and rhythm of convergence between the South American and global systems, it is worth drawing attention to the Antarctic Treaty system, which at first sight would seem an ideal type to be emulated in structure, procedure and institutional fitness. That system, however close geographically to South America and however tied to the global system by virtue of its membership, is historically *sui generis*. It is notable that the Antarctic Treaty system, whatever one might think of the equity of its proceedings, has displayed high degrees of flexibility in accommodating itself to new situations. Above all, by concentrating on technical issues – if only willy-nilly – it would appear to have managed to contain the highly political and potentially explosive issue of territorial sovereignty. It seems inevitable, therefore, that the Antarctic Treaty system should affect both South America and the global system, and in turn be affected by them.

Notes

1. Victor A. Belaunde, *Bolivar and the Political Thought of the Spanish American Revolution* (Baltimore: Johns Hopkins University Press, 1930).
2. Arthur Whitaker, *The United States and Argentina* (Cambridge, Mass.: Harvard University Press, 1954) pp. 86–7.
3. Robert N. Burr, *By Reason or Force. Chile and the Balance of Power in South America, 1830–1905* (Berkeley and Los Angeles: University of California Press, 1967).
4. Pope G. Atkins, *Latin America in the International System* (New York: Free Press, 1977) p. 95.
5. Only Britain still led the United States in the volume of investments in Latin America. However, 'not only was Britain's lead narrow, but most of her investments were concentrated in South America, and above all in a single country, Argentina'. See Arthur P. Whitaker, *The Western Hemisphere Idea: Its Rise and Fall* (Ithaca: Cornell University Press, 1954) p. 113.
6. For a detailed treatment, see Mark T. Gilderhus, *Pan American Visions: Woodrow Wilson in the Western Hemisphere, 1913–1921* (Tucson: University of Arizona Press, 1986).
7. Wilson was only reluctantly agreeable to the insertion of Article 21 into the Covenant of the League of Nations which referred to 'regional understandings like the Monroe Doctrine' for securing peace. See Whitaker, *The Western Hemisphere Idea*, pp. 121–5.
8. The United States was at first reluctant to be too firmly associated with a regional security treaty.
9. Whitaker, *The Western Hemisphere Idea*, pp. 148–9.
10. See Fred Parkinson, 'The Alliance for Progress', *Yearbook of World Affairs*, Vol. 18 (1964), pp. 96–127.
11. By far the best systematic treatment of the phenomenon of 'hegemony' is Heinrich Triepel, *Die Hegemonie* (Stuttgart: Kohlhammer, 1938). On the limits of hegemony, see Michael J. Francis, *The Limits of Hegemony: United States Relations with Argentina and Chile During World War Two* (Notre Dame: University of Notre Dame Press, 1977) and Gary Frank, *Struggle for Hegemony in South America: Argentina, Brazil and the United States during the Second World War* (University of Miami: Center for Advanced International Studies, 1979).
12. For illustrative figures, see Robert Keohane, *After Hegemony. Cooperation and Discord in the World Political Economy* (Princeton, New Jersey: Princeton University Press, 1985) pp. 196–7.
13. Manfred Wilhelmy, 'La Evolucion de la Multipolaridad', *Estudios Internacionales*, Vol. 20 (July–September 1987) pp. 379–80 and 384–5.
14. Helio Jaguaribe, 'Reflexiones sobre el Atlantico Sur: America Latina y el Brasil ante la Desarticulacion del Sistema Interamericano', *Estudios Internacionales*, Vol. 15 (October–December 1982) p. 445.
15. A case can be made for the assertion that NICs tend to throw up standard patterns of politics. See the stimulating comparative analysis

conducted by Nicos P. Mouzelis, *Politics in the Periphery: Early Parliamentarism and Late Industrialisation in the Balkans and in Latin America* (London: Macmillan, 1986).

16. E. Bradford Burns, *The Unwritten Alliance. Rio Branco and Brazilian–American Relations* (New York: Columbia University Press, 1966).
17. *XV Konferentsiya*, October 26–November 3, 1926 *Stenographic Record* (Moscow, 1927).
18. At the San Francisco Conference on the United Nations in April 1945, Molotov made some derogatory remarks about Ecuador and opposed the membership of Argentina.
19. As regards Latin America, see M. Bolkovitinov, 'Doktrina Monro – legendy i deistvitelnost', *Mirovaya ekonomika i mezhdunarodniye otnoshenya* (September 1960) pp. 22–6; M. Danilyevich, 'Dvizhushchiyeye sily osvoboditelnoi borba v Latinskoi Amerikye', ibid., pp. 90–94; and V.G. Spirin, 'Na puti k natsionalnomu osvobuzhdeniye', in V. V. Volski *et al.* (eds), *Latinskaya Amerika v proshlom i nastoyashchiem* (Moscow: Izdatelstvo Scotsialno-ekonomicheskoi Literatury, 1960) pp. 44–64.
20. Elizabeth Kridl Valkenier, *The Soviet Union and the Third World* (New York: Praeger, 1983).
21. On these points, see Valkenier; L.I. Reisner, *Razvivayushchiesya strany: ocherk teorii ekonomicheskovo rosta* (Moscow: Nauka, 1976); and Johan Lorenz Schmidt, *Entwicklungslander* (East Berlin: Die Wirtschaft, 1974).
22. Valkenier, *The Soviet Union and the Third World*, p. 82.
23. Peter Shearman, 'Gorbachev and the Third World: an area of reform?', *Third World Quarterly*, Vol. 3 (October 1987) pp. 1083–1117. Gorbachev's statement on the NICs was reported in *Pravda*, 12 March 1985.
24. Cole Blasier, *The Giant's Rival. The USSR and Latin America* (Pittsburgh: Pittsburgh University Press, 1983) pp. 146 and 6.
25. David Rock, 'Argentina's Quest for Stability', *The World Today*, Vol. 30 (July 1974) pp. 306–314.
26. Isabel Turrent, *La Union Sovietica en America Latina: el caso de la Unidad Popular Chilena, 1970–1973* (Mexico City: El Colegio de Mexico, 1984) p. 248.
27. Carlos Portales, 'Sudamerica: seguridad regional y relaciones con los Estados Unidos', *Estudios Internacionales*, Vol. 29 (1986) pp. 279–97.
28. For a severe, extremely well documented indictment of official United States strategic perceptions in Latin America, see Lars Schoultz, *National Security and United States Policy toward Latin America* (Princeton: Princeton University Press, 1987).
29. Carlos Portales, 'Sudamerica', pp. 284–5.
30. *Clarin* (Buenos Aires), 11 December 1983.
31. Carlos Portales, 'Sudamerica', p. 287.
32. Bryce Wood, *The United States and Latin American Wars, 1932–1942* (New York: Columbia University Press, 1966) p. 347.
33. Helio Jaguaribe, 'Reflexiones . . .', p. 456.
34. Steven Clissold, *Latin America. New World, Third World* (London: Pall Mall, 1972) p. 306.
35. Carlos Portales, 'Sudamerica', pp. 287–9.

36. Augusto Varas, *Militarization and the International Arms Race in Latin America* (Boulder: Westview Press, 1985) p. 56; Jack Child, *Geopolitics and Conflict in South America: Quarrels Among Neighbors* (New York: Praeger, 1985). There is room for the view that the fading hegemony of the United States in South America is having the effect of exacerbating existing intra-South American disputes.

37. Fred Parkinson, 'The Latin American Contribution to the Law of the Sea', in William E. Butler (ed.), *The Law of the Sea and International Shipping. Anglo-Soviet post-UNCLOS Perspectives* (New York, London, Rome: Oceana, 1985) pp. 139–72. Also Eduardo Ferrera Costa, 'La cooperacion funcional y la concertacion de intereses nacionales en el caso del derecho del mar', in Heraldo Munoz and Francisco Orrego Vicuna (eds), *La cooperacion regional en America Latina. Diagnostico y proyecciones futuras* (Mexico City: El Colegio de Mexico, 1987) pp. 579–610.

38. Fred Parkinson, 'Towards an International River Basin Development Law?', in Francis Snyder and Peter Slinn (eds), *International Law of Development: Comparative Perspectives* (Abingdon: Professional Books, 1987) pp. 215–20.

39. In 1960 Venezuela in conjunction with Saudi Arabia took an initiative with worldwide implications in launching the Organisation of Petroleum Exporting Countries (OPEC). See L. Vallenilla, *Oil: the Making of a New Economic Order. Venezuelan Oil and OPEC* (New York: Harper & Row, 1978).

40. Lucio Tomassini, 'Towards a Latin American Nationalism?', *The World Today*, Vol. 25 (1969) p. 545.

41. Lucio Tomassini, 'La desintegracion del proceso de integracion latino-americano: origenes y modalidades de la cooperacion informal en la region', in Heraldo Munoz and Francisco Orrego Vicuna (eds), *La cooperacion regional*, pp. 553–78.

42. Antonio Ortiz Mena, *America Latina en desarrollo. Una vision desde el Banco Interamericano de Desarrollo (BID). Exposiciones y documentos, 1976–1980* (Washington, DC: Inter-American Development Bank, 1981) p. 119.

43. Ricardo Davis-Ffrench and Ernesto Tironi (eds), *Latin America and the New International Economic Order* (London: Macmillan, 1982).

44. Sh. Sanakoyev, 'The World Today: problems of the correlation of forces', *International Affairs* (Moscow) (1974) pp. 43–4.

45. Nils Wessell, 'Soviet Views on Multipolarity and the Emerging Balance of Power', *ORBIS*, Vol. 22 (Winter 1979) pp. 787–8.

46. Yegor Ligachyov, Number Two in the Politburo until late 1988, still adhered to the old view. See *Guardian*, 6 August 1988.

47. *Guardian*, 3 August 1988 and *The Economist*, 22 August 1988. See also Lily Marcou, 'Reconnaissance de l'interdependence generale, le grand tournant de la diplomatie sovietique', *Le Monde Diplomatique*, May 1988, p. 5.

48. Lev Lvovich Klyuchkovskiy, *Latinskaya Amerika v sistemye mirovykh khozvyastvennykh svyazei* (Moscow: Mezhdunarodniye otnoshenya, 1984), contrasted with Nikolai Gregorevich Zaytsev, *Latinskaya*

Amerika b borbe za perestroiku mezhdunarodnykh ekonomicheskikh otnoshenii (Moscow: Mezhdunarodniye otnoshenya, 1987). It is to be noted that the term 'borba' (struggle) has undergone a subtle change in meaning, since in the present context it would no longer appear to refer to the class struggle (whether domestic or international) but to the struggle for the establishment of 'perestroika'.

12 Conclusions
Michael A. Morris

Each of the four parts of the book focuses on a different dimension of great power relations in Argentina, Chile and Antarctica, whose rationale was set out in the introductory chapter. Each part will be briefly reviewed in order to reiterate some highlights and most particularly to indicate some relationships between the various parts. Some overall conclusions emerge from the study as a whole.

BACKGROUND

The introductory chapter posited that a distinctive and important five-cornered relationship exists involving three great powers in interlocking issues involving Argentina, Chile and Antarctica. Subsequent pages of this volume affirmed and elaborated this proposition, so that it remains to explore some of the implications of the five-cornered relationship.

A recurring theme here in great power–lesser power relations has been continuity tempered by change. Changes at the regional and global levels have resulted in part from the emergence of new powers and the decline of established ones, while fundamental national weaknesses have continued to lock still other countries into subordinate positions in the international power hierarchy. In addition to the juxtaposition of upwardly mobile and declining powers, gaping disparities in power between countries have remained. In fact, Brazil's emergence as a major power has tended to accentuate disparities in the South American hierarchy. The international position of Argentina and Chile has declined relative to that of Brazil, while that of Chile has tended to decline with respect to Argentina. At the same time, Argentina and Chile remain important in South America and they have been the leaders in the region in forging a presence in Antarctica.

Rapid changes in regional and global international relations are likely to continue to affect the status of the great powers in general and their access to and influence in Argentina, Chile and Antarctica in particular. The great powers may not be as influential in South

American countries as previously, especially in the larger ones, but their influence there is likely to remain substantial. The five-cornered relationship therefore constitutes an element of continuity in the rapidly evolving diplomatic constellation of Argentina, Chile and Antarctica.

Some recurring problems of great power relations with South American countries in general and Argentina and Chile in particular may be identified. Relationships between strong and weak states tend to be stressful, especially when, as here, an historical legacy of great power–lesser power interaction has conditioned responses on all sides. Rodriguez Berrutti traced the generally negative UK and US impact on Argentine borders including Antarctica, while de Hoyos observed that these two great powers have been considered in Argentina, rightly or wrongly, not only in nationalist sectors but in public opinion at large, as responsible for causing national problems. Fermandois noted a counterpart populist tendency of Chilean resentment towards the United States, which has been largely suppressed during the years of military government although recent bilateral problems have given rise to a conservative version of this resentment within governmental circles and supporters.

Domestic resentment of longstanding dependency on and manipulation by the great powers has been expressed in the international sphere through attempts to develop a more autonomous, independent foreign policy. Diversification of foreign relations has been pursued to counterbalance US influence, although the form this has taken has varied from country to country. For example, Argentina's development of an important commercial relationship with the Soviet Union has not been available to Chile, which, with some exceptions, has suffered from international isolation. Great Britain has constituted one of these exceptions for Chile, while Anglo-Argentine relations have remained severed since the 1982 Malvinas/Falklands war.

Continuing dependency has constrained these efforts, but Black heralded the passing of Pax Americana. Greater leeway or space in the international arena has resulted, especially for those countries in the region with fairly sizable national capabilities. The decline of traditional US hegemony in the Western hemisphere has been especially evident in South America, and in the Southern Cone geographical remoteness and a tradition of resistance to great power pressure have accentuated the relative decline in US influence.

At the same time, great power relations continue to pose problems for Argentina and Chile as well as other regional states. The United States has attempted to maintain its control over Latin American states, even where weakening of the levers of its traditional hegemony has been pronounced as in the Southern Cone (Black). Chile has continued to feel threatened by the Soviet Union and Argentina has regarded Britain's military build-up in the Falklands as provocative and menacing.

GREAT POWER RELATIONS

Great power relations in Argentina, Chile and Antarctica tend to be conditioned by the five-cornered relationship, even though each of the five parties would wish to have greater control over events. While Britain enjoys the status of a great power, any stable, mutually acceptable settlement of the Falklands/Malvinas dispute must necessarily involve outside powers and most particularly the United States (Calvert). Both Argentina and the Soviet Union may have wished to fashion a bilateral relationship free from outside pressure, but the dynamics of Argentine–Soviet relations have tended to be triangular in nature in so far as the US presence has conditioned actions and reactions (de Hoyos). The United States has tried to pressure Chile to conform to its preferred standards and policies, but the military government has exhibited considerable autonomy (Fermandois). Fermandois adds that new transnational relationships have emerged between Chile and the United States during these same years of military government with attendant alterations in attitudes and coalitions on each side. Further complicating US policy, British aims towards Argentina and Chile have increasingly begun to diverge from American ones (Morris, Chapter 9).

At the same time, the five-cornered relationship has tended to be confining for Argentina and Chile. While the Argentine–Soviet relationship may develop a military facet, the core commercial dimension on which such military relations would rest has been decaying (de Hoyos). Argentine efforts to diversify and intensify foreign relationships in pursuit of pressing national needs tend to be diverted by the British presence in the Falklands/Malvinas and Antarctica. Apart from the merits of the Argentine case, disproportionate Argentine attention is absorbed by the hostile Anglo-Argentine relationship. Chile, in spite of having friendly relations with one great power (Great Britain), has suffered from increasingly strained relations with another great power (the United States) and hostile relations with the third (the Soviet Union), which has helped sustain the country's international isolation. Brazil has had much more success than either Argentina or Chile in diversifying its foreign policy and forging an influential role regionally and globally (Watson).

ISSUES

While Antarctica is a global issue, the five-cornered relationship is evident there as well (Calvert). Some of the frictions from that relationship in South America have been transferred to Antarctica, but all five parties have collaborated through the Antarctic Treaty system. Parkinson argues that the tradition of Antarctic co-operation could interact positively with the increasing convergence between the South American and global systems. Amidst these multifarious tendencies, Argentina and Chile have been able to sustain distinctive Antarctic policies including territorial claims.

While important co-operative strains exist within the five-cornered relationship, discord has predominated. The dependency of Argentina and Chile on the great powers has been a recurring source of friction. While the former have made concerted efforts to fashion more autonomous, independent foreign policies, their ability to lessen the impact of the great powers has varied by issue. While the five-power relationship has been constraining in Antarctica as elsewhere, both countries have managed to sustain their territorial claims there. Antarctica is *sui generis* with regard to Argentine and Chilean prospects for surmounting dependency, but so too are the other issues analysed – the external debt (Alagia) and conventional military and nuclear affairs (Morris).

In spite of a crushing debt burden, Argentina has been able to maintain some bargaining power over the short term although the overall impact of the foreign debt has constrained Argentine foreign policy. While creditors and/or debtors eventually may alter present conditions perpetuating the external debt crisis, so far this problem has been worsening with time for Argentina. Alagia warns that if mutually acceptable solutions to the debt crisis cannot be developed, a major casualty will be relationships between the creditor and debtor states and most especially between the United States and the larger Latin American states. In contrast, US policy-makers have praised the Chilean approach to its external debt, while condemning the political policies of the military regime.

While great power leverage has tended to increase over time on the external debt issue, at least with regard to Argentina, this has not involved an across-the-board return to US hegemony. Since dependency has varied by issue, considerable great power leverage on this issue has been counterbalanced by more autonomy of local states on some other issues (i.e. Antarctica and military affairs). A variety of changes, including a less prominent US presence in the Southern Cone foreign policy panorama, also has thrown up new limits on US interference.

Argentina, Brazil and Chile all remain dependent on the great powers for weapons transfers as well as for technological transfers for national armaments industries and nuclear programmes. However, particularly for Argentina and Brazil, this military or military-related dependency has been decreasing over time. Both countries have responded to great power pressure by diversifying conventional military and nuclear suppliers and stressing eventual autonomy for national military industries and nuclear programmes. Some weaponry imports and technological transfers will need to continue for the foreseeable future, but for most purposes military autonomy is a realistic mid-term goal for Argentina and Brazil.

COMPARISONS AND CONCLUSIONS

The five-cornered relationship extends beyond the South American continent to Antarctica (Beck), thereby contrasting in this and other respects with local power–great power relations in Central America and elsewhere in Latin America (Black). While these and other comparisons throughout the pages of this book bear witness to the distinctiveness and importance of the five-cornered relationship, the comparisons in Part IV relate particularly to the continent of which the Southern Cone countries form a part, South America.

Like the five-cornered relationship, Brazilian relations with the great powers are distinctive and important (Watson). In contrast to Argentina and Chile, Brazil's emergence as the most prominent Latin American state and her longstanding pragmatic foreign policy have coloured relations with the great powers. Brazilian policies as well as her relations with the great powers will be influential in shaping the emerging South American order. The evolving regional order could lead to the eventual replacement of US with Brazilian hegemony, although this kind of new order would be as stressful as the old one.

Possible evolution of a more collaborative regional order will depend to a considerable degree on how the Southern Cone states adapt to Brazil's emergence as a major power and how Brazil manages its own rise. While the transition from the old regional order towards a new one has not been easy, intra-South American collaboration has been easing the change. The new order will in any event surely be more autonomous than the previous one, although the great powers have been influential in the transition and their relations with the local states will likely remain important in the new order.

Global change affects regional change and vice versa, but again both positive and negative trends may be discerned. Greater convergence between the regional and global orders may emerge from simultaneous change at both levels (Parkinson). While this could be a positive development for South American states, increasing regional autonomy has been accompanied by a resurgence of traditional security concerns. The great powers will continue to affect the transition both regionally and globally, although Parkinson shows that Soviet policies towards South America and the developing world as a whole have often been as inappropriate as US ones.

This book has identified specific areas of friction without neglecting existing and potential areas of co-operation and harmony. On the one hand, there is an historical legacy of stressful great power relations with Argentina and Chile, while, on the other, changes with positive potential are occurring at multiple levels – the Southern Cone, South America, Antarctica and the global system. The five countries in question have influenced the transition towards a new order at the sub-regional, regional and even at the global levels, although often at cross-purposes to one another. None of the actors in the five-cornered relationship consequently are wholly satisfied with the direction of change affecting them individually or as a group. Since the five-cornered relationship is likely to be present in the new order as in the old, it is hoped that greater understanding of its dynamics will help promote more harmonious local power–great power relations.

Index